DEEP DARK BLUE

DEEP DARK BLUE

POLO TATE

Feiwel and Friends
New York

A Feiwel and Friends Book
An imprint of Macmillan Publishing Group, LLC
175 Fifth Avenue, New York, NY 10010

The names and identifying characteristics of some persons described in the book
have been changed.

Our books may be purchased in bulk for promotional, educational, or business
use. Please contact your local bookseller or the Macmillan Corporate and
Premium Sales Department at (800) 221-7945 ext. 5442 or by e-mail at
MacmillanSpecialMarkets@macmillan.com.

Library of Congress Cataloging-in-Publication Data
Names: Tate, Polo, author.
Title: Deep dark blue : a memoir of survival / Polo Tate.
Description: New York : Feiwel and Friends, 2018
Identifiers: LCCN 2017041558 | ISBN 9781250128522 (hardcover) |
    ISBN 9781250128539 (ebook)
Subjects: LCSH: Tate, Polo. | United States Air Force Academy—Biography. |
    United States. Air Force—Women—Biography. | United States. Air Force—
    Women—Crimes against. | Women military cadets—Colorado—Biography. |
    Women military cadets—Crimes against—Colorado. | Rape victims—United
    States—Biography. | Rape—Colorado. | Sexual harassment in the military—
    Colorado. | United States Air Force Academy—History—21st century.
Classification: LCC UG638.5.M1 T38 2018 | DDC 362.883092 [B]—dc23
LC record available at https://lccn.loc.gov/2017041558

Book design by Sophie Erb

Feiwel and Friends logo designed by Filomena Tuosto

First edition, 2018

10 9 8 7 6 5 4 3 2 1

fiercereads.com

For my darling Sary.

Thank you for gifting me the full spectrum of human emotion.

Playing with you always in my heart, pinkie swear.

And to my parents,

I have never felt more inspired, more supported, and more loved
by any other souls alive.

If only you could know the depths of my love and appreciation for you.

It's an honor to be your daughter.

DEEP DARK BLUE

PART ONE
WADING IN

1

THE ACADEMY

POLO REO TATE
USAFA, 15 MAY, O-NEG
NO ONE CAN TAKE YOUR JOY

The words were under my thumb from the very beginning. From the time the bus picked us up, until the time its brakes squealed to a halt and exhaled their deep and final sigh, my thumb ran back and forth over each tiny raised letter on my junior dog tags, like a worry stone.

Po-lo Re-o Tate. *Rub.*

U-Saah-Fa, U-Saah-Fa, U-Saah-Fa. *Rub.*

No-one-can-take-your-joy. *Rub.*

After a two-year wait for a senatorial appointment, an application process, and a lifetime of preparation, I had earned the chance to pursue superior academia, to train militarily, and to play Division I volleyball. All while becoming the newest member of the team in charge of protecting our nation. I was living my childhood dream, sitting on a bus that was taking me in to start my first day of basic training at the United States Air Force Academy.

Holy shitballs.

The bus's hydraulics expelled the rest of their air over each wheel, lowering its enormous frame one side at a time. As if kneeling down to pray in the loaded, quiet calm before a storm. Bloated, visceral silence. I sat perfectly still, except for my thumb, rubbing, rubbing, rubbing the dog tags.

I stopped rubbing, afraid the friction was contributing to sweltering heat inside the stuffy bus. I stole the moment to wrap my junior dog tags around and around my arm for good luck and tuck them under the thick leather cuff that hugged my wrist.

This was both one of the happiest days of my life, and one of the scariest. I had always preferred to live on the shiny side of life, and yet I knew that where there was shine, there could also be shadow. I had just turned eighteen. And I had already experienced the extremes of tragedy, loss, and love enough to know that none of us, no situation, was just one thing or another. As I sat on the bus to basic, I had a sneaking suspicion that for better or worse, USAFA was going to force me to see both sides of life's coin. I held my breath.

The energy, like the trapped, stagnant air inside the bus, pulsed to the beat of my accelerating heart, throbbing it like a bladder.

USAFA.

USAFA.

USAFA.

Silence.

BOOM.

The bus doors *blew* open, startling even the driver, and a wiry young man bounded up the stairs, blowing a piercingly shrill whistle. *WHEEE!*

"GET OFF THIS MOTHER-CHUCKING BUS RIGHT NOOOW, BASICS!"

For such a small man, his lung capacity was awe-inspiring. *Wait . . . mother-chucking?*

"I SAID *MOOOVE*, PEOPLE!"

He was gesticulating wildly, as if bringing in a 747 jumbo jet, sans the supercool orange lightsabers. One windmilling arm took a break to point a finger at the Heisman Trophy's bigger, badder younger brother, sitting next to me. I hoped to God that this mountain of a boy was a USAFA football recruit, because our Fighting Falcons could really use this Mack truck of muscle mass barreling down our opponents.

"LET'S GOOO, BOY. . . . GET THAT BIG ASS A-MOVIN'!"

Basic Cadet Trophy Boy grabbed me by the arm and hoisted me up like a tackling dummy. He dragged me past the roaring mouth and windmilling arm to the bus's exit.

From my perch one step above his broad shoulders, I could see the utter chaos that met each of my classmates as their feet hit USAFA pavement for the first time. God, I wanted to grab the back of Basic Cadet Trophy Boy's shirt and hang on for dear life. A second later, we were both yanked into the chaotic swell below. I sucked in my last breath of free air and stepped down onto the perilous pavement.

I almost overlooked the small cadet waiting for me off to one side, wearing a perfectly pressed blue uniform and a large hat that looked as if he'd just swiped it from his father's closet. Before I could turn to look at him, he stuck his face so close to mine that I felt his nose dip into my ear. *His nose just went inside my ear.* Instinctively, I grabbed the side of my head and doubled over with ticklish laughter. I instantly regretted it as I straightened myself up. Too late.

"OOOHH, WE GOT A *LAUGHER* OVER HERE! SHE CAN'T MAINTAIN HER *BEARING*! YOU THINK THAT'S FUNNY, BASIC?!"

Umm, yasss? Not that I would say it out loud, but OMG, yes. It was hilarious. How was I supposed to maintain my bearing—whatever that was—when this little and loud Jersey-sounding stranger had just stuck his *nose* inside my *ear*?

"YOU THINK THIS IS FUNNY, BASIC?! YOU THINK WE ARE HERE FOR YOUR *AMUSEMENT*?!"

Damn, he is ferocious. I bit my lip to keep from nervously laughing. Two other uniforms answered Cadet Itty-Bitty's mating call.

"AWWW, GIGGLE-PUSSS, EH?? YOU THINK THAT'S FUNNY??"

"WHAT. THE. MOTHER. CHUCK. ARE. YOU. FRIGGIN. LAUGHING AT, SHIT-CAN?!?"

Fear had shrunken my sphincter to the size of a shriveled currant. Perhaps it was my coping mechanism, or a fear response, that was allowing giggle bubbles to surface from deep inside of me. Either way, I had to answer.

"No, sir!"

I wondered if laughter was considered an honor code violation. I didn't think so, technically, considering we had not yet taken any kind of oath—unless that was one of the 14,000 papers that I had signed that morning.

"OH, YOU DO *NOT* THINK IT IS FUNNY, BASIC?? BUT YOU WERE LAUGHING, SHIT-FOR-BRAINS?!"

My body froze like I was buffering, and the upperclassmen just stared at me for a beat, impatiently waiting to refresh my URL. I wasn't sure of anything. They took my silence as a concession.

"THEN YOU *DO* THINK IT IS FUNNY?!"

Shit. I started to gesticulate.

"No, no, no, sir! I mean, it's *not* funny, sir!"

"WHAT ARE YOU DOING, BASIC? GET YOUR ARMS DOWN! ARE YOU ALLOWED TO USE CONTRACTIONS?! GET BACK AT ATTENTION, YOU DUMB LOOSEY-GOOSEY!"

Wow. The insults so far had sounded like my grandparents trying to speak emoji . . . barely comprehensible, but definitely awkward and insulting. However, unlike my grandparents, the cadre—the cadet officers assigned to train us—had *meant* to insult, and they hurled their language with enough velocity that it stung.

Four more cadre members descended. Each one fired off a question that added to my own personal hell.

"Yes, sir!"

"No, sir!"

"No, sir!"

Okay, I'm starting to get the hang of this.

"Yes, sir!"

Silence.

I looked into the eyes of the uniformed cadet I'd just answered. *She* was pissed.

"Yes, ma'am!"

"YOU THINK I LOOK LIKE A BOY, BASIC? HOW WOULD YOU FEEL IF I CALLED *YOU* A BOY, BASIC?!"

Hmm. How would I feel? Well, I'd feel like I was back in elementary school. Back when the elf shelf, pixie, or as my father liked to call it, "Don't you wanna look like a girl, goddamnit" haircut was sweeping the nation and I was its poster child.

If there was anything I understood, it was how shitty it felt to be mistaken for something that I was not—and I had just done that very thing to one of the women in charge of my training, on my first day of *college*.

TOP GUN.

"Pardon me, sir, I'm finished. May I give you back the form for my dog tags?" I handed the grizzled gray-haired vet behind the counter back the form he had given me. His wool baseball cap said ARMY in gold letters and was adorned with various combat pins along the sides, hiding most of a jagged and salty sweat ring wrapping all the way around. He squinted at the completed form, then at me.

"Startin' a little early, aren't ya, son?" His eyes pinged off me and landed on another older gentleman sitting behind the register. "Don't think they're gonna believe you when you go to report for duty. . . ." They laughed and shook their heads. I ran my hands through my long pixie haircut and tucked it behind my ears, accentuating my *gold earrings* in each ear. I was finally starting to grow my hair out and dress more femininely; this wasn't supposed to keep happening.

The army/navy surplus store was empty except for my good friend and teammate, Munny, and me. She was over looking at army jackets, and when I looked over at her, embarrassed, she was mouthing something forcefully at me. I shook my head and waved her off. Mr. Army Vet took the form that I had filled out over to a metal press.

"Um, excuse me, sir, she's a *girl*," Munny said, more strongly than I'd hoped.

"It's okay, Munny, he didn't mean—"

"Is that right? Well, pardon me—wow—are these for your boyfriend, then, sweetie?" He started to press the tags.

"No. They're for *her*." Munny folded her arms and popped her hip, her blond ponytail punctuating her every point.

Munny was three years older, six inches shorter, and twice as loud as I was. We had been playing basketball together since I was eight. Now that I was eleven, I had been playing in her age bracket for a more competitive traveling league, and we had both just found out that we'd made the All-Star team out of all the fourteen-year-old girls in our region. We were celebrating.

I had *loved* sports since tumbling out of my mother's womb. I'd played catch at thirteen months and ridden a bike without training wheels at two and a half. Every team that I had joined, and every sport that I had played, just reinforced to me more and more that athletics incorporated almost everything that I adored about people, problem-solving, math, science, and communication. I had instantly felt at home on the playing field or court. And I was going to practice as hard as I could to be able to play Division I volleyball, basketball, or soccer in college. It wasn't until we had started our All-Star team practice that I'd found the "even more" I'd been looking for.

Munny's dad—Coach Munny—was a smart, funny teddy bear of a man, whom I adored, and who had become our assistant coach. Our whole team went back to their house for a slumber party after our first practice. After dinner, we watched one of the movies for which Munny's dad had written the screenplay, called *Top Gun*. The moment the credits rolled in their home theater, we were up on our feet, high-fiving, cheering loudly, and ready to totally *crush* our first tournament. Not only did we choose *Top Gun* as our team name, but we watched the movie before *every* tournament. A tradition had been born within our team, and an unknown world had just revealed itself to me.

Beyond being a romantic, action-packed blockbuster, *Top Gun* sparked the flint to my kindling thoughts of the future, immediately igniting a wildfire inside my gut.

As I watched the screen pilots train, work, play, and study, I knew what I wanted to do when I grew up. For the first time, I saw that work could be both an academic *and* a physical challenge. I didn't have to choose a job that only used my brain—like the jobs my parents had—or one that only used my body, like those of professional athletes.

To me, the flyboys of *Top Gun* challenged themselves in every way, each day. Obviously, it was a movie—not real life—but I'd immediately talked to Coach Munny and found out just how much of it *was* based on reality, so I added books on navy and air force aviation to my reading list. I had already been reading books about the FBI, and was completely fascinated by profiling and forensic behavioral science, so books on the military were a natural next step.

I had loved seeing how the military honored and encouraged the mind-body connection. I wanted that challenge. I wanted that training. I wanted to be a part of that elite team. Flying planes while getting to learn and work seemed like it would be the ultimate bonus. It was the air force that actually felt like a perfect fit on every level. My friend Munny knew I wanted to get a pair of dog tags, and even though she didn't want any, I knew that she wouldn't tell anyone about mine. It was a promise that I was making to my future self. A commitment to work hard. To go all in. A promise that was *to* me, *for* me, *by* me . . . just *private*. She also knew a friend with a car, and a penchant for

Jersey Giant sub sandwiches. Which allowed me to finally get my very own set of dog tags made that pressed my goal—my hope—into metal, and further into its fulfillment:

POLO REO TATE
USAFA, 15 MAY, O-NEG
NO ONE CAN TAKE YOUR JOY

"Welp—there ya go, hon! Say—where'd that quote come from on the bottom, there?" Mr. Army Vet said as he handed me my shiny new dream.

"Just . . . someone close to me said it when I was seven." I reached for the tags.

"Hmm . . . They for a Halloween costume or something, darlin'?" Mr. Army Vet pried.

"Um, no, not a costume. Thank you." I took them from him gingerly, holding my dreams close to my heart and my cards close to my vest. I held my money out to Mr. Navy Vet at the register.

"She is gonna be a *soldier*. Like, an *amazing* soldier!" Munny couldn't help herself; her heart was ever on her sleeve, and the chip protecting it was ever on her shoulder.

Mr. Navy Vet at the cash register raised his eyebrows, pursed his lips, and nodded. Mr. Army Vet, on the other hand, grimaced.

"Naww, even if you *could*, why would you wanna go and do that? . . . It's no place for little girls like you. Screws with a man's head, seeing women in a place like that. You don't wanna do that, do ya?" His face was gnarled, trying to set us straight. Munny's ponytail started bobbing like a prizefighter's feet before a knockout. I put my hand on her shoulder and gave her a look. Mr. Navy Vet gave me my change. I took it and looked at Mr. Army Vet.

"Why did you go into the service?" I asked, truly wondering.

"Well, back then we didn't have a choice—I had to. Guess it turned out all right, though—had a good career." He crossed his arms, rocked back on his heels.

"Wow—you didn't have a choice?"

"Well, it was a different time back then—old-school—"

"Old-school. Kinda like you still want it to be for us . . . *women*?" I smiled, looked into his eyes. "Wouldn't it have been nice for you to have had a *choice* . . . ?" I put the change in my pocket and stood there for a beat.

Mr. Navy Vet's eyebrows went up and he crossed his arms and nodded over at his buddy, throwing his head over his shoulder at me and chuckling. Mr. Army Vet grimaced at his buddy's razzing, and squinted for a grizzled, contemplative beat. Munny had her hand over her mouth, but took it down, revealing a giant smile, held her head higher, and took my arm as she spun on her heels and pranced back out the door. I turned before getting outside.

"Thank you for my dog tags!"

The moment we were out of eyeshot, Munny spun around.

"Holy crap, Popo!" She had her fist in front of her mouth. "That was just . . . *bomb*!" She looked up, enjoying it. "Ha—oh man, his *face*! Epic."

I was looking at my dog tags, rolling them over in my hand. I put them around my neck, and felt the cold metal over my heart, the rubber silencers absorb their clank. *Yesss.* My goal. Declared in metal, protecting my heart.

2

THE ACADEMY

"**M**a'am, I am sorry!"

"WHAAAT?! YOU ARE *SORRY*?! IS THAT PART OF YOUR ALLOTTED VOCABULARY, BASIC?!"

Buffering.

Ahh . . I don't know . . . is it?

"No? . . . Ma'am?"

"THEN WHAT *ARE* YOUR BASIC RESPONSES, BASIC?!"

Shitballs. It was the first time I had ever been called *basic.* In any way. I still didn't know the answer to her question. In fact, I had never not known so many things in my entire life.

The only thing I did know was that I had to give it my all. I knew that if I gave 200 percent all day, every day here at the academy, success would find me. This was the standard I'd set for myself before, and it only made sense that it would carry me through military training and beyond. It was about time I, once again, started to appreciate the power of leaving everything out on the floor. I wrapped up my train of thought, in time for Cadet She-Not-He to go one more round with our eardrums.

"ALL OF YOU BASICS: LISTEN UP!"

The audible chaos stopped.

"FROM NOW ON, YOU ARE NOT ALLOWED TO ANSWER WITH ANYTHING OTHER THAN THESE SEVEN BASIC RESPONSES:

"YES, SIR.

"NO, SIR.

"SIR, I DO NOT KNOW.

"SIR, I DO NOT UNDERSTAND.

"SIR, MAY I ASK A QUESTION?

"SIR, MAY I MAKE A STATEMENT?

"AND FINALLY: NO EXCUSE, SIR.

"YOU MAY NOT USE ANY VARIANCE IN TONE OR INFLECTION WHEN RESPONDING. AND BE SURE YOU KNOW THE DIFFERENCE BETWEEN *SIR* . . . AND *MA'AM*. TRUST US WHEN WE SAY THESE ARE ALL OF THE RESPONSES THAT YOU WILL NEED FOR THE NEXT SIX WEEKS . . . IF YOU EVEN MAKE IT THAT LONG."

Her eyes burned a hole into me as she finished her speech, and like a perfectly timed tag team, her compatriot then jumped into the ring to verbally wrestle us to the ground.

"FAAALLL INNN, BASICS!"

I stopped midbreath like a game of freeze tag.

"ROOMMM, TENNNCH-HUTTT!"

I felt a few classmates make sharp movements like mimes locking themselves into imaginary phone booths. Their muscles locked tightly, perfectly still. The rest of us looked like a bunch of deer in headlights.

"PATHETIC! ABSOLUTELY PATHETIC, BASICS! FROM THIS POINT FORWARD IN YOUR CADET CAREER STOP

EVERYTHING AND SHOOT TO ATTENTION WHEN YOU HEAR THIS COMMAND. NOOOWW, PEOPLE!"

The gaggle of cadre bobbed in and around our novice group shouting commands like DJs at a bar mitzvah guiding us through an aggressive "Chicken Dance."

"STAND TALL!

"TUCK THOSE CHINS!

"ROLL THOSE SHOULDERS UP, BACK, AND DOWN, THEN HOLLLD!"

Cluck, cluck, cluck, cluck . . .

"CLENCH YOUR HANDS INTO FISTS, WITH YOUR THUMBS ALONG THE SEAMS OF YOUR PANTS!

"HEELS TOGETHER, WHILE YOUR TOES FACE OUTWARD AT A FORTY-FIVE-DEGREE ANGLE!"

I turned my head slightly to make sure I was doing everything quickly and correctly, and a very tall upperclassman appeared in my blind spot like an apparition, to correct my form. I swallowed my shriek.

"Well, well, wellll, Basic Cadet *Tate.*"

He made my name sound like an accusation.

"LOOK at that CHIN, just FLAPPIN' IN THE BREEEZE . . . EYES ROAMIN' ALL AROUND, WILLY-NILLY!"

We may have all downloaded this new USAFA "keyboard" into our brains' settings apps, but I had no idea how to translate it yet. I grimaced, anticipating a Mad Hatter ending to what felt like his creepy Alice in Wonderland–style poem.

"TELL YOU WHAT I'M-ONNA DO, *TAAATE!*"

Yikes. His Southern drawl deconstructed my "Chicken Dance" into McNuggets with each drawn-out syllable.

"I'M GONNA TAKE THOSE PRETTY LIL' EEEYES OF YOURS, TATE, AN' I'M 'ONNA LOCK 'EM UP IN CAAAGES AND THROW AWAY THE KEEEY! FROM NOW ON, WHEN YOU STAND AT ATTENTION, YOUR EYES ARE GONNA BE *CAGED*. THAT MEANS LOCKED. STRAIGHT AHEAD AND UNMOVIN'!"

The hairs on the back of my neck started standing at attention one by one.

"YES, SIR!"

I choked out my response and followed Cadet McNugget's orders, feeling instantly trapped. If they wanted us to learn quickly, I wondered why they would take away our observational ability. I needed to quickly figure out a way to peripherally compensate for my lifelong habit of learning by looking.

A chill crept up my spine shooting every follicle on my body to join the ones on the back of my neck already at attention, as if the energy around us had screamed, *ROOOM tench-HUT!* It felt like we were just . . . *wrong*. Everything we did, said, thought was just . . . *wrong*.

I had always been extra sensitive to the vibe of any room, or that which each person emanates. Much of my love for people comes from the curiosity between immediately feeling their magnified emotions, and the challenge in figuring out why they felt that way. Being empathic can be positive when allowing me to read people and connect with them, but the refraction can be unnerving when the vibe is angry or aggressive.

As the cadre hovered over us, the energy swirling around us was total chaos. There was intrigue, fear, aggression, excitement, and anger. The *Top Gun* scenes wherein Maverick and Goose get in trouble started rolling through my head. It was a short reel, and spaced out in perfect Hollywood time, so that each disciplinary action was immediately followed by a chance for redemption and success. I could handle any discomfort or feeling of doing something wrong, as long as I knew that there would be a chance to get it right. As long as I had the chance to prove myself. But that had yet to be confirmed. The trend in this weird new world seemed to be "elimination of all that was familiar." So, along with any preconceived notions we might have had about how to sit, stand, walk, and talk, every bit of our self-confidence quickly began to crumble.

I took shallow breaths while we treaded there, in the choppy waters of the unknown, hoping that at least this initial agitation was temporary. . . .

Basic training had begun in a *big* way.

OUTLIER.

"Congratulations, you guys!"

I eagerly passed out the cards that I had drawn for my basketball teammates the night I signed my letter of intent to USAFA, each one designed with their respective colleges and hobbies.

"Order's up for number twenty-five!"

The White-Hat Hottie behind the counter of our favorite lunchtime Greek deli shouted out our order. None of my teammates flinched. For the first time. Ever. We only had forty minutes for lunch, and they let the call go so they could look at their cards. I stared at BT, head of the White-Hat Hotties and adorable walk-on for the Michigan State University hockey team, shell-shocked for a beat before we accidentally plowed into each other trying to grab and serve our food.

"Ooooop! I finally caught you, Popo."

I was suddenly eye level with his beautiful white picket fence of teeth, surrounded by rugged day-old scruff. The butterflies in my stomach flocked to every place on my body that had run into his.

"Something told me you were up to the challenge." I tried to be chill, er, coy, er . . . God, IDK.

Ugh. Really, Po? I've literally never been easy to catch. I'm nearly six feet of solid muscle. Which—even though the scale had reflected more than my clothing size—still weighed heavily on my mind. I would love for someone to be able to catch me. For the love of God. I'm surprised he didn't bounce off me and go flying to the ground. The fact that he was bigger, stronger, and more solid than I made my heart swoon. I was sure he could see its pounding beat making bigger bulges in my shirt than my boobs!

"Your salad, Mee Lady." BT placed it in front of me, half bowing. "You don't ever want any chicken or something on that salad?"

"Oh, no, no, no—thank you." I recoiled.

I loved animals—so much so that I had become a vegetarian as a small child, and vegan thereafter, as soon as I had made the association between the adorable living, breathing beings among us, and what had been sitting on my plate. The meme of the toddler bawling after finding out that his hamburger came from a cow . . . might as well have been me. It felt so wrong that I've since never even considered consuming meat again.

"Vegan?" BT asked, putting napkins on our table. I nodded. He picked up my wrist, and pointed to the leather cuff I was wearing, sending thrill bumps all over me. "You know that's leather, right?" He smiled, winked.

"I know." I, too, touched the smooth, supple leather. "Sometimes leather makes me feel comforted, protected. Like, at one with nature and the earth. Probably seems, like, bizarrely contradictory . . . but, for some reason . . . it makes total sense to me."

"Well, you're just full of contradictions, aren't you?" He tousled my long brown hair as I nodded.

I *was* full of contradictions. I was both right- and left-handed, a jock and a scholar, a tomboy who modeled, boho on the inside, preppy on the outside, an artist who excelled in math and science, and a vegan who wore leather. I suffered the indescribable loss of my only sister as a child, but maintained an unwavering belief in the fundamental goodness of the universe. I adored people, yet I'd spent much of my life alone. A myriad of contradictions, impossible to fit under one label.

"I mean, I guess just don't eat your bracelet and you're good!" He laughed and looked over at the card in the hand of Spuds, our point guard and five-foot-three replica of NBA anomaly Spud Webb. "Ahh! Another Polo Tate original, I see," BT said, snatching her card.

He leaned back behind the counter and plucked a card wedged between framed, autographed shots of MSU greats Magic Johnson and Bubba Smith.

"Aww, that one's cute, too, Po!" Spuds looked at the card BT took off the wall.

"I figure it's just a matter of time before we'll see her children's books on display at Barnes & Noble." BT thumbed sideways at me. "Eh, Popo?"

He held up the card stock festooned with "T-H-A-N-K Y-O-U" spelled out in bright, hand-drawn, Prisma-colored pieces of baklava, kalamata olives, spanakopita, condiments, and various other menu items. I'd given it to them two months earlier as a thank-you for making our lunchtime so amazeballs. He turned back to the card I'd made for Spuds and leaned up close to it.

"Wait—she's going to University of Michigan??" He mugged. "I'm sorry!" He winked, revealing his white picket fence again for his loyalty to their biggest rival. God, he was cute. Spuds yanked her card out of BT's hand. Still laughing, he retreated back behind the counter to take orders from the line that had started to form.

"What about that, huh, Popo?" Spuds spat. "What about the fact that your art should be out there for the *world* to see . . . ?"

Her tone was a familiar preamble to many of my friends'

broken-record rants that I was crazyballs for attending a military academy instead of one of the more liberal Ivies.

"You guys . . . it's gonna be fine . . ." I stammered.

"Seriously. Po. I mean, what the hell are you thinking going to that place?" Hoffy, our team's power forward, jumped in. "Don't you wanna enjoy college?!"

Our other teamie, the center we called Knobs—because of her knees—shot her arm out in front of Hoffy's body like a soccer-mom seat belt.

"You're picturing yourselves going there, Hoffy and Potato Head. . . ." She then leaned in and rolled her eyes while talking out the side of her mouth to both of them. "I mean . . . look who we're talking to. . . ."

She thumbed in my direction. Unsubtly. *Where is this going?* I shifted in my seat.

"What time did you get up this morning, Popo?!" asked a suddenly chipper Knobs.

"Um . . . at five forty-four . . ." I said hesitantly.

"So you could go to the gym before school?" Knobs.

"Mmmaybe." It was my turn to speak out of the side of my mouth.

"For your own self-imposed basic training?" Spuds.

"I just want to be ready—"

"Ha! See?!" Knobs pointed at me, then Hoffy and Spuds.

The exchange was like a verbal Milk-Bone lobbed into a pack of puppies. Their words got louder and faster as they jumped and landed all over one another to make their collective point.

"Mm-hmm, predawn workouts—"

"Then our team practice after school—"

"OMG, giiirl!"

"Wait . . . is tonight National Honor Society, too?"

"Or are you struttin' yo asss down the catwalk tonight?!"

"Ha. Ha. Suuuperfunny, guys. I'm no stranger to sarcasm," I deadpanned.

"Yeah! Which one is it, Angelina, modeling or saving the world?"

OMG. "Ha. Ha. Hardly." I shook my head.

But they persisted.

"It's a good thing you're nocturnal, Batgirl, otherwise how would you keep your grades?"

"Or be voted Most Likely to Succeed?"

"Holy four-point-oh, Batman!"

"Yeah right, you guys!" I half stood, hunching with embarrassment, trying to tamp down their voices with my outstretched hands.

"Most Popular Girl!"

"Most Loved by Teachers!"

"Shhhh! That's . . . not even true!" I whispered, hoping they would get the hint.

"Oh, it is sooo true, girl!"

The other patrons had stopped talking and were now staring at our table.

"OhmyGod. We're *so* gonna get kicked outta here. . . ." I muttered futilely as I crept toward the restroom. BT yelled from the register.

"Polo Pile-On?! Hells yes!"

His fist pump was quickly interrupted by a woman two tables over.

"Hey!"

Her booming voice put my chortling teammates to audible shame. The entire restaurant fell silent. I had to clear my throat to coax my voice out of hiding.

"I'm so sorry, ma'am, we will be quieter."

A beat.

"Weren't you just on the news? Player of the Week, Channel Six?!" A beat. "Yeah! That's you—congratulations!"

I closed my slack jaw. I nodded and smiled graciously, truly touched. I thanked her, put my hand to my heart, and as I shook my head, my gaze was intercepted by three shit-eating grins plastered across the faces of my teamies.

"Yeaaah, Pile-On Polooo!" BT yelled and raised his Styrofoam cup in a toast while everyone broke into applause. Naturally, our table got in my face to rub it in. They obnoxiously high-fived, hollered, pounded fists, and smacked my ass repeatedly.

My embarrassment made me want to run, but the generosity of everyone's spirit made me tingly. I was still blown away by my teammates actually looking at and liking their cards, let alone . . . everything else. The entire lunch sent my appreciation to the next level. I hadn't eaten a bite of salad, but it felt like I had swallowed a box of sparklers. I blew kisses to the White-Hat Hotties on our way out the door, and BT jumped the counter.

"Congratulations, beautiful." He pinched my blushing cheek and handed me a white paper bag full of Greek cookies and baklava. All I could do was smile as I looked into his sweet baby blues. God, he was cute.

My teamies made me swear on a basketball that I would at least keep doing artwork if I had to go to *that place.* I took their oath. Everyone grabbed for pistachio cookies while my synapses fired away. *What is it going to be like at USAFA, a place I've been dreaming of attending since I was little?* I had been a total weirdo for so long that the thought of jumping into a crowd of people more like me was enough to make my head explode.

What will it feel like to be in the majority for the first time ever?

3

THE ACADEMY

Moving between the bus and USAFA base exchange, we learned how to march to the cadre's guttural cadence call. There was something so primal—a camaraderie so visceral—inspired by their rhythmic guidance. Like a tribal call to arms. The driving rhythm started pulling our disparate crowd together. In front of me was a broad-shouldered, skinny Wiffle ball of a boy wearing a Notre Dame shirt. I had the same shirt, though I knew not to wear it on the first day of starting a rival university. To my left, there was a boy wearing a gold chain, Michael Jordan basketball jersey, shorts that sagged below his waistline, and an angled baseball cap that barely hid his red-cheeked and snarled attempt at bravado. Allegedly, USAFA was 11 percent female, but the girl to my immediate right was the only other female I had seen thus far in the sea of new cadets surrounding me. She wore a tank top, Daisy Dukes, cowboy boots, and a cowboy hat that shaded her peaches-'n'-cream face from the summer sun. Within the first five minutes of "instruction," the cadre moved right past Notre Dame Boy, and spanked both Basic Daisy's and Basic Bull's hats off their respective heads with such force that they UFO'd their way to the middle of the terrazzo. We all watched openmouthed and wide-eyed, while the beat thumped on, and we strove to answer the call toward cooperative competence. We were in our infantry infancy, but we were definitely becoming part of something much bigger than ourselves.

Being part of a large group of synchronous soldiers felt powerful. My skin buzzed as the collective current of kinetic energy grew in size and speed.

Soon, we had remastered the art of walking and looked as if we were playing a game of human centipede. An upperclassman with a blinding array of silver on his uniform swooped down on me to correct my form. Following his booming earthquake of a voice came a tsunami of saliva that drenched my neck and shoulder. *Eww.*

"GET YOUR CHIN INNN, BASIC!"

He whipped out a credit card from his wallet and shoved the hard plastic under my chin like the blade of a guillotine.

"MY CREDIT CARD SHOULD STAY IN BETWEEN YOUR DOUBLE AND TRIPLE CHINS, BASIC!"

Double . . . TRIPLE chins?! My mother had reminded me how to minimize the appearance of such a horrific feature my entire life. I was pretty sure that he had just called my neck fat, but I was too confused to be offended. So I did the only acceptable thing: I smashed my *multiple* chins together like an accordion, then jammed everything against the back of my spine. I answered Sir Spits-a-Lot as best I could through my flattened airway.

"Yes, sir!"

I sounded like a flight attendant making a nasally announcement over a plane's PA system.

"WE TUCK IN OUR CHINS, BASIC, BECAUSE IF YOU NEED TO EJECT FROM YOUR AIRCRAFT AND YOU DO *NOT* TUCK IN YOUR CHIN, YOUR HEAD WILL SURE AS SHIT *SNAP* OFF

OF YOUR BODY! YOU WILL *DIE* IF YOU DO NOT TUCK YOUR CHIN IN, BASIC! DO YOU UN-DER-STAND?!"

"Yes, sir!"

I scanned my mental inventory of *Top Gun* and every other military movie for an example of soldiers tucking in their chins. I could not think of a single one. I had never seen it, most likely because no A-list actor or his A-list agent would want an accordion of chins under his firmly squared, bankable jaw. I sympathized while I fought the urge to massage my *fat* neck.

The cadre granted us permission to be "at rest" (free to move without marching or falling in at attention—provided that we adhered to verbal etiquette) throughout our next inprocessing errand. I breathed a sigh of relief. I let my eyes out of their cages, unglued my chin from the back of my spine, and rubbed my décolletage. I still felt the three-inch credit card imprint on my skin.

A finger poked my shoulder blade.

"Let us move it, Tate."

The required robotic, contraction-free speech pattern made the upperclassman behind me sound like a Transformer toy. I felt his hand again, so I responded.

"Yes, sir."

He nudged me toward the back of a short line of somber girls next to a long line of rambunctious boys. The spacey tingle of premonition crept around the base of my skull. I turned around to find Cadet Optimus Prime winking at me above a sly grin. My heart sank.

Haircut.

I had known this moment would come. Ninety-five percent of me had been looking forward to the transformation, but I had not expected to feel so crushed by the objecting five percent. I had spent the last several years trying to grow out my short hairdo, trying to live down my ridiculous tomboy moniker. It had taken me a long time to do both. The obstinate five percent of me was afraid that the little girl who had disappointed her daddy by being mistaken for a boy would reemerge at the end of this line. I shook my head from side to side, surprised by the regression of my psyche.

Suck it up, Popo. . . .

The closer I inched toward the front of the line, the more fuzzy tennis-ball heads I saw emerge from beyond the partition of the make-shift barbershop. Those who had chosen to get their hair cut short before arriving at the academy seemed to have suffered only a slight trim.

Maybe I should have done that, too . . . but then again, nope. I needed to experience this moment for my own complete transfor-mation into Soldier Girl. The life that I had chosen required a substan-tial commitment. I was willing to commit. And I truly believed that there could be no subtle transition into the life I was about to lead.

I stepped up to the door like a soldier reporting for duty. *Er . . .* perhaps more like a teenage girl reluctantly choosing duty over van-ity. Over identity.

It was a start. *Bring it on.*

Once I was inside, a woman with a poorly dyed bouffant hairdo impatiently waved me into her empty barber's chair. Her colleague—sporting a beehive hairdo—was already in the middle of cutting another girl's hair. Neither woman paused or looked up at me as I filled the open seat.

"Hand me my cape, wouldja . . . ?" Ms. Bouffant asked.

Ms. Beehive grabbed a black plastic cape with her scissor hand and whipped it over at Ms. Bouffant, who snapped it a little too tightly around my neck. Before I could speak up, she had gathered my long hair into a ponytail at the base of my skull and lopped it off. She just . . . *lopped it off* without thinking, flinching, warning, waiting, or even pausing in her conversation with Ms. Beehive. Thirteen inches of my life. Lopped off.

The air flew from my lungs like wind from a punctured balloon. I felt light-headed. Literally. Ms. Bouffant didn't skip a beat.

"Oh my *God*, you would *not* believe who I saw at Citadel Mall yesterday!"

Snip.

"Uh-huh, that's right! Can you believe he had the nerve to show his face?"

Snip, snip. Ms. Beehive never answered Ms. Bouffant. She was either mute, or was actually concentrating on the hair that she was cutting. *God . . . Did I get into the wrong chair . . . ?* My heart started to race. My identity was cascading to the floor in huge chunks. There was no mirror in sight, so all I had to measure the devastation was the time it took . . . and it took a *long* time. Ms. Bouffant didn't seem like the type to take a long time to do anything, but she was sure as shit taking a long time to cut my hair.

"There you go, sweetie pie," said Ms. Beehive, breaking her silence. She took her girl's cape as if she was expecting a tip. The cadet simply stood and walked, shell-shocked, from Ms. Beehive's chair to the tiny mirror in the corner of the room. She began to sob—softly at first—plummeting quickly into a full-out ugly cry. She fell to her knees, her face crumpled. She threw her hands upward in apocalyptic fury. My eyes widened as I watched silently.

Dear. Snip. God. Snip. Panic. Snip. Panic. Panic. Panic. What am I doing here?

Ms. Bouffant's shears finally stopped their staccato beat. Before she could even take off the plastic sheath, my hands were running fiendishly through my hair. I didn't have any. She pulled at the cape.

I hung on to what was left of my hair for fear that her shears might find their way back to my fuzzy skull. She yanked and we ended up tangled in a tug-of-war of plastic/arms/head/plastic until she literally whipped me out of the chair. I spun and tumbled all the way over to join Basic Ugly Cry in the corner. I looked into the mirror.

It was a drastic change. A solitary tear escaped its duct and inched its way down my right cheek, but I promptly smeared its campaign. There would be no pity party. This was the beginning of a new challenge . . . a new me. This half a moment was all the time I would give myself to mourn the loss of something that didn't define the whole of me. It wasn't my entire identity, and I knew it. Half a moment. It was all I'd give.

I dragged my short hair, my huge bag, and my transformed self toward an older civilian gentleman at the last station.

"Looks like you may need a hand with that thing, *missy!*"

"No, sir, but thank you, sir!" I smiled, still feeling a bit clunky with the *sirs*. The five-year-old inside of me sighed with relief that he had addressed me—with my plushy head—as female . . . no matter how condescendingly. I picked up my bag and threw it over my shoulder to prove I wasn't a weakling . . . in case this, too, was a test. It spun me one and a half times around so that Mr. Missy's next comment was directed at the back of my head.

"Welp, here ya go!"

Mr. Missy pulled three sets of camouflage battle dress uniforms (BDUs) up from under the countertop and slid them over to me. I stared at the bundle of clothing like a bundle of gold bricks. A chill shot up my spine. I was being issued new skin.

In this skin, I can get as dirty and as sweaty as I want. In this skin, I can work and play as hard as I want. In this skin, I will not be judged for wanting to run outside and play in the dirt with the boys. In this skin, I will not have to worry about what I look like. In this skin, I will not be called a tomboy. In this skin, I will only be encouraged to give 200 percent, to leave it all out on the floor.

I opened the top of my Santa sack and laid the BDUs neatly on top of my new shirts, pants, sweat suits, boots, shoes, hats, gloves, underwear, socks, deodorant, shoe polish, and other unidentifiable miscellany, the purpose of which I had absolutely no idea. I smiled. I felt as if I were Tiny Tim taking a huge gulp of steaming hot chocolate, following its heated trail down to my stomach, then deep into my soul. My physical transformation into a soldier was nearly complete.

God bless us . . . every one.

By the time we arrived at the dormitory barracks, the majority of the incoming class had been divvied out among Lego-like buildings along the terrazzo. USAFA's cadet wing, mirroring an active air force wing, included 4,417 cadets broken down into forty squadrons, each one numbered and labeled with a corresponding mascot. Ten squadrons formed a *group.* For basic cadet training purposes, however, each squadron was broken down further into a series of *flights*—the smallest organizational unit—and named with letters of the alphabet. Those of us in Demons E-Flight eventually found ourselves standing in front of our new home, Vandenberg Hall.

"DEMONNNS, FORWAAARD HAULT!"

Our flight leader's command stopped us from marching straight into the building. I recognized the dorm from my recruiting trip.

"LISTEN UP, BASICS! THIS IS VANDENBERG HALL."

Nearly every building and landmark on academy grounds was named after a fallen hero or hallowed soldier. Much like Vandenberg Hall, which was the first of two cadet barracks on campus. It housed squadrons one through twenty, whereas Sijan Hall—on the opposite side of the cadet inner sanctum—housed squadrons twenty-one through forty. Each squadron had a name and mascot attached to its number. For instance, the wing's first squadron, Mighty Mach One, was known for being *stract* (soldier who keeps the most fastidious uniform and strictest military decorum) and keeping their number one ranking in all things military matched with their position in the wing. Unsure of our school-year housing, we had stopped at the stairwell leading up to the Tough Twenty Trolls of squadron twenty for the summer.

I snuck a peek at the vertical line of windows above my head as we walked into the building. They'd all been painted to look like the colorful squadron patches adorning the upperclassmen's jackets. Accessories. Exactly what my parents had overtly hinted to be the "appropriate" amount of collegiate creativity: a morsel to feed my inner artist, but, dare I try to make it my whole life's meal, they feared I would become another starving artist on the street. The swirled brushstrokes on the glass curled up the corners of my mouth. *Did cadets paint these? Could I paint these . . . and more?* I'd need at least one artistic outlet to fully thrive here—after all, I had promised my high school teammates.

"BASIC CADET TATE! YOU AND SMALLTOWN ARE IN THERE!"

Once we landed on our floor, our flight leader pointed to an open door down the hall.

CHILDHOOD.

"Shhh!" A beat. "Maybe he's going down the hall. . . ."

My older sister, Sary, whispered past the finger she held pressed up to her little mouth, and covered mine with her other hand. We held in our giggles until my father's wedding ring stopped dinging against the brass banister as he made his way to the second floor of our white Dutch Colonial. My sister and I were hiding inside an epic fort we had built out of chairs, bedsheets, and pillows in the guest bedroom. It had grass-green carpeting, which was perfect to "feed" our vast collection of Breyer horses. We held our breath until his footsteps passed us by.

"Okay, Rhoda and Guy are in the ring warming up so we can jump. All the others are out in the field eating." She pulled up the bed skirt behind her. "Well, Hickey and Dough are in the stables . . . like, duh."

"Ha—yeah. Like, duuuh." I rolled my eyes, too, but had no clue why.

She dropped the skirt and pointed to the Appaloosa and palomino inside a ring of Popsicle-stick fences I had glued together the day before. The rest of the floor inside our fort was wall-to-wall horses feeding in the pasture. If we moved a muscle, they would all fall like dominos.

"You're riding English on Rhoda, Popo. Remember to post up when you're trotting so it's easier when you start to canter. . . ."

She galloped Rhoda—hind legs to front—around in the ring.

"Last time you jumped, you landed in front of the saddle one time—"

I rubbed my right butt cheek with the memory and protested.

"But! My foot came out of the stirru—"

"Shh. Listen, Popo, so you can get even better than you are right now."

I shut my mouth and let her use the model horses to coach me. She had been coaching me in the game of life since I was an infant. Among many other profoundly important lessons, I'd learned what raw passion meant through my sister's love for horses. She knew and adored everything there was to know about them. About a lot of things. She was an avid reader, even at ten. I didn't have the academic breadth that Sary had yet, but I had a physical intelligence that allowed me to keep up with much bigger kids. She saw that, and rounded out the rest of me with anything and everything she could impart. She had knowledge way beyond her ten years, and seemed to perpetually be three years and a lifetime beyond me.

"Sary? Popo?" my mom called from outside the door. We screamed, startled, having been so deep into our lesson.

"Can we come in?" My dad was with her, already opening the door. We froze, wide-eyed and giggly as their feet crested the bottom of the striped cotton 550-thread-count wall. The fort's perimeter was breached by a giant arm, like a dragon, reaching for anything human.

"Ahh! Daddyyy!" I squirmed just out of his reach.

"Roooarrr!" His deep voice came like a thunderclap, making us scream again. My sister threw herself like a shield over me as his hand grabbed her leg and pulled her out.

"The horses! Daddy!" Sary warned.

Two dragon hands came for me next, pulling me out upside down. I squealed and dropped from his chest-high talons into a perfectly executed back walkover. Sary climbed onto my dad's feet, arms around his waist, and he walked her over to the bed. They were two peas in a pod. Shaped the same, introverted in the same way, same inflections and sensibilities. I ran, jumped up, and belly flopped to join them. My mom joined us on the bed, holding a picture that Sary had drawn entitled *Home*.

Sary was a prodigious artist as well, and it was expertly drawn. Our house stood front and center, like a novice architect's rendering. Inside, my parents could be seen in the dining room eating dinner. Sary and I—clearly having been excused from the table early—held hands and played upstairs in our bedroom. She held on to a bridled horse with her free hand, while I held on to a soccer ball. It was detailed, colorful, perfect.

"That's my favorite soccer ball! Look, Lommy!" I poked my mom's knee and pointed to the perfectly drawn Adidas Italia red, white, and green pentagons within. I had tongue-twisted calling my mom "Lommy" the year before and Sary started doing it, too, so it stuck.

My mom enveloped me with her arm, tousled my hair. My dad held my sister on his lap while she took us through her drawing's every detail. We sat there, a family. The sum of which was much greater than our four individual parts. Detailed, colorful, perfect. The last and truest sense of home I would feel.

4

THE ACADEMY

"**G**O, LITTLE GIRLS!"

Our flight leader's voice snapped me to attention, ordering me to follow his finger down the hall. There were only five female basics out of about forty basics in our squadron; however, engendered insults were ubiquitous. Today alone, some cadre members thought every basic had "run like a girl," had "huge-ass hips like a girl," sounded off like "Sallies," "cried like a chick," and "been a pussy like you'd gotten your period" at one point or another. Apparently doing something "like a girl" was bad enough to insult both males and females. However, something told me severely outdated insults were not going to be the most offensive thing we'd experience today. So I let it motivate me to do things better and quicker, and shelved the rest of the implications for later.

I stepped out from the line, bag in hand, and turned a sharp ninety degrees to march behind Basic Cadet Smalltown. She was way shorter than I, so my caged eyes landed squarely on top of her head. I had a bird's-eye view of her bobbing bangs surrounded by the vestiges of a small-town haircut and frosted highlights. My brain moved her small town to the Midwest the moment she spoke.

We both ducked into our room and out of the cadre's line of sight as quickly as we could. She toppled over her bulging standard-issue laundry bag, which had to be more than half her body weight. She went down. Hard. But bounced up just as quickly, embarrassed and avoiding eye contact. I laughed. She narrowed her amber irises at me.

"Hee-hee—Oh, no! Sorry, I wasn't laughing at you, I just thought for sure *I* would bite it first!"

I cleared my throat, devolving my giggle into nervous laughter as I lowered my head. I would never intentionally try to make someone feel bad. *Ever.* After a few seconds, she disengaged her tiger-eyed laser beams and we both took a deep breath and a look around our new room.

Like everything else on campus, the room was rectangular and fastidiously maintained. Aside from the fact that you could eat off every single surface, it sort of resembled a typical college dorm room, minus the ubiquitous weed-centric blacklight poster—probably a felony here. The white walls met dark blue thin-pile industrial carpeting. There were dark wood built-in wardrobes on either side of the door. On opposite sides of the room stood matching "bed units" consisting of a desk, a computer cubby, and a series of shelves set below a lofted mattress. The wall opposite the door was made of two large rectangular windows five stories up from a rectangular quad below. Two identical chairs straddled a cube-shaped bookshelf/end table below each window. There was a built-in sink under a three-sectioned mirror that could hardly be described as a vanity.

Every fabric was the same deep shade of blue, every piece of wood stained with the same dark varnish. The effect was austere, firm, metric—but quite soothing to me.

I looked down at my new roommate, who was sitting on her heels next to her Santa sack. With her round cheeks, short, pear-shaped frame, and frosted bowl haircut, she totally looked like a snow-topped elf making toys in Santa's workshop. She pulled out the *Basic Cadet Handbook* for instructions on how to put our room together, which completed the adorable-IKEA-elf-prepping-for-the-Christmas-rush vibe.

I promptly followed suit by dumping my bag out onto the floor alongside hers. Neither of us realized how much we had been issued until it was sitting in two giant heaps in the middle of our room. I wanted to dive into it like a puppy in a sea of gifts under the tree.

Smalltown placed the handbook between us, open to a page of instructive hieroglyphics. She was already folding her underwear into a square smaller than a sixth-grade school note. I picked up a pair of enormous, white, industrial-strength underwear issued to me. *My God.* They were huge; not what I was used to. I was a volleyball player, after all. My very first high school team had practically handed out thongs on day one of practice, so we didn't embarrass ourselves in front of the crowd—VPLs were unacceptable in our sport. It was the women's volleyball culture. Each sport had one. Of all the sports for which I had been recruited to play—basketball, volleyball, and soccer—the volleyball teams at the colleges on my recruiting trips had resonated most with my desire to both wear a bow in my hair, be as feminine as I want to be, *and* kick some ass on the court. Femininity and athleticism were no longer oxymoronic or mutually exclusive. The thick white tablecloth I held in my hands could've easily passed as our away-game uniform.

When I showed Smalltown the tighty-whitey origami swan I had folded, she broke into laughter for the first time. *Finally.* The cool flash of her eyes a few minutes earlier had made me fear that we were in for a long year. I laughed, too, and stuck out my hand.

"How do you do? My name is Polo."

"Oh, hey—yeah, no, call me Gabby—everybody does—I like to talk."

It felt good to hear our first names. Warm and human. She shook my outstretched hand.

A booming voice shattered the moment. "YOU HAVE NINETY SECONDS TO STRIP OFF AND SURRENDER ALL OF YOUR CIVILIAN CONTRABAND. DRESS YOURSELVES IN THE PROPER UNIFORM AND GET YOUR LAZY ASSES OUT INTO THE HALLWAY! GET TO IT, BASICS, NOOOW!"

I threw a look over to Gabby. She was grabbing two white-and-navy USAFA ringer T-shirts off the floor, along with two pairs of rumpled camo pants. The clothes on our backs had officially become civilian contraband, as well as everything we'd carried onto campus. We had to surrender all of it for our entire first year, presumably so that we could assimilate into a cohesive group and so that we could come to appreciate life's luxuries much more. I watched Gabby dig through her pile.

"I'm a preppy," she said when she noticed my gaze.

Oh . . . Is this something we're doing? I couldn't even begin to codify my own social circle. She clarified.

"I went to USAFA Prep School—I didn't get in here on my first try, so they sent me there for a year. . . ."

"Ohhh, okay, cool . . ."

She smiled and it made me want to stoke her embers into a full-blown belly laugh just to warm up the room a bit more.

"Here, put this on," she said, chucking a wad of clothing at me.

"Sweet! Thank you!"

Ninety seconds did not allow for modesty of any kind. Nor did it give me time to mourn the last glimpse of the supercute outfit I wore here for the next . . . who knew how long.

Gabby was almost fully dressed already and hastily trying to shove her watch into a rolled-up pair of socks. The watch was beeping and ticking and putting up a fight. Taking her cue, I considered the personal items that I wanted to keep with me. Gabby went practical with her illegal article that kept time; I went sentimental with items that were home to me. *Home* hadn't been a literal dwelling for me since the age of seven. It had become amorphous in the blink of an eye; a memory, a smell, a feeling deep within, a certain quality in another person, a child's drawing. To survive this six-week journey into the unknown, I figured I would need perseverance, clarity, and items to protect my open heart: the dog tags that I had had made when I was eleven, my perfumed body lotion, a Swiss Army knife engraved with initials SBT, a few carefully selected pairs of thong underwear, and one last very personal item. I hoped that these weren't really considered contraband, since I wasn't much of a rule breaker—but they were definitely things I did not want others to see . . . so I stuffed them all into a large tampon box from the issue warehouse. Gabby looked over at me, smiling.

"Whatever gets us through, right?"

"Hells yes." I winked back.

"Zip up your bag and put it by the door," she said, "cuz they're gonna collect our civvies and contraband soon. And here—I think we have to put these on."

She flung a set of elastic-and-metal thingamabobs over to me that looked like some sort of BDSM device. *Wowza . . . Where do I even put these on my body?*

I watched as Gabby clipped one end of her set to one cuff of her T-shirt and threaded it through to the other side, attaching it like the string we used to hold our mittens in place in kindergarten. Even in my cluelessness, that didn't seem right.

"Umm, are you sure—?"

Gabby's elastic thingy got caught on her belt loop, then flung free and whacked me in the face midsentence. She froze, wide-eyed, until I spoke through the hand over my face.

"Soooo . . . *that* happened."

A sizable welt started forming underneath my eye, but we were laughing way too hard to care. The welt, our folly, stood out even more hysterically from the seriousness of what we were beginning. I held my eye while Gabby held her stomach and belly laughed.

Totally worth it.

"YOU HAVE GOT FIVE SECONDS TO GET YOUR BUTTS OUT HERE, BASICS! FIVE SECONDS!"

Shit. Shit. Shiiit!

I turned in circles trying to stuff the rest of my civilian belongings into my civilian bag. My uniform pants were still unbuttoned, my shirt still untucked, and I had no idea how to assemble anything else. Gabby had missed three belt loops with her navy-blue uniform belt. I didn't even know there *was* a belt to our uniform. Her shirt was untucked as well, and she had only one sock and one boot on.

OMG! We are so dead.

"ALL RIGHT, BASICS! OUT IN THE HALLWAY NOW! NOW! NOWWW! WHAT IS TAKING YOU SO LONG?!"

Gabby was bent over, pawing at the pile of clothes between her legs, like a dog covering its poop.

"Where is my boot?" she wailed.

"I got it! I got it! Where is *my* belt?!"

"Ooo! There's a belt right there!"

"IF I DON'T SEE SOME BASIC *BUTTS* OUT HERE THIS SECOND, THERE ARE GOING TO BE *SEVERE* CONSEQUENCES!!"

"Shiiit!"

This time we said it in unison. I was bent over, putting Gabby's sock on her foot and tying her shoe. She was bent over me, shoving my belt through my belt loops and fastening it together. Both of us were so scared of the austere baritone in the hallway that all we could do was collapse into a crippling gigglefest that eroded our already pathetic motor skills and made us drool while trying desperately not to pee our pants.

"TATE AND SMALLTOWN, WHERE THE HELL ARE YOU LITTLE GODDAMN GIRLS?!"

That sobered us up instantly. We hopped to our feet and rushed into the hallway. Our classmates (forty of us now, but we were told we would probably lose ten before the end of the first semester) were flung up against one wall, and we immediately packed ourselves in tightly next to them. I peeked at everyone else's equally pathetic attempts at assembling their uniforms. Shirts were hanging out of pants and poking through unbuttoned flies. Boots were untied and on bare feet, or hanging limply at sides. There were belts. There were no belts. Boys and girls had on different-colored pants. It was ridiculous.

About fifteen cadre members let us know how ridiculous it was. They let us know at the top of their lungs.

"PATHETIC!"

"WORTHLESSSSSSSS!"

"YOU NOW HAVE THIRTY SECONDS TO GET IT RIGHT, FOR GOD'S SAKE. GO NOW, GO!"

Everybody scattered. Gabby and I returned to the scene of our fashion crime, but this time, there was no laughing. We tucked in what was untucked, we stuffed in what was unstuffed, and we pinned together what was unpinned. Gabby put her hand on my shoulder.

"Dear God, I hope we have it right this time."

I high-fived her.

At the door, I looked at my civilian bag, stuffed full and closed. I knew it was ridiculous, but I felt vulnerable without my civilian armor. I sniffed the perfumed lotion on my wrist. I inhaled what remained of my civilian identity.

Gabby looked at me. "Ready? Let's do this."

We braved the dark blue hallway as if we were jumping into the Arctic Ocean. The cadre were just as displeased with our second attempt but, fortunately, scheduling took precedence, and we were swept off to dinner.

Meals were served in Mitchell Hall, an enormous, open building that could accommodate over 4,400 cadets, officers, visitors, and dignitaries three times a day, seven days a week.

For those of us in basic, meals were glorified training sessions with an edible garnish . . . or so we felt, since we could rarely ever *taste* the food. I looked upon dinner as an exercise in letting my hunger go. Hunger was really just a state of mind . . . right?

All kidding aside, I had actually spent the majority of my life teaching, molding, and rewiring my brain and body to squelch their organic responses and replace them with a default of my choosing; something more efficient, unemotional. The trick was to bypass tears, fear, and pain. I never asked myself, *How do I feel?* but rather, *How should I feel? What feeling might serve me best in accomplishing what I desire in the long or short term?* Hunger was precisely the type of innate response that I had worked hard to short-circuit.

I close my eyes without closing my eyes. I plug my ears without plugging my ears. I retreat without retreating. I take my hunger and

I ball it up in my hands like the unwanted rough draft of a letter. I crumple it. I throw it away from me. I crumple it and throw it away. It is outside of me now, and I feel better.

I opened my eyes, unplugged my ears, and resurfaced from the depths. Some food had finally reached the highest-ranking cadet at the opposite end of the table through the proper channels. We basics were finally granted permission to eat exactly *two bites of food*. We were allowed to chew each bite exactly seven times before swallowing. That way, if we ever found ourselves at a meal with high-ranking officers or dignitaries and they asked us a question, we would be able to respond quickly. Having been raised by Emily Post's biggest fans, I was used to etiquette as justification. I actually felt fortunate to have gotten the two bites that I did: two glorious mouthfuls of salty, cooked—though cold—canned green beans.

At that moment, I started training myself to treat knowledge as my sustainable fuel, anticipating that this would be my primary form of nourishment for the foreseeable future. By the time we left Mitchell Hall and returned to our squadron, most of us were deaf, tired, deconstructed, still hungry, and not happy about it.

Back in our room, Gabby took off her shoes, stuck a piece of contraband gum in her mouth, and climbed under her covers to get some shut-eye. Fully clothed. Five minutes later, there was a stringy glob of drool oozing from the corner of her mouth onto her pillow. Her ability to give in to basic needs instantly amazed me. Gabby was tired; therefore, she went to sleep. Uncomplicated. No overthinking. Simple cause and effect.

I, on the other hand, executed a version of my nightly routine, albeit abbreviated. Instead of 515 stomach crunches, I only did 232. I washed my face, brushed my teeth, and analyzed each scenario of the day to note what I could improve upon tomorrow. I ran through the growing list of things for which I felt appreciation. And only then did I finally allow my cheek to hit the pillow.

The softness against my head was a comforting contrast to the hardness inside of it. I was hungry and tired, yes, but that feeling of incompletion and need was not new. Part of being an overachieving perfectionist was making sure that I was in shape physically as well as academically and athletically. I had always been athletic, so my clothes and style had been more of a concern to me than the size of my body. Until our first volleyball game my freshman year.

We got new uniforms: bun huggers. Which are basically bikini bathing suit bottoms. It threw me. I was expected to stand up off the bench in front of my entire school, and our entire crowd, in . . . bathing suit bottoms. I had not had to wear them yet, and having that first time be also at the time of profound change while entering high school, new and wanting to make a good impression socially, it threw me. Starting then, my disciplined schedule included a calorie cutback. Until the weight loss started to affect my vertical jump and stamina. I came back up to a healthier weight, but it set up camp in the back of my mind. Just as it had in every one of my teammates'. And most of the young women in our high school. The pressure to adhere to the classical standards of beauty was palpable, whether you had a skimpy uniform to wear or not.

So I had known that feeling of hunger—both physically and metaphorically—intimately. I had always been faintly afraid that if it receded, a part of me would be unsettled by its absence. Sometimes that feeling was my only friend. As if a little bit of struggle were some-how honorable. That didn't seem completely kosher. But it was where I was. And I couldn't get where I wanted to go, unless I knew where I was . . . or something like that. *Enough analysis for the first day.*

I am hungry. I am tired. And, therefore, I am with old friends. Enough.

I was excited as well. I had left it all out on the floor today.

As a reward, I let my mind wander over to its softer, sweeter side. After one day of being stripped of nearly everything familiar, I had become Hollywood's stereotypical soldier on a cot, thinking of their great love back home. Such a cliché. But it was so true . . . my memory, my imagination had become tonight's most decadent dessert.

I am here. He is not. So I think of him.

I inhaled deeply and I thought of him. Booker. He was my brain's screen saver. I thought about his smell. I thought about burrowing my nose and lips into the nape of his neck, breathing in and out, and in and out. I thought about the tiny droplets of condensation my breath would create, how the scent of his cologne would come away on my nose and lips. I breathed deeply and tried to inhale him once again from memory. In and out. In and out. I thought of his hands, strong and heavy, light and soft and big. I felt the butterfly in my stomach move south. It fluttered. I exhaled.

I thought of him. I breathed him in and out. I thought of him and I was gone.

5

THE ACADEMY

I came up hard and fast to the surface of morning as if I'd just yanked the emergency-inflate rip cord on a life jacket while free diving deep in the ocean. Heavy fists were pounding swiftly against our door. I shot out of bed and landed on the other side of the room as a deafening bugle riffed at lightning speed over the PA system. Guns N' Roses' "Welcome to the Jungle" started blaring through the hallway. Gabby was dead to the world.

I scurried over and shook her shoulder gently. "Hey, buddy, we gotta get up—like *now*."

No sign of life.

"Hey, babe—they aren't kidding—we have like thirty-five seconds to be out in the hallway with our clothes on."

Movement. "Huh? Oh. Right. Right. I'm coming."

Yikes on bikes. She was totally unfazed by the lunatic cacophony surrounding her. I had never been one to oversleep, but even a deep REM cycle hadn't stopped me from shooting out of bed as if I'd been fired from a slingshot.

We somehow got ourselves together, exited the room, squared a sharp turn to our right, and followed the cadre out the door, down the stairs, and onto the terrazzo. It was still dark. The sky was the deep royal blue of a racquetball. Near the horizon, a layer of green hinted at the impending sunrise.

By the time we finished a grueling squadron run following the power lines up and down the foothills of the Rocky Mountains, the sun had woken up. Our cadre allowed us to catch our breath on the terrazzo. They rewarded us with two full minutes "at ease," free to look around silent but unencumbered, to witness Colorado Springs in its full glory. Like the first sleepover in a relationship, the mountains awoke blushing. We peeked under the covers at their raw and rosy vulnerability splayed against a spectrum of color from the rising sun's rays. Our chests rose and fell as we caught our breath. Our glistening faces couldn't help but show naked emotion to the grandeur before us. It was more revitalizing than an orgasm. It was a *soulgasm*. Right there on the terrazzo.

We changed uniforms quickly, followed the cadre's orders, and performed an endless, grueling series of tasks all day long: two loud and hangry meals, long and tedious marching practice, massive amounts of academy and military knowledge to learn, cleaning and shining our rooms, folding and pinning our uniforms, followed by more physical training, shortened—only in name—to "PT." After dinner, we were actually granted a choice of activities. I chose to go to chapel. The upperclassmen that I had met on my volleyball recruiting trip had told me to *always* attend church during basic training if given the opportunity, because it was the only place to experience a few minutes of uninterrupted peaceful relaxation . . . while *sitting*.

A small group of Screamin' Demons headed out across the terrazzo, and I followed. Stark-white, pebbled tile bordered by smooth, alabaster marble strips formed a wide, rectangular border around the massive grassy field that separated the two cadet dormitories. Basic and freshmen cadets were required to run along the narrow strips at all times. Running the strips behind three of my classmates felt like running on a balance beam. We sprinted along the perimeter in boxy patterns, hoping that we would not pass any upperclassmen who would decide to stop and train us before we reached our sanctuary.

The famed USAFA chapel grew in size as we neared it. I was eager to sit down and revel in the quiet. The sun was beginning to set. For the second time that day, I was bowled over by the breathtaking surrounding grandeur. The mountains blushed a fiery, deep shade of red, as if they, too, had been through a hellish day.

We stepped over the line marking the chapel grounds and were finally at ease; allowed to slow to a walk. I took my eyes out of their cages, swiveled my head far left and far right without fear of punishment. It felt good. I looked up at the sky, where the starlight was unfettered by city lights. There was no pollution, no smog, no man-made interference. The canopy of constellations in the clear night sky had to have been the same view that inspired Michelangelo.

I had never been comfortable with organized religion. It felt like a man-made hierarchy that put middlemen in the way of us realizing our own divine power. I understood the attraction to rituals and a feeling of belonging, but I had yet to find any religion that could answer all of my questions without hypocrisy. Looking up at the starlit mosaic, I realized that nature—this God-given place—*was* my church. Humbled by everything around me, I said a prayer of appreciation.

I walked around to the chapel entrance. There were two staircases, one leading up to the Protestant chapel and the other down, below ground, to the Catholic chapel. *OMG.* This picture was fit for Reddit/r/funny.

I laughed, deciding on the Protestant service. Catholic ceremonies were a workout; up, down, kneeling, shaking hands, sign of the cross, repeating verse, Communion. We had already had enough of a workout for one day. I would have much preferred to stay under the present, starry cathedral. But my superiors would definitely have had trouble conceiving of it as a viable church.

I ascended, and entered a breathtaking space. The astounding height of its beamed apex made me feel like I was walking down the aisle under a giant saber salute at a military wedding. In between what resembled massive blades were slivers of magnificent stained glass. As impressive as it was that night, in the light of day I suspected it would be even more magical.

Whenever I'd felt scared as a little girl, I would look up wherever I was and find Orion among the constellations. His presence had always made me feel safe. I had often imagined marrying the colossal warrior, and thereby ensuring his protection for eternity. Walking toward the altar of the USAFA chapel had thrown me back to that giddy feeling, as if I were finally getting to fulfill my childhood romantic fantasy.

I scooted into a pew near the back. The minister tending the service began sermonizing, gesticulating, but all I wanted to do was breathe deeply, meditate, decompress. I hadn't realized how tightly wound I was until I tried to relax. I started to pull in a deep breath, when someone tapped my shoulder.

"Face forward," the voice oddly instructed.

I flinched.

"Count to ten and meet me in the bathroom at the back of the chapel."

I moved only my eyes, whispering, "Seriously?"

"Just do it. It's okay." The voice unsuccessfully tried to soften.

Nothing about this felt okay, according to my stomach. But my brain overruled my biology and I started counting. *One-one thousand, two-one thousand, three-one thousand, four,* I whispered to myself, trying not to rush.

I hadn't recognized the voice or the energy of the mystery person.

When I got to *ten-one thousand,* I shuffled out of the pew, still bent at the waist, to the rear of the chapel. Just beyond the sanctuary doors I stopped to face a wall made of vertical wooden slats effectively hiding the restroom door. It was an optical illusion worthy of a Bond film, much like the clandestine meeting set inside of it. I unfocused my eyes until a small brass doorknob revealed itself. Then I opened the door and walked timidly through.

"Hey there, Tate. How you holdin' up?"

An angular upperclassman with a blinding row of silver on her shoulder boards leaned against the sink. She had mousy-blond hair pulled back into regs, but not too tightly; a uniform tailored to fit her frame, but not fastidiously; and shoes shined well, but not mirrored. She was by the book, but not, as I'd heard it called, *stract.* I started to look at her name tag, but she covered it with her hand, tauntingly. My eyes skipped back to hers. She was a difficult person to read. I felt multiple energies coming from her. A beat passed.

"I'm your captain." She kept her hand over her name tag.

Air force captain? Too young. Cadet captain for basic training? I would've already met her. Wait, ohhh . . .

"Oh my God! Our *team* captain!" *C1C (Cadet First Class) Tip Attila.* "I'm so sorry! We missed each other on my recruiting trip. . . ."

"I know! The other girls said I missed a *whole lot* when you came to visit." A beat passed after her words.

"Ma'am, that sounds ominous. . . . A whole lotta what? Wait . . . do I even want to know?!"

I was kidding, but she barely cracked a smile. Which made me genuinely curious. *Should I be worried . . . ?*

She stayed silent, opening her two palms to reveal a peanut butter cup and a Tootsie Roll. My stomach reached out with a hangry growl. I didn't even eat chocolate . . . but it had been so long since I had had candy . . . or *food . . .*

"Ma'am . . . ?"

I held Tip Attila's gaze, fighting the urge to check for an upperclassmen sting operation. She nudged the candy toward me genuinely. I grabbed both pieces, tore open the wrappers, and munched happily. The pure joy of my sugar high momentarily hijacked all of my other senses like a sneeze.

"Holy shitballs, ma'am, THANK YOU. Thank you SO much."

"No fuckin' problem, freshhie. And you don't have to call me ma'am, dipshit."

I cocked my head, unsure if she was being mean . . . or if that was just her sense of . . . humor?

"Yes, ma—yesss. Thank you again! I cannot wait for practice to start!"

"Stay strong, and remember, bright lights make big targets. The key is to blend in. Just make it through first and second beast flying under the radar and you'll be fine."

I heard her words, but it would take much more time to process a sentiment so antithetical to my nature. I started to step in for a hug, usual teammate behavior, but it felt . . . weird.

"Yes, ma'a—whoops, I mean . . . YAY! Thank you for the sugar!"

Instead, I offered a high five. She took it, then slipped out of the bathroom. I stayed lost in thought a moment longer. What a strange interaction. But what a nice surprise. My new team captain's mannerisms and words played on a loop in my brain. What can only be described as an unsettling undercurrent ran the length of my spine, making the hairs on the back of my neck stand straight up. Though I couldn't pinpoint why.

"Oh well—whatever, Popo," I said out loud to get myself off of the analytical merry-go-round. I smiled, feeling the sugar course through my veins. It was nice to finally meet our team leader.

I snuck out of the bathroom and the chapel to find Orion in the night sky. He was as bright as I'd ever seen him, and assuaged any feeling other than appreciation inside of me. I stood on the chapel wall, overlooking USAFA, under Orion's watchful eye, with fresh insulin beating my full heart. I hadn't experienced a better Communion.

The upperclassmen were right about freshman year—always choose chapel.

6

THE ACADEMY

The schedule varied little during the following days. We awoke to the sound of heavy fists against our doors followed immediately by the blaring hard-rock chords of an electric guitar. The songs differed, but the startling effect was the same. I wasn't a huge fan of heavy-metal hair bands before basic, but after having them blow up our mornings repeatedly, I liked them even less.

We exercised, got trained, ate. Well, sometimes we ate and sometimes we served food to the cadre and then stared forlornly at our place settings. We rifle drilled, got tested, exercised, got trained, sat . . . near food. The days passed. The further and deeper we dove into basic training, the more I felt myself acclimating to the altitude. I felt myself losing fat and gaining muscle. I felt my skin turning various shades of camo green. I felt my blood turning air force blue.

We celebrated our first cadet Fourth of July in Arnold Hall, per tradition, during which our wing commanders played songs out of which they would eventually choose our class song for us. We danced—awkwardly at first, then like a full-blown exorcism, finally understanding what it meant to "Work hard, play hard."

Afterward, we were ushered out to the balcony to watch fireworks and catch candy thrown to us by civilians who made it an Independence Day tradition to picnic outside the wall below. It was like feeding time at the zoo, and we were the animals, though none of us took offense—or resisted sugar or kindness in any form.

We weathered many firsts. Both negative and positive. We began to bond tightly to one another, to work together as we prepared to hit the midpoint in our pre-cadet education.

"GET YOUR BASIC ASSES OUT INTO THE HALLWAY NOOOW, PEOPLE!"

The predawn began with a torturous PT session, after which we moved to Mitchell Hall for a torturous—and foodless—breakfast. We never even got the chance to roll the aluminum serving cart to our *table*. After "breakfast," we moved to the terrazzo for a torturous—and repetitive—drill session. But it hardly mattered. Because shortly thereafter, we were escorted to the field house parking lot in droves so that we could escape into the blissful freedom of Doolie Day Out.

Depending on who you asked, *Doolie,* one of the many terms for freshmen at USAFA besides four-degrees, smacks, shit cans, etc., derived its name from either Doolittle Hall—our first stop during basic training inprocessing—or from the Greek term *duolos*, meaning *lowly subjects*. Regardless, Doolie Day Out meant Halle-freakin'-lujah! As this was the *free day* between first BCT and second BCT—basic cadet training, aptly pronounced "beast." On this day we were taken off grounds for a whole afternoon. It felt like Christmas, Halloween, and our birthdays all rolled into one.

Most Doolies were waiting for their "sponsors"—local C-Springs persons or families that volunteered to offer a surrogate sense of home, warm meals, and laundry to those cadets away from everything familiar. Since I had signed my letter of intent to play volleyball for USAFA, and our NCAA Western Athletic Conference season started immediately following basic training, the volleyball coaches were my sponsors. They were sponsors for the other three freshmen players as well, and the rest of our team. I had met other basics who were varsity athletes, and most of their coaches were their sponsors as well. There is an honor in getting to play NCAA Division I athletics . . . not to mention, big money involved for the school and athletic staff. Coaches at every university in the country—not just service academies—often offer parenting, counseling, tutoring, and life coaching to their players. They keep tabs and give whatever they can to ensure a successful team, season, and, hopefully, beyond that, a successful individual. Knowing that we were going to see our coaches felt good—it was great to anticipate something familiar during beast for a change.

As I stood in the parking lot, waiting to be smuggled out of the USAFA gates, familiarity found me. I felt a pair of lanky arms wrap around my waist: Quinner, a tall, willowy surfer girl from Southern California who had no doubt been born with her tattoo, "Chill. Live and let live." A moment later, the two of us were tackled by a giddy little defensive specialist power pack: Mo-Mo, a short, black-haired spitfire from Hawaii. The three of us had met on our recruiting trip and had hit it off instantly. Mo-Mo and I did our secret handshake, which had by then turned into a short hip-hop music video in which Quinner made a guest appearance. Our fourth and final freshman teammate, Linny—a member of superstract squadron one—walked stiffly up to the outskirts of our growing mosh pit and offered a stract nod. That is, until we yanked her into the center of the circle and tickled the Mighty Mach One–ness out of her. Linny warmed up shortly thereafter. Teammates in general, and volleyball girls specifically, are an ebullient and often physically emotive bunch. There are exceptions, of course.

Our upperclass teammate, Lassy—dubbed so because of her kilt and tartan-clad childhood Scottish dancing troupe—took us to meet the rest of our team at our coaches' house. The car ride was heaven. Laughter, friends, sunshine, non-death-metal music, laughter, nature, laughter, laughter, laughter. Perfection. We pulled into the driveway, sandwiching our car between others already parked out front. *Something's up.* The hairs on the back of my neck instantly stood on end. This seemed like more than just a team gathering. Out of habit, we basics marched like a weary centipede in a single-file line up the driveway.

Before we reached the porch, all our mothers flew out of the house, swooping down like hawks pulling apart our centipede.

"WE'VE BEEN CONSPIRING FOR MONTHS!"

"WE WANTED TO SURPRISE YOU!"

"OH MY GOD, YOUR HAIR!"

They couldn't help their decibel level as they fell all over themselves and one another to dote on us. I was more thrown seeing them than I would've been seeing our commandant of cadets standing there. I loved, admired, and appreciated my mother infinitely and without reservation. Yet I would've discouraged her from coming out, had I known. The distance from my family and Michigan had allowed me to establish USAFA, basic training, Colorado, volleyball, teachers, coaches, and friends as my *own* undertaking. It felt different, empowering. But even more than that, I was afraid to let my guard down in this new environment. There were vulnerabilities that parents inevitably pulled out of their children—especially my mom—and letting that show during basic training was like strapping raw meat to your body and jumping into a tank full of piranha. Not something I had wanted to test. But . . . too late! My mom held on to me tightly with one hand while the other ran through my glorified mullet.

"Oh, I can't *believe* your *hair*!"

I just surrendered to it, as my teammates had already done within their first nanosecond. I could feel fatigue sweeping my legs as Coach Wifey—the female half of our married coaching duo—met the gaggle of us at her door.

"Thank you, ma'am, for letting us come over today." Spoken from my heart.

She smiled and returned the sentiment with an armful of soft, supple brushed cotton. *My own clothes!* I had longed to feel something other than scratchy polyester against my skin for the last three weeks. I hugged her tightly before running to change.

Mo-Mo and Quinner did the same, then met up with everyone else in the living room. Linny—a Mighty Mach *shock*—had opted to stay in her USAFA uniform, for which Mo-Mo and Quinner poked her. I kind of understood, again, not wanting to give in to vulnerabilities.

––––––––––––––––

An epic feast had been laid out for the four of us freshmen, our mothers, several of the upperclass players, and coaching staff. We had started beast early in the summer—almost two months before my friends had to report to their Ivies or state schools, a little less so if they were going to play ball. USAFA summers were split up into three different sessions, two of which were required, meaning most cadets only had a few weeks off each summer. And those whose time off coincided with Doolie Day Out were nowhere to be found. Our team captain was in session, but unable to come to the coaches'. However, pictures of her with them abounded throughout the house.

Coach Wifey pointed to a bevy of riches.

"Help yourself to whatever you want, girls—we've got burgers 'n' dogs, mac 'n' cheese, salads, and side dishes galore—Po, there are condiments for you, since they're your *fave* and freshmen aren't allowed to use 'em—and cookies, cuppies, and ice cream sundaes for everyone else. You all look like you have lost some weight, so dig in!"

Coach Hubby put his hands up.

"Well—droppin' a few LBs is not such a bad thing . . . at least for some of you, right?! Heh!"

Tank, an upperclassman middle hitter, and Lassy both made eye contact with Coach Hubby. Tank guiltily returned half the items on her plate to the buffet table. Lassy presented her plate with a burger, salad, and half a cookie to Coach Hubby for approval. Instead of looking at her plate, he looked at her narrow hips, smiled, and patted her shoulder. Quinner, who had been watching, reached around Tank's waist and put her surrendered burger back on her plate. Then a cookie. Then another cookie. She winked at Tank—who was, BTW, a *beast* on the court. Coach Hubby left for the kitchen.

His comment had made my ear canals itch. I wanted to shield Tank's and Lassy's hearts from feeling any impact of what he said. Sure, someone with an unwaveringly healthy ego and a bulletproof body image wouldn't have even *heard* those words. A room full of college-aged girls, however? *Blech.* I had tried to shake off insensitive comments like his before, but my being a perfectionist had made it difficult not to internalize them. And always to my detriment. Words like his just *reminded* me to worry about what I looked like, and how I should perform, and wonder if there would *ever* be a time when I wasn't self-conscious about some aspect of my body. I didn't know a single person who hadn't felt too fat, too short, too this, or too that. And my heart broke for everyone, girls in particular, who had been told to watch their weight instead of their *health*. I fixed myself a plate, then retired to the living room floor with the others.

Quinner, gifted with beautifully Teflon self-esteem, was out of heartshot from Coach's comments. Linny and Mo-Mo were out of earshot—having each piled high multiple plates of edible treasure that their moms had to help them carry. We dissolved into delirious laughter at the absurdity of it all as we sank down into the plush carpeting of the living room. By comparison, our squadron carpet was steel wool pulled over concrete. I sat and picked delicious food off of my plate with my hands—just because I *could*. It was one more thing, in a long list, to appreciate during this all-too-brief field trip to the outside world.

"Hey, Po . . . Why don't you have any *food* on that plate?!" Coach Wifey stood over me with her palms up. I looked down at the colorful array of veggies in front of me, then back up at her.

"Pardon?"

My plate was totally full . . . to me.

"Ohhh . . . I'm a veggie."

Record scratch. Coach's eyes widened. Everybody else stopped and looked up from what they were doing.

"It's . . . all good." I shrugged pathetically. Every cadet, coach, and mother familiar with USAFA knew it was a big deal there. My militarily naïve Mom was looking around, increasingly worried.

Quinner pointed at me and laughed with her whole body. My mom further furrowed her brow. Not wanting to stop eating, Quinner just covered her mouth to speak.

"LOAD MASTERRRS!"

Linny and Mo-Mo reflexively flanked Quinner and me, bringing their plates with them, as they mocked our daily Doolie duties during each meal. Load Masters, mirroring ones in the active duty air force, loaded the cargo (in USAFA's case, food onto plates, and in my case specifically, *meat* onto plates) and start the serving process. They put all their burgers, hot dogs, chicken, and cold cuts on one plate and sounded off at the top of their lungs one by one, starting with Linny.

"Cadet Fourth Class Tate! Please pass this SCRUMPTIOUS plate of CARCASS, filled with CUTE, FURRY ANIMAL GRISTLE, to the HIGHEST-RANKING OFFICER at the table, while REMINDING US ALL THAT YOU ARE WASTING GOOD FOOD THAT THE GOVERNMENT PROVIDED FOR YOU BY CHOOSING NOT TO EAT MEAT!" The girls put on this "training session" for a solid five minutes before our coach interjected.

"Yeah, any sort of vegetarianism doesn't really work too well here."

Coach Wifey spoke as if my socks didn't match and I should just run upstairs and change them. My mom ran her hands through my hair, the energy of her maternal instincts seeping through her fingertips. I half expected her to drag me away from this wretched place that, in her mind, had sheared her daughter's identity to within an inch of her scalp, made her talk ridiculously, and punished her for being a vegan. But instead, she encouraged me to get more food.

Once our bellies were full, we broke into smaller conversations. My mom pelted me with questions. I censored my answers, knowing there was only so much information she deserved to hear. I focused on the praise, accomplishments, and bonding moments that I had experienced thus far. I told her that everything was fine, just fine. I told her how nice it was to see her. I told her this because it was true and also because it felt like she needed to hear it. She smiled, shed loving tears, and hugged me tightly. I felt her holding something back, but I didn't want to upset her by prying. So I just thanked her. For everything.

As soon as we had started to feel remotely comfortable, it was time to return to the belly of the beast. We tearfully and fearfully said good-bye to our moms and our coaches, completely appreciative for our snippet of the outside world.

By the time the cadre stopped yelling at us that evening, we had burned off every single calorie from each forbidden food we'd gobbled up during our afternoon away. We had burned off even the *memory* of our recent taste of freedom.

Gabby and I did not even trade stories about our respective afternoons before folding our crumpled, exhausted bodies onto our bed units and falling fast asleep.

7

THE ACADEMY

The next morning, I awoke sitting straight up, feeling like some poor bass on the end of a fishing pole. My arms were at my sides, my chin tucked, and my eyes caged. I had never fallen in so well during my waking hours. Ten seconds later came the thunder of pounding fists against our door. I flew off of my bunk and smacked my knees against the built-in desk below my bed, just as I had done the previous morning. And the morning before that. And the morning before that. *Damn.* I bent over and rubbed the mosaic of bruises that adorned my knees and shins. *Double double damn damn.*

As Gabby and I listened to the Uniform of the Day (UOD) announcement calling for camouflage BDUs for the first time, every hair on my body stood fiercely at attention, then did "the wave" up and down my spine. We looked at each other—me smiling from ear to ear, her wincing. I went over and hugged her.

"Together?" I pulled back offering my high five.

"Together." She smacked it—not being the most physically adept cadet, Gabby worried for our next phase. But I had her back, and she had mine. And our squadron would all be in it together.

Until this point in our training, we had been completely immersed in campus life at USAFA. We had learned how to maintain our dress blue uniforms, execute intricate rifle and marching drill patterns, and arrange our dorm rooms in the strictest Saturday-morning inspection, or SAMI, order. We had been schooled and tested in the conduct becoming a USAFA cadet, learned our way around the inner sanctum, acclimated to the altitude, and taken placement exams in preparation for the school year. We had spent half our summer concentrating on our academic and intellectual side. And we had gotten in shape. But now it was time to get *physical*.

I could feel a visceral shift in mission and mentality as I stepped inside the heavy cotton camouflage skin. We were migrating toward a new challenge loaded with positive potential.

We packed our footlockers full of uniforms and standard-issue essentials, then met the rest of the wing on the terrazzo to embark upon the mysterious march out to a place about which we'd only heard lore . . . a place called Jacks Valley.

Five miles and a world away from USAFA's inner sanctum, we set up camp for second BCT, the last half of basic training. We Screamin' Demons found ourselves treading unfamiliar waters as our entire chain of command was replaced with all-new upperclassmen cadets and officers during the changing of the guard ceremony. We were stunned. As much as our first BCT cadre had beaten our civilian selves out of us, they had also started to build us back up into stronger, stracter soldiers. And, strangely, we loved them for it. Once again, it was reinforced to us that beast was all about structure and routine mixed with incessant change.

Our new squadron commander introduced himself to us after the ceremony. He was a tall dirty-blond with a pronounced chin and a whiny, rambling voice, who bore an uncanny resemblance to film director Quentin Tarantino. He introduced the rest of his staff in a verbal hailstorm and then ordered us into the next phase of our adventure—we hoped it was not going to be as bloody as Tarantino's films.

The closest I had ever come to roughing it overnight in the wild had been falling asleep on a chaise lounge between the front yard and rocky beach of our summer place in Northern Michigan. But—as usual—I was all in.

We hugged and high-fived each other for successfully erecting our olive-green waxy-canvas, metal-poled, and wooden-platform-tented living space with the gusto of an Amish barn raising. We were assigned a tent according to gender, then ordered to assemble our cots and organize our footlockers. Since there were so few women in our class, the females from every flight in the whole Screamin' Demons squadron were all housed in one tent. It was the first time since arrival that we had seen twenty women in one place. Or at all, for that matter. Though the boys felt far away, it was nice to feel less outnumbered . . . if only while inside our tent.

By first nightfall, before reputations attached to their source, and the rumor mill reopened, before competition set in, and the claws came out, we enjoyed a good old-fashioned slumber party atmosphere; complete with sleeping bags, ghost stories, pillow fights, makeovers, and girl talk.

Well, okay . . . the sleeping bags were olive drab; there weren't ghosts so much as there were angry cadre members and Jacks Valley border patrol *ghoulishly* equipped with scent dogs and pepper spray; there were absolutely *no* pillows; and none of us was allowed to possess or use makeup, nor did we have any hair left on our heads to braid. Although if we waited just a little bit longer we would definitely be able to braid our *leg* hair. And, finally, as we'd learned the hard way in first beast, anything we said after taps—which was played over the loudspeaker signifying the same wing-wide bedtime each night, just as reveille was played in the morning to wake us up—would surely be eavesdropped upon by one or more cadre members and lorded over us for what would probably be the rest of our careers. Our first night in Jacks Valley may not have been the beginning of a three-week-long *slumber party,* but it did mark the beginning of a wild ride.

———————————

The first of many mornings like it out in the valley, I shot out of my cot at the first bugle note, just as I had done on campus—only now, I was zipped so tightly into my little olive drab cocoon that I fell face-first onto the floor. I wiggled back over to my cot, propped myself up, found the zipper, and eventually broke free. The cadre shouted their good mornings in the form of orders at the top of their lungs. Their voices were urgent, unfamiliar, and sounded MUCH too close through the thin tent walls. We quickly dressed in our UODs and ran to meet the rest of our squadron.

After morning formation, we went on a weapon-clad run over the rough terrain of Jacks Valley. It was difficult, but left each of my cells with a powerful, visceral sense of accomplishment. Being athletic was a tremendous asset in second beast. Our whole flight had to make it through each PT session, and each run. Often, those who started to wheeze, puff, and hack midway up the mountain would pass back their utility belts, canteens, and weapons to those of us who weren't, in order to make it through. When that wasn't enough, we'd wrap our arms around them and carry them to the finish line. I was the tallest girl in the squadron, and the only female varsity athlete. I had vowed to do whatever it took to always finish strong, and make my team proud. Some of the stronger basics rolled their eyes resentfully, or complained behind the backs of those who were weaker—especially if those "weaker" were women, making all of us especially aware of performance vs. gender. But overall, we were becoming a team, supportive and willing to sacrifice our own comfort to ensure that no member was left behind.

After morning PT, we marched to breakfast. Meals in second BCT were served on individual trays in buffet lines. We were actually allowed to pick and choose what was put on our plate. Mine often consisted of fruit or cereal, but occasionally I would score something hot, like *vegetables*. I caught so much flack for it, but I didn't care; it felt amazing to have choices. Verbal castigations were fewer and farther between during second beast meals. We required much more endurance, so the cadre often ordered us to eat and hydrate. None of us questioned it . . . our mouths were too full.

Each day we were assigned a new obstacle course. The courses were gauntlets intended to highlight, test, and train different skill sets. We had to push everyone in our squadron through each obstacle as fast, correctly, and responsibly as we could. And we were held accountable by the barking, pounding, pushy cadre who led us. We went over, under, around, and through every construct that was put in our path. To me, it was a beautiful lesson in being fully present and available in each moment. All that mattered was whatever lay directly in front of us. We had no control over where we were, when we were there, or what was next. All we had was the present moment. So I gave myself permission to narrow my focus. I conquered, built, memorized, shouted, lifted, ate, supported, and surmounted every challenge placed before me. Instead of worrying about the big picture taking place on 18,000 acres of USAFA land, I allowed myself to only do my part to the best of my ability. And it paid off. Hugely.

I was able to set the curve ahead of every girl and most of the boys in our entire squadron. Our bodies were used up; our minds were used up. My heart was still full. I finished each contest dirty, wet, whipped, and smiling from ear to ear. It was amazing.

After one such contest, I shuffled the trail to the restroom with a sense of accomplishment in my head, heart, and voice, and lead in my feet. I had felt something—or someone—follow me past the communal showers and into one of the stalls. I whipped around as soon as I could to find Tip Attila, the volleyball captain from chapel, locking the door behind her.

"Wha— Ahh!" I yelped, garnering energy from my last reserve tank.

"Shh! Shut the fuck up, shh . . ." She pushed me against the wall of the stall—a little too hard, *BTW*—and put her index finger to her lips.

WTF, dude??

"What happened? Is everything okay, ma'a—er—Tip?" I whispered, trying not to fall in the toilet.

"What? Yeah—everything's fine, this is just the only place we can talk—*freshie*."

A beat passed.

"Um . . . okay." I guessed that made sense, since there was—hopefully—no one in the lavatory at the time.

"Hey—I heard you're kicking some major ass out here." Her tone was almost accusatorial.

I shrugged. "I don—"

"You know why I know that? Cuz you're not staying under the radar! Bright lights make big targets, remember?" She was patting my shoulder.

"But, I thought it was a good thing . . ." I couldn't help but start to tear up. My body was so tired. And her words felt like a slap in the face to my entire sensibility. She softened.

"Aww, jeez—hey, no, I mean, I just heard the upperclassmen talking about you—in a good way—and I wanted to keep an eye on you, that's all. Gotta take care of my team." She smiled and handed me a small bag of organic jelly beans.

I felt like I was on tape delay from this conversation whiplash. But I took the candy and thanked her. She held my shoulders with both hands.

"Hey—you're doing really well. Just know that it's okay to be average, too." She put one hand up to her mouth like she was divulging a secret. "You can get away with more stuff. . . ."

She laughed, gave me a hug, then punched me in the shoulder. She slipped out the door.

I stood there for a moment before locking the door again and sitting down.

Weird.

I wasn't even totally sure what being average meant. I was never in competition with other people anyway. My sole competition had always been with the idea of perfection. The idea of executing a textbook maneuver, or having the perfect form, or being able to reach every ball on the court, or figure out the right answer. My brain was starting to become as sore as my body. I opened the bag of jelly beans and poured a few into my mouth. I meditated on the fruity, chewy goodness until I could walk back to my bunk.

Weird. Once again, weird.

I climbed onto my cot, squeezed a dollop of perfumed lotion onto the inside of my wrist, and basked in the glow of having crushed it on the assault course earlier. I allowed my brain to default to its screen saver, Booker. It was dark. I smelled him. I tasted him-home-him. I closed my eyes and reveled in the sweet darkness. Not a scary darkness, but rather, the darkness in which love, passion, and creativity flourished. The closing of one sense opened up my heart, and I was able to see him, feel his skin, to smell him, breathe him in. I felt his chest beneath my cheek. I felt his musculature rise and fall, his strength hiding in his coiled muscles under his smooth and vulnerable sun-kissed skin.

I shifted in my cot, and my own aching muscles, cuts, and bruises attempted to vie for my attention. So I focused harder on the feeling, the memory of Booker's skin under my fingertips. I ran over the slightly embossed, pink, infantile skin of his scars in my mind. I could feel the sport, stupidity, or accident that had caused each of his markings and I read them like a braille memoir. Taps provided a sultry soundtrack to the scenes projected onto the back wall of my psyche until my reward for another successful day in basic training fell asleep with me.

BOOKER.

"Hey." Booker's deep, gentle voice pulled me to him like gravity. His straight white smile, his chiseled chin obscured by day-old scruff set my soul on fire. He put his hand on my cheek, meeting me halfway over the center console of his SUV. The dark night air outside his truck made the inside our own little world. Nothing else existed. His pale green eyes, like fresh hot springs, offered endless depth. And I couldn't help but fall into them. Again. Each time as if it were the first.

"Hey." Almost a whisper as I moved closer.

I could feel the heat coming off of him as I nestled perfectly into his arms. I lifted my cheek off his chest, not wanting to break contact with his pale green pools, peeking out from beneath the kind of lashes that women pay good money to affix. I was in free fall. I had been for two years. We had had a connection the instant we were introduced. It was undeniable. We had talked all day long at an off-season basketball tournament that our mutual friends were coaching. And by the end of their team's first game, we were sharing a pop and calling each other by new nicknames. He loved that I wanted to go into the FBI. I loved his passion for football. He had set multiple records while playing for Michigan State.

We could talk for hours, about anything. By our third time hanging out, we'd sat in his truck talking before I had to go home.

"I don't know, you just seem . . . older—like, way older than just in high school."

"Wow. I can't hear *that* enough . . . ! Every girl's dream . . . to be called old," I ribbed.

"I didn't say you *look* older! Although, actually, you totally do—"

My palms flew out, facing the roof of his car indignantly. I made a digging motion with my hands and threw my lower jaw at him.

"No! I mean, like, in a beautiful way—in a more-mature-for-your-age kinda way—like you're already in college! I mean—I would never date someone in high school. Er, just *anyone* in high school. You're . . . just way chill, way cooler than your age. You're super smart, and funny, and focused, and gorgeous—hell, sometimes I can't keep up with half the shit you talk about. You just . . . I'm just . . . You challenge me. And I think you're amazing. I don't know . . ." He shook his head, exasperated and adorable.

My cheeks gave off a warm glow that I hoped the low light of his truck's interior didn't give away.

"Booker . . . God, I think you are incredible. You know so much, and you have such a gift for football. And I don't mean just that you're strong and crazy fast, and incredibly coordinated. You *are* all that. But I mean that you are an incredible teacher. You understand how your body does what it does—and how others react to that—and you are able to break it down and describe it to people. You have such a mind for strategy and a total talent for getting teammates inspired to do the right thing for each circumstance. You're incredibly intelligent. Both academically and socially. That might be weird to say—but I can see it, I . . . I feel it. I love watching you do what lights you up. It's . . . *you* . . . are just such a gift." Lighter. "It also doesn't hurt that you are totally hot."

His eyes were alight, and for a split second, stripped of any swagger, of any game, any guile, he was even more handsome for revealing it. A beat passed. I poked his shoulder.

"Besides. If it's any consolation, sweet Booker . . . you'll *always* be older than I. Much, *much* older." I started to giggle.

He broke and grabbed my knee, sending me into a ticklish fit. He'd stopped and kissed me for the first time right there.

I sat in that same position now as I had then.

"You know I'll always love you . . . don't you?" His raw vulnerability, again, made his eyes dilate as he spoke. Flecks of gold, woven through his green irises, caught the reflection of the streetlamp over the parking lot in which we were sitting, making them twinkle like their own constellations. "Always. No matter where you are . . . or . . . who you're with . . ." His eyes dropped for a millisecond and he shook his head, as though trying to erase that thought off of the Etch A Sketch in his mind. "Or—whatever. I just . . . I'll always love you, my little Fed." He smiled, a twinge of sadness showing briefly, for the larger implications of this moment. I smiled at his smile.

Booker held my face in his hand and kissed me deeply, passionately. He pulled back as if to say something, but didn't. Instead, he just kissed me again. And again.

"I love you, too, Book." I put my hand on his heart. "This. You. Will always be a piece of home to me."

He put his hand over mine and stared into me. Into my soul. And I stared back. Free-falling in an endless pool of pale green and gold.

"Do you really have to go?" His own words surprised him, as if he hadn't expected to say them out loud.

"I could ask you the same question." I rubbed his heart, feeling energetic sparks from his chakra. "But we both know the answer."

He held my gaze. And just as he opened his mouth to protest, I felt a rush of heat radiate between my hand and his chest. Instead of talking, he took a deep breath. He exhaled with his whole body, then kissed me. A bit more relaxed. He was more than six years older than me, and in a completely different phase of his life. We had already spent some of our relationship as long distance, and as much as our love was a fiery ember that burned deeply in both of us, our relationship wasn't . . . *practical*. While he was on the road playing professional football, our love stayed in a state of suspended animation, still breathing, still beating, and ready to pick up right where we had left it. But it was not easy to be apart; our love for one another, our soul connection, existed independently of the lives we were both meant to live. And it was time for us both to go and live our new lives. Freely. And 100 percent all in. Without feeling like we should be elsewhere.

I had to leave the next day for volleyball nationals and basic training. He had to leave the next day for a coaching job down south after injury had forced him to retire early from the NFL. I was just starting my *college* career. He was already on his *second . . . career* career. He had asked me to marry him, and I had said no. I was not ready for marriage. I hadn't even established myself as an *individual* yet, let alone as somebody's *wife*. My future was waiting for me out west.

"I have something for you, lil' Fed." He popped open the glove box and took out an expensive black leather jewelry box. I whipped my head back around to him. "Shhh." His finger was already reaching for my lips, immediately assuaging my concern that it was another ring. He leaned over, took out the box, and handed it to me.

"Baby . . ." I touched his face. Traced his adorable dimples with my thumb, grabbed his scruffy chin with my hand.

"Open it!" He nudged it toward me excitedly. I looked at him while breaking open the leather, exposing rich, gorgeous velvet . . . and a beautiful gold chain. Centered in the gold, keeping together the ornately patterned rope, was a stunning miniature pair of . . . handcuffs. Handcuffs. Studded with two diamonds where the key would go. It was beautiful and hilarious and generous and totally . . . him. Him, handsome him. I clutched it to my heart.

"God, I love you. So much." I kissed both of his cheeks, then his lips.

"Lemme put it on you!" He got out of the car and ran around to my passenger door. He opened it, offered his hand for me to climb out, then took the necklace. I swung my long hair out of the way as he fastened it, then spun me back around. I felt for it with my hand while he acted as my mirror. "It's perfect." His eyes were alive.

We stood in the shadow of his truck, wrapped in the pitch-black calm of night. The temperature, having dropped, had turned too cold for what we were wearing. As if nature had conspired to give us yet another reason to stay pressed against one another. My hands ran under his shirt, over the warm bare skin of his stomach, and then around his torso to his lower back. We hung on so tightly, afraid of what might happen if we let go. My nose fit like a jigsaw puzzle into the nape of his neck. I opened my mouth slightly and took in a deep breath. His musculature, his strength, his lips, his safety, his smell . . . they were *home* to me. The condensation pulled his woodsy, amber-spiced liquid gold onto my nose and lips, capturing his essence as a souvenir. Slowly, we breathed. Together.

He was my first. My first love, my first . . . of many things, of everything. And my body had never allowed me to forget it, both in and out of his presence. Finally, after shaking from the cold and rocking from the pain of having to say good-bye indefinitely, I reluctantly pulled myself away from Booker. I left with a pit in my stomach, and a pair of golden handcuffs over my heart.

8

THE ACADEMY

For the majority of my life before the academy, my extracurriculars had often left me heavily outnumbered by guys. I'd always played football with the boys at recess and had gone on to be the only girl on an all-male All-Star soccer team, the only female pitcher in all-male baseball league, the lone female in math, science, and aviation classes and competitions, and in many of my groups of friends. Basically, in just about every area of my athletic, academic, and social life growing up, I had become accustomed to being radically outnumbered. I had, of course, received plenty of ribbing, name-calling, mud-slinging, and pressure. But my discomfort had never overshadowed the joy of participating in something important to me, nor had it ever felt like I was infiltrating a seriously hostile camp. After all, I wasn't thinking about gender; I just wanted to partake, have fun, and play. Not fight. Usually, all I had to do was prove I was good enough to belong, and I was able to continue without too much friction. Much like it had felt to apply and to start USAFA: radically outnumbered.

Jacks Valley accentuated gender differences more than first beast. Perhaps one of the reasons was because instead of being woven into rooms next to each other, the boys had their own two tents, and we had ours. For us, living with girls from other squadrons helped us talk, share, study, and prepare communally. From what I had heard, the boys seemed to be enjoying their communal lifestyle as well. The only problem seemed to be exactly that: We were enjoying them *separately*. Much of our downtime was now spent inside segregated tents. From everything that we had been learning about creating a tight-knit, cohesive military unit, trust seemed paramount. And the most profound way to create a strong, trustworthy, tightly woven body of soldiers willing to live and die for one another was to spend off-duty time getting to know one another.

Gabby and I usually volunteered to act as messengers for this very reason. We would get or give information, or simply reach out. One afternoon, the two of us scurried over and rapped our *supersecret* four-degree knock, "Shave and a Haircut, Two Bits," on one of the boys' flimsy tent doors. The ridiculously obvious code of ours was supposed to alert those inside that there was no need to hide any contraband, or leap to attention. I'd been joking when I had suggested it, but it had stuck. So far, the cadre hadn't usurped it.

Gabby and I could hear the noise inside the boys' tent drowning out our knock. Rather than risk even more exposure to any passing cadre, she rolled her eyes, grabbed my wrist, and dragged me through their door.

"Gabby, I don't know if we should just walk i—"

"Shh—we don't have ti— Whoa." She cut me off with a harsh whisper.

"Whoa." I honestly wasn't sure if I had said that, or if my subconscious had.

Holy shit.

We froze, wide-eyed, midstride, gaping at the scene in front of us. A ring of our boys stood facing each other in a circle. Each one, having dropped trou, was standing ankle deep in a camouflage puddle. It looked for a second like we were in line at Panera, staring at a row of pumpernickel, white, wheat, and the dreaded hairy-cranberry *buns* squished against one another. Only these buns hovered above the bare legs of our squadron mates. The decibel level rose as they cheered, jeered, laughed, and moaned while comparing the size of their . . . *breadsticks*.

"NOmyGod!" Gabby, never one to censor herself, chortled so hard that she snorted, which sent the boys to try the bumbling, stumbling, uncoordinated task of *bagging* their . . . *bread.*

They hopped, yanked, zipped, shoved, and spun around.

"I can't—"

Gabby, too flustered to speak, shoved the wing staff list we'd brought them against my stomach.

"Mmbyeeee . . ." I turned to leave, but she grabbed my arm.

"We were given a direct order," she whispered harshly. A beat.

"Fine," I responded through pursed lips.

"Ahh . . . guys?" I shook my head and tried to look at anything in the tent *but* them.

The decibel level fell.

". . . So . . . Cadet Second Class *Burns* is actually our wing-wide *training* noncommissioned officer . . . er . . . NCO. . . . We had it as . . . *Buns* . . . on the other sheet. . . ."

No pun intended, but holy shitballs. My cheeks hurt from trying to stifle my urge to laugh, making my words come out flat, tight, and wonky. I held out the paper for them to take.

"Here, we fixed it for you. . . ." No one took the paper.

"This is all Danno's fault!" came an accusatory voice from the back, followed by a retaliatory headlock.

"Hey, fuck YOU, Beansy! *You're* the one who insisted on *proof* that I was telling the *truth*!"

Aww, God, please don't reopen . . . Panera's box. Danno flicked Beansy's crotch with his hand and broke free from the headlock.

"Oh yeah?! Well, at least *my* fucking story was *true*!"

"Do you *really* want me to show you who's the fuckin' *bigger* man, *again*?"

I raised my voice above the rumblings.

"SURE . . . LIKE *ANY* OF YOUR . . . *STORIES* ARE TRUE!" I teased, trying one more way to get their attention and give them the paper before leaving.

The tent exploded in protest.

"Awww! You gonna take that from a *girl*? Like you're some kinda *pussy*?!"

"Shutcherhole, Paulson!"

Several of the guys started unbuttoning their flies, until one of them lobbed a question, like a grenade, into the space between us.

"Hey, how many men does it take to do the wash?!"

The rest of them clamored for the proverbial floor.

"None! It's a *woman's* job!"

The energy in the tent changed palpably. Uproarious laughter sliced the air like a razor. Then came another voice. Another cadet. Another . . . question.

"Hey, why'd the woman cross the road?"

To get to the other side . . . Please say, To get to the oth—

"Who cares!? What the fuck is she doing out of the *kitchen*?!"

Their guffaws macheted the air. Gabby and I exchanged uneasy glances.

"Whaddya call a woman with ninety percent of her intelligence gone?!"

Swing. Slice.

"DIVORCED! AHHH-HAAA-HA-HA!!"

Wow. WTF is happening? This felt horrible. *Should we protest, laugh, or leave?* I didn't want the boys to say another word. I was afraid that they were telling me how they really felt. And who they really were. I was afraid that I was losing respect for them with every word they hurled out of their mouths. And that they had no respect for me to begin with. Usually, I would just migrate away from someone who didn't respect me. In order to prevent unnecessary and incendiary trespassing into radically differing worldviews. Everyone is entitled to their opinion. But I lived, worked, and would conceivably *die* for these guys. This was different. The stakes were much higher. And I desperately wanted them to just. Stop. Talking. My feet couldn't move. As if my heart, heavy, had fallen into them.

"Why did God invent lesbians?"

"So feminists wouldn't BREED! HOO WOO-HOO HA-HA!"

I winced. The room had grown rowdy; the semicircle of boys around Gabby and me felt more like the sharp crescent of a sickle. The more the boys said, the more doubt as to our capability as a gender bled through their sarcasm. This wasn't a sports team competing for points anymore. The stakes were infinitely higher.

"You guys are assholes!" Gabby yelled.

"Why do women have periods?!"

"Because they DESERVE THEM!"

My stomach tightened. *How do we get TF outta here?*

"I don't trust anything that *bleeds* for seven days and doesn't *die*!"

Wow. We couldn't storm or sulk or shimmy out of that tent. We had to maintain our position—whatever *that* was—and make the conscious decision to leave . . . on our own terms.

"What does PMS stand for?!"

I intercepted the lob and raised my hand in jest.

"Oooh, wait, I know this one, umm . . . *PUTTING UP WITH*

MEN'S SHIT?" I chucked the wadded-up wing staff list at Beansy, grabbed Gabby by the arm, and pulled her out the door.

I could hear Gabby telling the story to the rest of the girls as I left for the showers that evening. Topping off the room full of laughter with one final thought.

"God—guys will be guys, right?" Gabby said.

I hustled down the wood-chip path, eager to wash the entire encounter off of me.

SARY.

You could hear a pin drop.

Four adults, a bevy of children ranging in ages from six to eleven, shuffling dinner and drinks between the dining room and kitchen, and all the commotion, the conversation just . . . stopped.

And you could hear a pin drop.

It was my fault. The adults had gathered around the kids' table to take a look, and the children started to inch toward their parents' legs in fear. But I was stuck. It was my fault.

My parents had invited our closest family friends, the Raymonds, over for dinner. My sister and I had been stepping-stones in between their three girls, and we all had grown up together. My dad was best friends with their dad, and my mom with their mom. My parents were trying anything they could to find some normalcy . . . a foothold in this scary, uncharted territory. Friends, neighbors, strangers, had been bringing over food all week, and since my parents hadn't had an appetite, they wanted someone to eat it. Otherwise it would just sit there, in the kitchen. A graveyard of casserole dishes with cards propped above them, like headstones.

It was always my job to set the table. That was one of my chores. I set the table; Sary cleared the table. And then we'd both do the dishes together. Alternating between washing, or drying and putting away. Out of habit, I had set the kids' table. Like I had always done at our house. But instead, I had made the world stop. And now you could hear a pin drop.

My parents came in from the kitchen to see why the world had stopped. And they looked where everyone else was looking. Down at the table. At five perfectly placed, beautifully symmetrical place settings. One, two, three, four . . . five.

Stop.

Pin drop.

I looked up at my parents. Their faces crumbled. Their lips trembled until the earthquake of grief caused an avalanche of pain to cascade from their faces onto the perfectly smooth tablecloth. My face was next to erode.

"I'm so sorry, Mommy. I'm so sorry, Daddy. I'm so sorry. I forgot. I didn't mean to, I forgot."

Today, I had made their faces drop.

My mother collapsed around me, hugging me so tightly that I didn't know who was supposed to hold up whom. My father leaned on the dining room table over us, and cried so hard that his tears ran down my cheeks, too.

The Raymond girls were hiding in the forest created by their parents' legs, holding on to one another, and wailing, while my parents' best friends held each other and sobbed before clearing what used to be Sary's place setting.

One week earlier she had been thrown from a horse and killed instantly.

Our world stopped.

Our pin dropped.

And from that day on, I've tried to pick up the pieces and put our family back together again.

9

THE ACADEMY

In my dream, I am fractured. I am the stractest military commando with brute strength and unyielding ruthlessness. I am the most gracefully soft aristocratic woman of refinement and peaceful calm. I am a starving artist covered in a spectrum of painted chaos, living out my dreams with Da Vinci–esque resourcefulness. I am book smart with no common sense. I am socially advanced with no formal education. I am logical. I am theoretical. I am fractured, like fingers off the same hand, a perfectly fluid piece of brilliant bionics when bonded together—but worthless when torn apart. All of the other mes surround the me who's having the dream. We walk through the world together and apart. And when reveille starts to play, we hold hands around the flagpole and salute.

Walking into the boys' tent with Gabby the previous day had apparently whipped my subconscious into a bit of a frenzy. I had tried to push it from my mind, but by taps, the experience had ping-ponged from cranial lobe to cranial lobe, provoking internal questions of gender construct, labels, cages . . . Clearly, it had upset me. It had forced me into a box with only one label: GIRL. I'd felt restricted, stifled, confined. We—women and men—were so much more than just one thing. *We are all so much more.*

─────────────

During the next few days, the cadre took components from days prior and tossed them like a salad, mixing in a few new ingredients for good measure. Time passed with similar speed and intensity. I woke up in combat boots—an effective time-saving tool that I had accidentally discovered after passing out fully clothed one night—then hurried to fall in with the rest of my squadron. We ran like hell, ate, hydrated, crawled, climbed, pushed, pulled, lifted, threw, screamed, and carried. We ate, hydrated, read, and memorized. We were tested and trained mentally, emotionally, and physically. We were broken down and built back up. We deepened our relationships, and felt like we were building trust with one another, at least in service of the task in front of us, but went home to separate quarters where who knew what—after our tent run-in—was being said. We were both together and apart. But we *all* ran the gamut from doubtful to hopeful from horrid to happy from angry to ecstatic. We barely showered. We barely slept.

At the end of a particularly long day, I donned my uniformed robe and rubber flip-flops for a walk to the showers. I left our tent as quickly as possible. It was going to take more time than we were ever allotted underneath the shower head to wash off the salty, sweaty, grimy remnants of the training sessions we had, that day, weathered.

We were required to walk to the showers at attention, with our towels folded in half and hung over our left arms, as if we were cater-waitering some weird pool party. I hurried along the path, feeling every wood chip and pebble through my flimsy foam-rubber soles. After my shower, I brushed my teeth, rubbed lotion into my dry skin and fatigued muscles, then cater-waitered my way back to our tent.

The sun had long since set by the time I started home, so the trail was virtually pitch-black. I tried to walk quickly, but the uneven terrain under my flimsy flops forced me to tread carefully. Halfway back to the tent village, I felt the whispering wake of soft wind as something passed by me. I paused momentarily but saw nothing. So I resumed walking.

"BASIC!"

"Fuck a duck!" The words escaped in a frightful yelp before I could stop them.

Shitballs. That was an upperclassman. My stomach plummeted. I stopped midstride and did an about-face. I squinted hard, trying to force my pupils to dilate enough to decipher the identity of the large, muscular man in front of me. Slight nausea kicked in as I considered the possibility that I may get trained, alone, along the darkest stretch of woodsy path. Fight-or-flight adrenaline forced my words out much louder than I had expected, sending nearby bats out of the trees.

"YES, SIR!"

I drove my chin into the back of my spine.

"Basic . . ."

A familiar rich Southern baritone poured over me like blackstrap molasses. *NOmyGod. That voice . . .* I knew that voice. That voice was attached to the biggest, baddest, stractest cadet NCO in charge of training the entire wing. *Training.* As in, he was literally responsible for enforcing the curriculum on how to yell, break down, and destroy cadets before building them into soldiers. He was also the *captain* of the *honor guard for all of USAFA.* They called him the Punisher. And I had just breezed by him with nary a greeting.

The moonlight illuminated his white teeth like an ultraviolet lamp. I wondered if mine looked as bright or if his teeth were just that perfect. They disappeared and reappeared in an instant, and I braced for what he was going to force past them.

"Basic . . ."

I could see much more of him as my eyes adjusted: his high-and-tight haircut, the *substantial* brass attached to his fastidious uniform, and the bright-as-hell reflection of the moon over his *entire* mirrorlike boot.

Oh God.

"Basic . . ."

I'm gonna pee.

". . . what is that *MAGNIFICENT* SCENT?"

Huh? I cocked my head. Then immediately straightened back to attention.

"Sssir . . . ?"

Please don't take my lotion. Please don't take my lotion . . . Cadet Punisher . . . whose JOB it is to confiscate contraband . . . Please don't take my sweet-smelling last vestige of home.

"BASIC?"

Welp. I guess this is something we're doing. Shit.

"Sir! It is Amber Romance by Victoria's Secret!"

A beat.

Another.

The corners of my mouth couldn't help but leak a tiny smile at the ridiculousness of what I had just said. I might as well've sent up a flare so that my roommates would know where to send the rescue dogs in the morning, cuz it was going to be a long night of training. I was locked up so tightly that my boobs had started to sweat. Which, iron-ically, perfumed my scent even more.

"BASIC! IT. IS . . ."

Fuck. A. Duck.

"... *ENCHANTING!*"

A beat.

Umm. Pardon? Does that mean I can unclench ... ? I stayed silent. His teeth showed again in a large, albeit stract, smile.

"From now on I shall call you ... *VICTORIA!!*"

His eyes softened into happy half-moons as he threw his head back with a resounding belly laugh. I almost jumped up and down for this to have been the ending to such an emotional roller coaster.

"YES! ... SIR!"

"You have a WONDERFUL evening ... *VICTORIAAA!*"

"Yes, sir! Thank you, sir!" *You, too.*

He tucked one hand behind his back and extended his other toward me while he bowed good night.

What is happening ... ?

Well, USAFA definitely didn't do anything half-assed. In the span of two days, I had seen the furthest the pendulum could go to both sides regarding my interactions with academy men. Those who were supposedly my brethren had lacerated me because of my gender. A man called the Punisher had liked the way I'd smelled, and bowed to let me pass. Were they polar opposites of one another? Or had the pendulum swung so far in each direction that they had landed in the same sinister place ... ? *Have I turned into a horribly jaded person who questions everyone's motives now?* I couldn't allow my mind, my heart to go even close to that cynical, skeptical place. My interaction with Cadet Punisher may have been unexpected, but it felt infinitely better than the situation in the boys' tent the day before.

I traded all of it for a smile that lit the wooded path back to my tent.

PARENTS.

I was trying to follow the map of USAFA grounds from the back seat as my mother set out to prove that our family minivan—as much a performance vehicle as our lawn mower—could take the academy's cursive pavement like it was on rails. It was the last stretch of road from my national club volleyball tournament to basic training. My father made a show of holding on for dear life in the passenger seat.

"Tssssk. Okay. OKAY—there's no need for *that* . . ." Dad grumbled.

"Oh, stop it. You're not driving!"

"Yes, well, *that's* obvious."

They continued spitting inaudibles at their respective windows until I pointed out the window.

"I think that's Doolittle Hall on our right—"

. . . Or, you know, the Grand Canyon, if you just wanna drive off it—

"I'm surprised you could even *see* it with your mother driving at warp speed," Dad griped—to her more than me.

"Enough already! We would still be in *Ohio* if you had continued driving!"

I buried my face in the map, still trying to figure out where we were and where we weren't. Clearly we were lost in Unhappy, Colorado—population: three. As much as I had tried during the last few years at home, I couldn't navigate a route out of it. Where was the *Emotional Waze: Family Edition* app when you needed it?

I peeked at the two of them, at odds in their bucket seats, an impassible and toxic moat filling up the cup holders between them. Disagreements over driving were, obviously, not the issue, though provided a convenient outlet. We had been through life-changing events individually and as a family—some small, and some enormous. The loss of my sister, obviously, being most traumatic. One thing that Sary's death did for me, immediately, was to elevate my concern for those around me—especially my parents, and people about whom I cared deeply—way above my own. Not only did I become hyperaware of how others were affected by things, but I desperately wanted to be able to soothe them. I wanted them to feel better, to feel happy and good. As an empath who felt things super strongly, it was scary and heartbreaking to see them sad. I didn't ever want them to have to cry again. I had tried to only bring joy to their faces, to only be a source of laughter and pride. But as much as I tried on my own to do the math, four minus one still equaled pain.

Perhaps after dropping me off at college, my parents would be able to rekindle some of what had brought them together in the first place. After all, they had been married for over twenty-five years—the largest portion of their lives. Whatever it meant, I hoped that they would decide to honor their history, my history, *our* history. I hoped.

10

THE ACADEMY

Mail call changed toward the end of basic training.

In the beginning of Jacks Valley, we would all gather in the boys' tent for our weekly ritual. Mail call was peppered with light-hearted jabs about the colorful, sticker-clad, and scented letters that mothers or girlfriends had sent to all of us during our sequestered time. The cadre would open our packages in front of us and take the obvious contraband out while occasionally letting a stick of gum, or a squished Circus Peanut or two in between some photos, slide by. We used to look forward to the potential of a treat making its way to us after a rigorous day of training . . . but not anymore. A few incidents in the valley had given our squadron a . . . ballsy reputation. Most notoriously, a "black-ops" mission henceforth dubbed by our squadron *and* wing-wide cadre as the "Roadrunner incident." Wherein one basic cadet by the name of Junior Jr., our lovably rowdy Alabaman squadron mate whose name had been the result of a typo on his birth certificate, and his trusted bestie from another flight, snuck out beyond the perimeter—beyond the scent dogs and border patrol of Jacks Valley—to steal contraband from a convenience store. The hijinks had given us a wing-wide reputation and had also inspired a significant change to the mail-call SOP (standard operating procedure).

Demons Squadron was officially on DEFCON-1 *lockdown*. Mail call was no longer a fun-loving, lottery atmosphere, but rather, a stoic checkpoint at which we surrendered our only remaining link to the civilian world.

One day, shortly after the Roadrunner incident, I heard my name called halfway through the stack. Our squadron commander, C1C Tarantino, held up the envelope for his henchmen—the roughest and toughest trainers on our squadron staff—to read. They both had begun chanting my name tauntingly as soon as they saw the stickers, glitter, and colorful marker covering both sides.

"TAAAATE!"

"TATER TOT! GET UP HERE, GIRL!"

"Who is it from . . . your mommy?"

Cadet Rougher and Cadet Tougher's tones were razor-sharp, not playful or bouncy. I walked toward C1C Tarantino's outstretched hand, anxious to move past the beast formalities. I reached out to take it from him, but he yanked it away like a fourth-grade bully and pointed to the floor.

"Let's go, Tate!! You know what to do, city girl!" C1C Tarantino crossed his arms and watched, rocking back and forth, seemingly eager for blood, sweat, and tears.

I pressed my hands against the dirty, splintered floorboards and pushed up.

"One, sir . . . two, sir . . . three, sir . . . four, sir . . ."

"HA! Fuckin' A, it *is* from your MOTHER!" Cadet Tougher read over Tarantino's shoulder.

I pressed against the floorboards, and against my embarrassment.

"Five, sir . . . six, sir . . ."

"Let's see what dear old *LOMMY* has to say to her *LITTLE BROWN BUNNY,* SHALL WE?! AAH-HA!" Tarantino was all in now.

For the love of God. Leave it to my mother to have addressed her letter to an air force soldier going through basic training, *"My Dearest Little Brown Bunny."*

"Seven, sir . . . eight, sir . . ."

Tarantino tore open the envelope.

"Nine, sir . . ."

He unfolded the pieces of paper.

"Ten, sir . . . eleven, sir . . ."

It sounded thick.

"Twelve, sir . . ."

C1C Tarantino cleared his throat. He was going to read it out loud. *Oh, shit.* My stomach sank. I usually looked forward to the flowery encouragement, to-do lists, or personal prose that Mom sent, but, not having vetted the letter first, I feared what embarrassments might lie within—beyond the nickname I had given her when I was five. "Fifteen, sir . . . Sixteen, sir . . ."

My stomach tightened.

"Dearest Brown Bunny . . ." C1C Tarantino began in a high-pitched, cartoony whine.

"Seventeen, sir . . . Eighteen, sir . . ."

"'Sorry about the Pony Express, but your father and I were *divorced* on Friday—now, Popo, not to worry about anything here, the weather has been a delightful mixture of sun and . . .'"

I stopped pressing. Tarantino stopped squealing. He cleared his throat and shifted his feet.

"Ahh . . ."

I stopped pressing and I held. I held.

"Basic Cadet Tate . . . ahh . . . you may stand up now . . . please . . ."

I stood and he shoved the cursive pages into my chest. They crinkled on impact. So did I. I stayed silent, my mouth dry.

My parents . . . divorced . . . ?

His bony, twitching hands spun me around and away. He shoved me toward the audience, hoping that my body would find an open seat like a pool ball finds a pocket.

Divorced . . . ? Really?

I found a seat in between Shiller and Pepe, next to whom I'd been marching since day one. We three had persevered—in a line—through training sessions, hellish mountain runs, and drill competitions. Shill was like a bestie girlfriend who had a biological pass into the good ole boys' club. Pepe—who was actually the one who had shown up to basic training wearing a Notre Dame shirt—was my comedy PIC (partner in crime). He and I would often do bits for the rest of our squadron during spare moments of free time. I clumsily dropped into the empty space between them. Eight ball in the side pocket. Shill squeezed my thigh. Roll call ended before my world stopped spinning. It was the end of an era, announced by a stroke of my mother's technicolor pen. I put my hand to my burning cheek as if the words on the paper, still crumpled in my fist, had physically reached out and slapped me across the face. The word *divorce* had never been put on the table, or used as a weapon in our household. I honestly had not quite seen this coming. And *especially* not during basic training.

I put my head on Shill's shoulder, closed my eyes, and flashed back to the first time the dam containing the powerful waters of our family had punctured. My sister's death. I remembered shoving my thumb into the hole in our family's dam, hoping that the churning water would not crack it wide open and drown us all. For days, months, and years thereafter, I pictured my thumb plugging the hole.

My humor and accomplishments would distract everyone from the pain and act as a sandbag to hold the foundation intact. Not that my parents didn't have busy, accomplished lives of their own—they did. I'd believed that my parents' marriage, like that wall, was sturdy enough to stand on its own. I certainly didn't think that when I went off to college, the dam would break wide open. I felt guilty. I had taken my thumb away.

Questions about my parents' divorce bubbled in my brain. Where would I stay when I visited my family . . . ? *Who took custody of our dog, Duffy? What TF is happening?*

I bit my knuckle hard, and swore to myself that my destructive train of thought would not last beyond reveille the following morning. I bit. I felt myself pulling back from the edge of my own personal abyss, filled with that which I could not control. Blood started to trickle from the teeth marks around my thumb.

Not functioning during basic training was *not* an option. So I wiped the blood from my hand. I took my parents' divorce—and all that it implied—and put it into a compartment inside the closet of my mind, next to the death of my sister, breaking up with my first love, and a few other boxes. I would deal with all of these unresolved feelings when I had time to do so properly, at a later—a much later—date.

In the time that it took me to pick out my uniform for the day, I had wrapped up thinking about the dissolution of my family as I had known it. Intellectually, I understood the absurdity of putting a cage around my thoughts, but I was at the mercy of someone else's schedule. I was required to rise up and perform brilliantly in short, demanding increments all day long. I did not have time for an emotional bloodletting. What if, God forbid, I allowed my walls to come down, allowed myself to feel vulnerable, to cry, to reminisce—and the next moment we were called off for duty of some kind? I could not afford the repercussions of letting go—so I locked the whole thing away.

For the first time, I looked forward to facing a lineup of angry cadre the next day. It was more appealing than thoughts of my broken family.

11

THE ACADEMY

The lengthy march back to campus from our dirty, noisy three-week communion with nature went quickly. We bobbed up and down like BDU'd buoys. We had survived Jacks Valley. We had experienced moments of utter brilliance and total disaster. We had fought hard, never given up, and—most important of all—we'd *never, ever* have to go through basic training again.

We arrived as the sun bounced playfully off of the threads of sparkling granite woven like tinsel through the marble of the terrazzo. We raised our right hands and intoned a solemn oath—*the* solemn oath of the United States Air Force Academy: "I will not lie, steal, or cheat, nor tolerate among us anyone who does. Furthermore, I resolve to do my duty and to live honorably, so help me God."

The unfiltered sun rays ricocheted in celebratory, angular patterns all around us, like a laser light show welcoming us as official USAFA four-degrees. I waited with my class to receive my first pair of cadet shoulder boards, thinking about how far we had come. These small, rectangular accoutrements came with their own center of gravity. Our first BCT squadron commander, C1C Ferris, ceremoniously fastened them to our previously empty epaulets.

Shoulder boards delineated rank and position. They were the element of every military uniform that communicated a soldier's present rank, while the ribbons, medals, and pins revealed his or her service history and experience. Until this pinning ceremony and the acceptance parade that followed, we had only worn name tags and U.S. pins on our light blue uniform shirts. Now we looked like cadets rather than delivery people visiting the academy grounds to stock toilet paper in the lavatories.

Shill tapped my thigh in his excitement, and Pepe nudged me with his elbow as C1C Ferris finished pinning them and moved on to me. My heart started to beat faster. I kept my eyes caged as he attached my rank and we saluted each other, but I couldn't help setting them free when he took a step toward me to shake my hand. The second we made eye contact, he winked.

"I heard you did very well out in Jacks Valley, Tate. Congratulations."

Really? My heart soared. I blushed at the compliment from our first fearless leader in this bizarre cadet world. Like a Ping-Pong ball, my mind bounced back to Cadet Attila's advice to avoid standing out, and strive for the middle of the pack, but I ignored the thought, not willing to give up the good juju inspired by this moment. Perhaps my definition of success would change, but as C1C Ferris stood before me, I allowed myself to bathe in the present sensation.

"Thank you, sir."

My mouth said it; my heart screamed it.

There was no time to celebrate, of course, because, in true USAFA fashion, the school year commenced immediately. Time for takeoff.

12

THE ACADEMY

By our first volleyball game, my academic, military, and athletic lives were pulsing along in a symbiotic rhythm that matched my heartbeat. Everything about my academy life was in sync.

"Sooo . . . rumor has it . . . that there might be someone . . . You see, I have this friend . . ."

Mickey, a two-degree (junior) and six-foot-five men's volleyball player, had lumbered over to me as I was warming up with a ball against the wall of our gym. I caught the ball and tucked it under my arm.

"Are you asking me . . . if I 'come here often'? *Really?*" I went back to hitting the ball.

"Wait. What? No! No—I really have a friend! *This* friend—and he—" he protested, getting animated.

"It's a he? Are you sure?" I winked, kept hitting the ball.

"Yes. He just wants to know . . . you know . . . what's up . . . ?" He exhaled.

I kept hitting the ball against the wall, visibly skeptical. Mickey reached his long, lanky arm out and snatched the ball out of midair without even looking. Like a frog snatching a fly with its tongue. It got my attention.

The USAFA men's volleyball team was responsible for calling lines, shagging balls, and taking stats for our home games. Since this was our first game of the season, I had finally gotten to do more than just greet Mickey formally on campus or running around the track. I had seen him practice once before, and his game was a thing of beauty. He had a *thirty-eight-inch vertical*. At *six five*.

"Yeah right." I gave him side-eye.

"Fine," he said, keeping my ball. "If you can't tell what a trustworthy, adorable, hilarious . . ."

He put an index finger in his dimple and twisted it back and forth to accentuate his alleged charm.

". . . insanely bright, adorable, honest . . . did I mention adorable . . . athletic, stand-up guy I am, well, then, I just won't tell you who it was who asked about you!"

"Wow. You drive a hard—and *very humble*, may I add—bargain, mister." I took my ball back. "Fine . . . let's say I believe you—"

"Everybody else does. Even the government trusts me. I have a security clearance."

"OMG," I laughed. "FINE! I believe you! Do you want to tell me who it is or not?!" I threatened to throw the white leather ball at him.

His brown eyes twinkled mischievously over his devilish grin. His teeth, untouched by braces, were the slightest bit crooked on either side, giving him the off-center beauty of a runway model.

"I thought you'd never ask!" He winked.

I shook my head, holding his gaze. I punched his shoulder. He reached out and palmed the top of my head with his enormous hand. I played along and swung at him with both of my arms, Three Stooges–style. We started laughing uncontrollably.

"SMACK!"

Tip poured her voice over us like her own personal Ice Bucket

Challenge, her tone—and reminder of my rank—sobering us up immediately. I nearly shot to attention out of reflex, but instead I gave my ball to Mickey, who put his hand up over his head for me to high-five. I jumped up and spiked it like I would a ball.

"She's ready," he said to Tip with a wink.

Tip glared at him, and he recoiled, then broke eye contact with her to bump my fist. It was time to play my first NCAA game. I had been working up to this moment my entire life. Tip yanked on my arm.

"I'll tell you later," Mickey called after me.

When the national anthem ended, the announcer called the names of each team's starting six . . . and I was out on the floor, *starting* in my *first* NCAA game. Ever. I had visualized this day since I was a kid. I went around the circle of our starting six, high-fiving each one. When I got to our captain, she put both hands up.

"This is all you, Popo. You're fucking amazing . . . show us whatchyougot, kid."

I smacked her hands with purpose, goose bumps shooting up my spine and out to my extremities. I reclaimed my position on the floor and looked down at the royal-blue paint under my feet. I kissed my hand, then touched my junior dog tags hidden in my sock. I took a moment of total appreciation for having made it here, after a decade of double seasons, double days, practicing alone into the wee hours, and unwavering persistence. I touched the paint under me as a reminder to bend my knees and dig deep on our first play.

Bring it, I whispered to the serving team, coaxing the ball into my zone. The whistle blew, the serve was up, and the game was on.

"GOT IT!" I shouted to alert my teammates that I was going to pass. I sank below the ball and held my platform squarely to the setter. I took the spin and speed off the opponent's serve and placed the ball perfectly above our setter's head.

"Got me one!"

"Got me two!"

Tip called ready for an outside hit. I called ready in the middle. The ball sailed beautifully on a low, outside trajectory. Tip was up and over, smacking the ball through a hole in the block and down to the floor. We had just scored the first point in the game *together*, in a beautiful textbook play. God, I felt *alive*.

"GO, AIR *FORCE*!"

Everybody gathered in the middle of the floor and put their hands in.

"AW, TEAM!" we all cheered, smacking each other's spandexed asses, and rotated for serve. *Holy shitballs.* Everything that I had been working for, that I had envisioned each night when I closed my eyes, was coming true . . . play by play by play. Everything.

"AIR FORCE!"

"WOOP WOOP!"

Quinner, Linny, Mo-Mo, and I were arm in arm, jumping up and down in a circle by the locker room door. Celebrating our first win as college athletes. It felt *amazing*.

"Hey!" Tip spun her warm-up jersey around in a circle and whipped me in the ass with it. "Go grab me a towel, will you, and meet me by our lockers—*Ace*."

I pulled my arm from around Quinner's waist and rubbed the growing raspberry where she'd hit me. It stung. I looked back into the eyes of each of my fellow freshmen.

"Great job, you guys!" I said, high-fiving each of them and then jogging over to the fresh towels. I grabbed two and headed back to where Tip had assigned me a locker next to hers.

"Congratulations, Popo. You were on motherfuckin' *fire* tonight," she said as I tossed her a towel. "I *told* Coach you had been working your ass off and you deserved to be on court, and you totally proved me right. Fuck yeah, girl. You'd never know you are a just a four-degree. . . . You played like a fuckin' PRO out there!"

It was high praise. "Aww . . . whatever, though . . . you *killed* it. Holy high scorer!"

"Ha—just wait . . . you'll be up there."

She put up her hand and I smacked it. She had totally looked out for me on the court during our game. And from what she had just said, it sounded like her input had helped lead to my starting position on the team. I had dreamt of my college career starting like this. And I wanted to do everything in my power to make it better and better.

Immediately after that first game, Tip picked me as her partner for nearly every exercise, workout session, and warm-up. She had asked if I wanted to make my mark on our team, in our sport, and I had said hell yes, without reservation. I wanted to push myself, and she stepped in, already highly invested, to mentor me. Not only was she a firstie (senior), but she was an amazing player, our team captain, and very close, personal friends with our coaches. She had her name up on the wall of our gym for records that she'd *already* broken as an outside hitter. To say that I could learn a lot from the only firstie on our team was an understatement. I wanted to get better, so of course I happily accepted her offer for one-on-one help. Wouldn't any player?

It had happened in almost the exact same way for me in high school. The best all-around athlete in our school had taken me under her wing. I'd learned immeasurably from her wisdom and example, then gone on to successfully lead our team after she graduated. She didn't drink, either, so she showed me a way to navigate high school while keeping my eye on the proverbial ball—or scholarship goal—as well. She proved to be a brilliant resource, teaching me much of what I needed to know about sports, leadership, attitude, visualization, and performance. So, when Tip stepped in to offer mentorship, I got excited at the advent of being groomed again, in an even bigger way. Yes, Tip was a different personality. Perhaps this more demanding environment required different personality traits.

She had started to open up and talk to me like a friend, not just someone she was mentoring. Time and friendship with a firstie outside of practice is a privilege. It doesn't often happen. Just like high school, once again, I had to prove myself both on and off the court. After our team dinner on the night of our first game, she rewarded my game performance with a vegan smoothie and time spent shooting the shit while driving around campus in her car. It allowed us to start fostering a friendship outside of volleyball.

On our bus trips to out-of-town games, she told me stories of what basic training was like for her, and her flying experience. During away trips, we roomed together, and she delved more deeply into her family and her friendships at USAFA. I could tell that she felt the need to impress me with stories of how her friends had partied here or there, or how she always had a good group of people around her at the firstie bar on the off weekends. I could sense she wanted me to look up to her academic and social résumés, on and off the court. I could tell that under her bravado was a shy, introverted, and socially awkward girl. I seemed like a gregarious extrovert compared to her, but I had confided that as much as I adored people, I had been alone a lot in my life. Especially having lived as an only child for so long. I felt deeply for other people, and though I had a ton of friends, sometimes I needed to take a break and recharge. It made for loneliness at times.

This seemed to make Tip feel more comfortable. She told me about her deepest friendships and fallings-out. She began asking my advice about people and social situations. Some of her questions—ranking fairly low on the social-IQ metric—made me wonder how she had earned such a high rank within her squadron, the wing, and even on the team. But I found that she was smart—very book smart—and accomplished, both in and outside the weird little world of USAFA. I was finding that many cadets at USAFA excelled at academics more than socializing. I learned a lot from Tip. She said she learned a lot from me. And I was getting better on the court. *Yay.*

13

THE ACADEMY

Heel. Sole. Heel. Sole. Heel. Sole.

I fell into cadence with the shiny black heels and gray scuffed soles pounding the marble in front of me. It was Friday night, midway through our first semester as four-degrees, and I was running the strips to Arnold Hall behind my squadron. We were official members of the cadet wing now, not basics anymore, but we were still at the bottom of the heap. And shit definitely kept rolling downhill.

Heel. Sole. Heel. Sole. Heel. Sole.

Each weekday of this year had begun in the exact same manner. Today was no exception. I watched the sun rise while starching and ironing my uniform, shining my metal accoutrements and shoes, and obsessively cleaning our room for inspection. I had read the paper and found three unique political, military, or impactful current event items to report on to my upperclass trainer. We had a different three-degree every week who was in charge of our military training. Meaning, I had homework to do—pages and pages of military knowledge, dates, names, events, battles, aircraft, and a whole curriculum to memorize, along with our uniform, room, and squadron chores, for which we all received an MPA score, or military point average, just as important as our GPA.

After readying my uniform and room, I stood at attention in the hall with my classmates to get feverishly trained before running to morning formation—where we watched the flag rise and got trained some more, before marching to breakfast . . . where we got trained even more. Nothing like getting the ever-living shit trained out of us first thing in the morning, before running the strips to class. It was more effective than coffee.

We four-degrees were at rest in and around Fairchild Hall—where we took the majority of our classes. It allowed us to focus on the academic task at hand before, once again, meeting the entire wing for noontime formation, and a hefty dose of training, before marching to lunch with our squadron. However, once inside Mitchell Hall at lunchtime, the varsity athletes were thankfully allowed to sit with their teams at rest, while the remainder of our class sat with their squadrons, at attention. And while they, perhaps, got an opportunity to get to know our squadron uppers more than the athletes, we got to bond with our teams. We actually needed to consume food at lunch to prepare for the intense afternoon practice.

After lunch, we ran back to Fairchild Hall for the rest of our classes, then down to the field house for a three-hour practice for varsity athletes, while all others either met with their extracurricular clubs, or went back to the squadron to take care of duties and get trained again before dinner. After practice, our team usually went to dinner together. So by the time I returned to my squadron it was usually time for ac-call (academic call to quarters) and two hours of scream-free silence in which to study.

Heel. Sole. Heel. Sole. Heel. Sole.

Gabby and I had continued the fun and compatible roomie

routine we'd forged in basic training. In fact, most of our classmates had kept the same roommates they'd had during beast, making it familiar and even more relaxed and fun to find moments throughout the day to talk or hang out as classmates. We snuck moments of levity, humanity, normalcy, into the in-between—laughing and joking as much as we could while we studied, worked, and readied ourselves— since those were some of our only times to be social. We did have a little bit more free time than in beast, but it was definitely not the same college experience that our civilian friends were having.

Heel. Sole. Heel. Sole. Heel. Sole.

Falling into cadence had become a meditative rhythm that allowed me to study schoolwork or military work while in transit, sort of like my own life-sized fidget spinner. Tonight was no different, except that it was Friday night. We all needed at least one night off from thinking in quotes.

Heel. Sole. Heel. Sole.

The U.S. Air Force vision is air force people building the world's most respected air and space force. . . . Global reach and global power for America. Heel. Sole. Heel. Sole. *The U.S. Air Force mission says to defend the United States through control and exploitation of air and space.* Heel. Sole. Heel. Sole. *The USAF core values are integrity first, service before self, and excellence in all we do.* Heel. Sole. Heel. Sole.

I sounded like a fistful of fortune cookies. I shook my head from side to side and did my best to rid my thoughts of military strategy, famous quotes, and how many goddamn chairs there were in Mitchell Hall. I stared at the feet dropping to the marble in front of me.

Heel. *Just.* Sole. *Have.* Heel. *Fun.* Sole. *Tonight.* Heel. *Po!* Sole.

My squadron mates were upset that my volleyball commitments had prevented me from spending more time with them compared to basic. Gabby referred to herself a "volleyball widow." And I missed them as well. What little free time I had was taken up by Tip. So I enjoyed the rare occasions when I had room to breathe and be with myself and other teammates, friends, and squadron mates outside of the duty day. Tonight was going to be fun.

We ran the last fifty feet to Arnold Hall as a race, crossing the invisible threshold with our arms outstretched in victory. It felt so good to finally be able to walk after having run all day long . . . all year long. Clearly, USAFA subscribed to the theory that quicker was better. Walking was now a luxury, and I would never again take tiny freedoms such as choice of clothing, accessories, speech, and hairstyle for granted. Hell, we four-degrees felt immeasurably grateful that we had choice. Over *anything*. Including how to spend our Friday night.

Our squadron buddies Shiller, Pepe, Ivy, and Jugs headed straight for the make-your-own-pizza bar while Gabby and I looked for a place to cop a squat.

"OMG." I nudged Gabby and pointed to our boys.

Shiller had put pepperoni on Pepe's eyes while Ivy put an olive in his nose and grabbed for the sauce.

"Shocking," I said.

We both laughed, then Gabby straightened and spun her finger in a circle.

"Let's take a lap before we commit to a location. . . ."

We looked at each other for a beat, and then dissolved into laughter again. Boys roughhousing, making a mess, and fixing huge plates of food; gratuitous *Clueless* references, music, and laughter . . . It felt good. Almost like college was supposed to be.

We claimed the seating area by the jukebox. Gabby ran over to a beanbag chair and jumped on top of it. I sank into an adjacent one. Everyone else filed in around us. Arnold Hall was filled with freshmen.

"You look shocked," Gabby said. "It's like this most weekends."

"Wow—I can't believe I've been missing this." I swiveled my head. I had spent most of my time at the field house. So most of the familiar faces I saw were fellow athletes who also had the night off. I waved at them while Gabby pointed out others she knew and gave me their abbreviated dossiers. She reached over and tugged on the sleeve of an adjacent boy.

"Po—this is a friend and fellow preppy. . . ."

I stood up and stuck out my hand by the time he turned around.

"How do you do?"

"Whoa—hey." He gave Gabby a look.

"He's not used to someone with *manners*." Gabby leaned over to me while poking her friend. He shook my hand, wide-eyed and mouth agape.

"Holy shit, you're tall!"

A beat.

"You're . . . *not* . . . ?" I shrugged, laughing. I pointed at his bicuspids in full view. "Careful or you'll catch flies with that thing." I poked him, too, and he laughed harder.

"Heh . . . yeah." A beat. He stared at me while calling out the side of his mouth, "HOTTAY! Hey—get over here!"

A sandy-blond Princeton haircut whipped around and held up his drink. He walked closer, revealing copper-colored eyes, a strong jaw, broad shoulders, and a confident disposition. Venus Flytrap smacked his friend's chest, then pointed to me.

"C4C Hottie, C4C Polo *Tate*." Flytrap said my name as if it should've meant something to Hottie, but we had never met.

Nonetheless, Hottie smiled a wide, strong smile. His intense gaze and athletic frame towered over me. He offered his huge hand.

"Cadet Fourth Class Hottie."

His name was salutation enough.

"Polo. It's nice to meet you."

He kept my hand. I kept his gaze. Time paused. I could feel Gabby and Flytrap looking at us and then each other, but Hottie wasn't letting go.

"Hi."

His voice was smooth. *Chemistry.* He was cute. He knew it, but I didn't care. *Sometimes cute is cute, no matter who knows it.*

"Hi."

I smiled from deep down as I said it. Gabby tapped my shoulder. The boys had finished making their pizzas and had come to save our seats while we got food.

"You coming back?" Hottie still had my hand.

"Will you be here?" I smiled and left with Gabby.

Hottie and Flytrap struck up conversation with our boys while we got in line. She turned to me and cooed the instant we were out of earshot.

"Sooo—whadya think of *Hottie*? You two had a moment—I saw it! Whadya think, he's totally hot, right?!"

This was literally the most amped I had ever seen Gabby.

"Phew! That boy is fine. . . . I mean, if you don't want him, I will *happily* take him."

Wowza. I said nothing. Just watching, wide-eyed, while she melodramatically fanned herself. She looked over at the boys.

"Mm-hmm! You two had a *moment*!" She bit her cuticles and nudged me unsubtly. "He's tall, too. Did you see how tall he was??" She turned back to me. "Girl, I'm telling you! If you don't want him—"

I shook my head, chuckling. The line moved forward. We moved with it.

"He *is* pretty cute, though," I added. "Wow."

Gabby pouted, folding her arms across her body. "*Fine.* I hope you guys are happy together."

SMH.

We finally made it to the front of the line. Gabby and I placed our orders. She got her fries and ran back to share them with Hottie, while I waited for my smiley-face pizza margherita. The next time I looked over at our group, Gabby was sitting next to C4Cs Hottie and Flytrap, laughing exaggeratedly and slapping Hottie on the knee. He was smiling coolly and looking over in my direction between slaps. Our eyes met momentarily, and I felt my cheeks flush red. The oven timer dinged, and I brought my pizza back to the group.

"Here, take my seat."

C4C Hottie stood up, pointing to his seat. *Wow.* The past two months had made me forget such chivalry existed. It was nice. He stayed standing until I agreed to share his oversized chair. Gabby watched the entire exchange impatiently, her micro-expressions hanging in the air between us.

"I'm sorry," I said quickly. "Did I interrupt your conversation?"

Gabby and Hottie answered at the same time.

"YES." Gabby, emphatically.

"No." Hottie, casually.

Gabby shot him a look as if he had dumped his icy drink in her lap.

"Umm, I was totally talking about my Pomeranian, Mr. Ridickles, back home!" she said. "Hellooo!"

Hottie hid his smile behind a nose scratch before offering a gentlemanly concession.

"I'm sorry, Gabby. You're right. Please continue."

Sometimes cute is cute, no matter who knows it.

The night wore on. I met more freshmen. Gabby lived up to her name. I relished eating my custom-made pizza at my own pace—which was slower than anything I'd eaten since arriving in Colorado. It was delicious. The cadets around me made fun of my toppings—or lack thereof—but it was so much easier to take on a full stomach.

C4C Hottie and I exchanged looks and laughs throughout the night. We ended up face-to-face by the jukebox, talking. Gabby had found another boy willing to engage in her stories, and they, too, were in a far-off corner of mutual infatuation.

It was nice to have my back against the wall without having to do wall sits. It was nice not to be sweating or yelling or trying to anticipate everyone and everything. It was nice to be looking at a cute boy instead of an angry upperclassman. It was nice to highlight the *girl* inside of me, instead of the cadet, or soldier. It was nice. He was nice. He was very nice and very cute. And he knew it.

We talked for quite a while without delving too deeply into our family histories or life before USAFA. This wasn't like a normal meeting between a boy and a girl in the outside world. It was different. *Here* was different. *We* were different.

Eventually, we left Arnold Hall and found a secluded spot outside the entrance, where we were technically only at ease, not at rest. In order to avoid scrutiny, we had to move quietly, communicate without talking. Our conversation evolved into a custom-created sign language. And then into body language.

I was leaning up against another wall, still face-to-face with Hottie. He shielded me from the night air, from the view of upperclassmen, from whatever threat there might be. I felt small, and so did the risk.

When Hottie took a step closer to me, my stomach felt him before any of my senses and it jumped slightly. My eyes made their way up his torso, neck, ears, and finally, to his dilated pupils. We broke our gaze only once to find each other's lips. We said things without saying a word. He leaned in. His lips touched my lips, his hand touched my hip. For the first time in ten weeks, I felt a man's strength being used for something soft and warm. I pressed my hip into his hand and my lips against his lips. Both felt good. He gained confidence. His hand moved to the small of my back without leaving my body. He pulled me in closer. The movement sent a hint of laundry and boy wafting up to my nose. My lips parted slightly and our tongues grazed each other's lightly, timidly at first, then more boldly.

We let ourselves play for just a bit longer before we both gently pulled apart. I could feel the genuine moments when he let himself get swept up and fully present in his connection with me, as well as the moments he was trying to *make* happen. It seemed a bit different from the usual nerves in kissing someone for the first time. He brought me in for one last kiss before he pulled away entirely—not offensively but responsibly. Almost scriptedly.

Do not overanalyze this situation. This is not a military operation; this is playtime.

Sweetly, he booped my nose with his finger. Sure, maybe it was practiced. But in that moment, I didn't care. The gesture was a sweet end to a fun and frivolous evening.

Voices punctured our silent conversation—male voices, slurring drunkenly, near the entrance of Arnold Hall. Four-degrees were forbidden to drink, so they had to be firsties. Hottie took my hand and led me around to the front of Arnie's—cadet nickname for Arnold Hall. It was cold, but his hand—his huge hand—kept my whole body warm. At the door, he whispered in my ear.

"I had a great time. . . . Let's do this again soon, okay?"

I smiled and looked into his copper-penny eyes. I put my lips to his and kissed him once more, quickly but thoroughly. We started to part ways, and he smacked my ass. Something about it made me pull up short and turn around. It wasn't playfully in the moment, it was . . . *IDK* . . . as if it had been written into a bad porn or something. *Do not overanalyze this situation.* He softened his face playfully, and I relaxed. *Phew—he must've been . . . joking?* He touched my cheek, then turned and ran toward his squadron. I touched my lips, my face. I closed my eyes and breathed. I could still smell him. *Sometimes cute is cute, no matter who knows.*

PERSPECTIVE.

"Great game last night, Po!"

High school, senior year. I spun around in Mr. Jax's physics lab, trying to find the man attached to the voice. I had arrived before class began, and he was in the corner, making a piece of toast over one of the Bunsen burners. I put my book bag down in my favorite seat and went over to high-five his outstretched hand.

"Aww, you came?" I asked, humbled and excited.

"I did! And I'm serious—I love watching you play!" He turned off the burner, propped his goggles up on his head, assembled the rest of his breakfast sandwich, took a bite, and winked at me while he chewed.

I laughed and felt the capillaries on my cheeks bursting like Fourth of July fireworks. I adored Mr. Jax. He was tall and muscular, young and brilliant. A doppelgänger of a young Mark Twain, or Da Vinci's Vitruvian Man. He cut his voluminous auburn hair—himself—twice a year and the rest of the time, just let it grow wild. He taught all my favorite subjects, and coached one of my favorite sports: football. I had taken every class that he had taught—all advanced math and sciences—and knew that we were kindred spirits from the first day of his first class. I had come to believe that there were just some people with whom we just vibed more easily. Regardless of age. Mr. Jax was one of those for me. Nothing inappropriate, simply kindred. I adored him.

"Are you going to that?" He pointed to the flyer, sitting on my bag, that I had been handed on the way into school.

"Homecoming? Probably." I shrugged.

"You were the first one voted onto homecoming court." He turned to face me, palms up. "If this school subscribed to a monarchy, that means you'd be homecoming *queen*. . . ." He smirked, but his sentiment was genuine.

"No, yes, of course I'm going—it's a huge honor—I just . . . don't quite know with *whom* I'm going." My eyes dropped to my desk. "Yet."

I didn't have a date. And I hadn't really found any guys at our high school super attractive since a few in the senior class when I was a freshman. I mean, there'd been some cute boys, and I'd had a couple crushes. But none that I resonated with enough to take precious time away from my other responsibilities. I had always gotten along better with, been more attracted to older guys. But that was weird, too, because it's hard to date college guys if you still have to adhere to a high school lifestyle. I pushed myself to be so high-achieving academically, athletically, and within the community so that I could have options. So that I could get out into a bigger pool, onto a bigger stage. However, in this particular area of my life, I had felt totally . . . in the greenroom, neither on- or backstage. Dating throughout middle and high school was frustrating. I could feel my cheeks ablaze again. I folded the piece of paper under my bag.

"Oh, wow—did you see the sunrise this morning?" I wanted to change the subject, but also asking a genuine question. Mr. Jax was still looking at me inquisitively. He cocked his head with the change of subject.

"Did *you* see the sunrise this morning, Polo?"

"I did. . . . It was stunning. The whole spectrum." I closed my eyes briefly, seeing it again.

"Mmm . . . do you know what causes that painter's palette at sunrise and sunset?" He smiled, ever the teacher.

After a beat, I shook my head. Sensing his excitement to tell me.

"Well, you know that the sun gives off light waves of all frequencies in the electromagnetic spectrum," he prodded animatedly.

"Of course." I nodded.

"During the day, when the sun is *above* us, the distance between the sun and us is *short*. When the sunlight hits the atmosphere, the air molecules spread the colors with the *shortest wavelengths*—the violets, blues, and a twinge of green—which create the blue-looking sky." His arms were above his head. "When the sun is low on the horizon, it is *farther* from us, which causes the air molecules to scatter the colors at the *longer* end of the electromagnetic spectrum—the yellows, oranges, and reds. Thus, at sunrise and sunset, we witness the sky's canvas splayed with a beautifully complex arrangement of hues." His arms were stretched out in front of him as his words hung in the silent space between us like Monet's *Sunset in Venice*. He swung his arm over to me and pointed, a little more serious.

"*You* are like that sunrise and sunset, Polo: far from where we are right here, right now. Your depth is wildly beyond high school. Our school colors are blue and white, right? Fight, fight?" He nudged me with his smile, but was quite intent on conveying his point. "You are a way more colorful palette than just blue. And not only that, but you have the arc of your whole sunny 'day' ahead of you, your whole life's trajectory. Trust me. High schoolers—dudes especially—don't have the first clue what to do with a color palette *that* diverse, vibrant, intense, brilliant." He shook his head. "Naw—high school is just your art supply store. Where you get the ingredients to round out the masterpiece that you are, to figure out what you want and don't want. Don't worry, Po. There is a prodigious artist out there just waiting for you. Of that, I am *positive*."

A beat.

I just sat there. Mouth agape. Eyes wet. Cheeks on fire from one of the best compliments of my life. I got up out of my seat and came around the desk to hug Mr. Jax with every color of appreciation I had. The full spectrum.

The warning bell rang, and students started flooding into the classroom. Mr. Jax smiled a modest smile, blushing, himself. From then on, every sunrise and sunset would be a gift from this man. I took my seat and exhaled, a bit more comfortable where I was in the greenroom. And even more eager to finish high school and go on to meet more prodigious "artists." When the final class bell rang, I was the last to head for the door. I turned back to Mr. Jax and leaned in.

"P.S.—you're my favorite. . . ."

I put my hand up to the side of my mouth.

"Don't tell the others."

We both started to laugh. I popped him a heart from mine and left for my next class. All joking aside, the spirit in which he had delivered his advice was like a big brother coming home from college and divulging the secrets to life. It was exactly what I had needed to hear to make the last of my high school dating experience bearable. And I was forever indebted to him for it. Two kindred spirits looking out for each other. Nothing inappropriate, simply kindred.

14

THE ACADEMY

I surreptitiously searched the back of each boy's head in Arnie's, looking for the dirty-blond Princeton haircut I had run my fingers through the night before. I had bribed Gabby with pizza and pop so that she would come with me again.

"I don't see him, either," she whispered.

"Whaaat? I'm not looking—okay, yes. I totally am. Ugh." Busted, I slapped my thighs. "Oh well! He's not here, sooo, what kinda pizza d'you want?"

I shook my head. *Smooth.* I couldn't help but look around again. After all, he was on the varsity baseball team, and they had the weekend free from practice, just like our team did.

I handed Gabby a wad of bills, and she went to order food. I checked my gig line—the alignment of my belt buckle and zippered fly—to make sure that it was straight. Then I mentally head-slapped myself for checking my *gig line* in preparation to see a boy. If we were at any other school, I would probably be applying more lip gloss.

My getting-ready routine for going out had turned into a routinie weenie. I had always been relatively low-maintenance, but even more so now. I no longer needed time to choose an outfit, style my long hair, or put on makeup or jewelry. I had only one wardrobe option, my makeup had to be imperceptible, and jewelry had to stay silent and hidden. The most time-consuming aspect of the process was working up the nerve to brave the cadre-laden hallway at attention in my bathrobe on my way to and from the shower. None of us wanted to get trained, least of all in our bathrobes. So much so that some of our guy classmates would rather *pee in their sinks* than risk going out into the hallway to go to the restroom.

I looked around at the boys and girls in Arnie's, each one unique yet adhering to the same regs outlined in the USAFA handbook. What I saw was a bizarre mixture of uniformity and individuality, work and play, duty and party, military and college. Wearing a uniform stripped everyone of the usual visual cues that denoted class, socioeconomic circumstance, social group, race, religion, and sect. I'd never worn a uniform to school before, so I wasn't entirely comfortable with it yet. I hadn't even realized that I was an emotional dresser until I got to USAFA. Whatever aspect of my personality that had been most dominant each morning in my civilian life was the one that had chosen my wardrobe. Some days I'd dressed super formally, some days were cuddly chic. Some days would be all-black rocker chick, some would be tie-dye and braids. It went on without my noticing it until I arrived at the academy, where I had only one choice. I suddenly understood why some people sported tattoos under their uniforms, just to have something on that was exclusively theirs and personal. Something that was not standard military issue. I hadn't yet reconciled all of this.

A tap on my shoulder.

"Hey! Tall girl!"

"Flytrap!"

He tipped his head back and laughed with a locker room nod. Next to him was his friend I'd seen the night before.

"So, you and Hottie hit it off last night . . . !"

What? *How much did Hottie tell him?* I gave him side-eye.

"I . . . guess. He's cool—anything I should watch out for?" I half laughed, only half joking.

Flytrap's friend smirked and then muttered under his breath, "Pffff—how 'bout your point value?"

He spoke so quickly, so quietly, that all I heard was his snarky tone.

"Pardon me?" I asked.

Flytrap elbowed him hard.

"Dude. Shut UP." He thumbed over at his friend. "He doesn't know what he's talking about." Flytrap changed the subject. "So . . . is Gabby here? I didn't see her."

A tiny red flag waved in the back of my mind, along with the hairs on my neck. I spotted Gabby in the corner and pulled her over with a look.

"Be right back," I said. "I'm gonna duck into the lavatory."

I needed to think. The bathroom had always been my sanctuary of choice. When I was younger I had used it as a bunker, a safe room, because it was traditionally the only room with a lock. I had just found a stall when the door opened and two standard-issue shoes poked under the metal partition. I recognized the shine style instantly, then mentally head-slapped myself for recognizing someone's *shine style. Yeesh.*

"Gabby? You okay?"

"Polo? Hey—can I come in?"

I unlocked the door.

"I'm okay—but I don't think you are. . . ." Her eyebrows were raised as high as a bad face-lift.

"Wait—why? What do you mean?"

Gabby paced around the handicapped stall.

"Sooo . . . I asked C4C Flytrap if he knew who was shipping who." She looked up. "I mentioned your name and he said that Hottie had wanted to meet you for a long time."

"But we had never met." I cocked my head.

"Yeah, well, Hottie's been dying to meet you, because you—apparently—have the highest *point value*. And if he . . . *collects* . . . your *points*, he wins their *game*."

Point value . . . That's what his friend mumbled.

My stomach tightened.

"Wait, so, it was . . . I mean, *I* was . . . a *game*? How are these—we—*points* . . . *collected*?"

"They made up a GAME, Po—a full-on *fantasy league*. Only, instead of sports, it's with *freshman girls*. Each girl's points are high or low depending on how hot she is, how many other guys want her, how easy she is to get with, and what she will do for them, etc. They started it all in beast and have been playing ever since. If Hottie *sleeps* with you, he wins the entire thing. He needs *you*, Po, for the *win*."

My mind was spinning. *I was nothing but a . . . BET? A literal score? Wow.* I'd seen guys create and play some ridiculous games over the years. Games like *who could pick up the most girls using different fake accents*, or *drink every time Matthew McConaughey says, "All riiight, All riiight,"* or *full-contact billiards*, or *full-contact darts/jarts/ croquet/monopoly*, or *strip darts/jarts/croquet/monopoly* . . . Boys could be shitheads sometimes . . . and I must admit that on some level I *loved* them for their . . . simplicity. Sometimes. But this felt . . . gross. Awful. My head stayed down. I took a beat to take it all in. Oh, *and BTW*, was I supposed to *jump for joy* that the boys had picked *me* for the win? Was having the highest point value something to cheer about in this twisted display of chauvinistic debauchery? Was I supposed to be flattered?

"What made him tell you?" I picked up my head. "Didn't he think it would get back to me?"

Gabby dropped her eyes and looked to her right. *Lie.*

"No—I pretended to be cool with it. I mean, I totally played along while they talked about different girls. I promised them I wouldn't tell you. But I had to tell you, Po—cuz you're, like, the nicest. And he—"

I closed my eyes. I rubbed my lips, my cheek. I rubbed them until I felt the memory of Hottie chafing off of me along with my first layer of skin.

Gabby bit her cuticles. "So . . . what are you gonna do, huh? Are you still interested?"

"Gabby!" My palms to the ceiling. "Eww. Why would I be nothing more than a number to *anyone*?" I sighed. "Even if he is a really good . . . well, great, actually . . . kisser. Damn shame." *Blech.*

If Hottie had sat me down to have an open, cards-on-the-table discussion about hooking up, I would not've been *much* more receptive, but at least I would have had a *choice.* I mean, I wasn't a prude. Guys underestimate the power of honest communication. Actually, people in general underestimate it.

"No! Yeah, *pshht*—you're right, of course!" Gabby babbled. "I mean . . . Damn, girl, I just thought you should know."

I grabbed her hands.

"Gabby, seriously, *thank you* for telling me. *Thank you.*" I stood up and gave her a hug, regardless of how she had obtained the intel. I couldn't help but be a little sad over losing something romantic to look forward to. I hated the fact that my instincts had been right about something being hinky the night before.

We walked back to the jukebox. "I think I'd rather take care of this on my own, if that's okay, Gab. So, play it cool—will ya? Act as if I don't know yet and you're still cool with it?"

I feared that might not be much of a stretch for Gabby. It felt like she enjoyed a little bit of drama for its entertainment value. Or for the excitement by proxy. But that was just my hunch.

"Oh, totally. I got it." She nodded eagerly.

Hottie had shown up in the meantime, right on cue, and stood up to greet me. Damn. It had been really nice to flirt with a handsome boy with old-school etiquette. He did have game.

I kissed him on each cheek, and he hugged me close. He offered his arm for a stroll.

"Thank you . . . Don't mind if I do. . . ." I looped mine in his.

He walked the long way around, but ultimately, he led me into a dark corner to make out. I turned my head as he leaned in. He missed my lips, kissed my cheek. He pulled back gently.

"I'm sorry—am I moving too fast for you? Maybe we could go back to my room—I'll show you how I short-sheeted my bed."

This made me genuinely laugh. It made him laugh, too, because that pickup line would *only ever* work on USAFA cadets. I mentally head-slapped *him* this time, for throwing away his likability on a bet.

"Wow. As *tempting* as that is . . . I'm gonna have to pass. I'm afraid you will have to snatch your last few points from someone else. You should try two girls at a time—or, hey, two *boys* at a time—you know, to raise the *point value.* . . ."

Hottie dropped his head, exhaling. He shrugged his shoulders.

"I—ahhh . . ." he stammered.

". . . You what?"

"Look . . . I'm not sure what you're talking about. . . ." He avoided my eyes.

"*Really?* Come on—at least nut up and tell me about it, now that I know." I said this without fire. I was honestly giving him an opportunity to explain, to say or do . . . something. He wagged his head, shrugged his shoulders, puckered his lips, and turned around and walked away. He just turned around and walked away.

I took a beat where I stood. And then I, too, turned around, and walked all the way back to my squadron.

PART TWO
RISING TIDE

15

THE ACADEMY

The evening started out like every other. I took my flight cap—our required uniform cover or hat—from underneath my belt and swiftly donned it before exiting Fairchild Hall after my last Friday class. I zipped up my athletic jacket, or A-jacket. When we didn't have to wear our service dress blues, we were required to wear A-jackets. Varsity athletes earned large, fuzzy *AF*s to put on them, and I had just gotten mine. It made my heart swell. I made sure my book bag was fastened and in my left hand so that my right was free to salute an officer if necessary. My bag was heavy. My head was light. I should have eaten more at lunch. *Oh well.* I kicked up my feet and ran across the tennis courts toward practice. I was in my element. I walked through the shiny waxed-concrete hallway of the field house, past glass cabinetry filled with plaques and trophies and busts and pictures of past teams. I realized, for the first time, that I—that our volleyball team—had the chance to earn our place under that glass as well. To win a national championship, and be part of history in the making. I floated down the hall in a sea of excitement.

I pushed through the locker room door and headed toward my

locker, stepping over a freshman member of the basketball team who was sleeping under the benches. She had her headphones on and her arm over her eyes to block the light. Our locker room was a safe zone, a place where all varsity athletes could be themselves without rank or worry. Her nap looked so enticing. I had always admired people who could sleep during the day. My mother could fall asleep in an instant and wake up just as quickly. She called these naps her little "Winston Churchills" because the prime minister used to attribute his brilliant ideas to the tiny power naps he would take throughout the day.

Putting all futile thoughts of a nap aside, I dug deep down into my book bag for a packet of vegan Jujubes and can of diet pop—or, hopefully, *jet fuel*. I squished a red and a yellow candy together and popped the new orange creation into my mouth. I munched happily as I changed into royal-blue spandex and a gray standard-issue air force T-shirt. I laced up my shoes, finished the can of pop, then closed my locker and headed toward the gym. I felt so free in my practice uniform, even though it was another type of standard issue. Our dress blue uniforms occasionally felt like a form of identity theft, but our athletic gear was like a second skin to me.

Practice flew by. We warmed up, went through four different drills, ran, and then scrimmaged. Done. We filed into the locker room and changed to go to dinner.

Tip was wearing my red Polo baseball hat. I had given it to her after a game so that she wouldn't get cold with wet hair, on the condition that she give my lucky hat back. That had been a month ago. I had asked for it back multiple times to no avail, so when she put it down to brush her hair, I grabbed it and stuffed it into my bag.

The minute she saw that it was gone, she lost it.

"Hey, what the fuck, Polo?! What, you're just gonna take your *friendship* back along with your cap?"

Tears began to stream down her face.

"You *gave* that hat to me. It was a gift. I thought you cared about me. I trusted you. I helped you, and this is how you repay me? By taking it all back?"

Whoa.

The locker room fell silent. Her emotions exploded all over me. Before I could respond, she was almost hysterical.

"You're not even allowed to *have* this fucking hat! God! I should fucking turn it in—hang it on your AOC's door—then *neither* of us would have it!"

Holy shit. I slowly took my hat out of my bag and slid it toward her.

"For the record," I said quietly, "I just . . . missed my favorite hat."

I missed my freedom.

Embarrassed, I peeked over my shoulder at the rest of the team, now staring dumbly at the two of us.

Tip pulled the red ball cap on over her forehead, stood up, and hugged me. I let her. I drove my frustration and mortification through my feet so that I would not run away and risk our team thinking that there was a weirder reason behind her over-the-top outburst. I had not done anything other than just take my hat back, yet her outburst made it seem like I had stolen her boyfriend or something. She let go of me, then cocked her arm and punched me, full force, in the shoulder. White-hot stinging pain shot down my arm, radiating all the way to my fingertips.

"Fuckin' jerk," she said, wiping her nose. "Don't fuckin' scare me like that!"

Me . . . scare *her . . .* ? I'd relinquished my hat. I would not ask for it again.

In her attempt at a mea culpa, Tip offered to escort all of us freshmen to a sit-down dinner together, rather than taking me separately for touch-and-go (USAFA's aeronautical pun for takeout dinner). As we walked, my mind turned to a few of the more disturbing exchanges I'd had with Tip. There were a couple times when Quinner and I had gotten down to the gym before anyone else, so we had started peppering together and playing together. Tip had been pissed the first couple times, then livid the third, saying that if I wanted her help, then she needed to see my progress. Therefore, I should be *her* warm-up partner. I guess I understood that, if she wanted to chart my progress—and I was improving.

She also didn't care for my friendly rapport with USAFA's guys' volleyball team, wanting me to ignore them more—which I had flat-out refused. I may take some orders in exchange for lessons, but I would never be rude to another person simply because someone asked me to. *No.* She could also be a bit rough, physically. Almost like a child who didn't know their own strength, but used it as a backup if their humor failed. Though I didn't think she *meant* it, it was still . . . rough. I would not have treated her like that, to which she had replied, "Pussy"—echoing our beast cadre—and then softened and apologized.

I tried to shake the loop of these memories off and focus on being grateful for my training from her, and for the group dinner ahead, which felt like relief. This, in turn, brought my mind back full circle—as feeling that it was *relief* was the most disturbing thought of all. Should it feel like *relief* when you have a night off from being alone with your close friend . . . ?

On the way home from dinner, I started to organize my academic assignments in my head. It was Friday, after all. Wow . . . how quickly things had changed. If I had gone to a civilian school, I'd be organizing my *social* schedule for the weekend, choosing between parties, walking around the mall, going out to dinner with friends, or seeing a movie. But, alas, I was not a civilian anymore. Like it or not, I had assignments that required weekend hours.

I used our secret knock to rap on Junior Jr.'s door. I needed to pick up a book from his roommate. The door slowly creaked open. The light from the hallway sliced his dim, candlelit room as I sidestepped into the sliver of darkness quickly and quietly. Junior Jr. had his index finger to his lips, and behind it, a sly smile. *Something is weird.* I squinted until my pupils dilated enough to see in the low light of the room. There were seven or eight members of our squadron spread about, listening to music and talking quietly. My heartbeat gradually slowed to the beat of the music. Junior Jr. walked over to turn on his desk lamp and missed the small switch at the base twice before I identified the faint but distinctive odor wafting around his room. Alcohol.

"All right, you fuckin' pussies, it's time to go, goddamnit."

Junior Jr.'s Alabama drawl was so loose that it sounded as if someone had replaced his tongue with putty. He adjusted his belt exaggeratedly, with both hands, like a cowboy having just hopped down from his horse.

"Hey, where're you all going?"

I had to ask him—given his condition. He was obviously rallying his troops to go for a *ride.* His glassy eyes found me, and he answered my question on tape delay.

"POPO-PALOPOPO!" drawled Junior Jr.

He swung his arm around my neck and semisloppily kissed my cheek, keeping us pressed against one another while he spoke.

"C4C Roadrunner's sponsor is outta town, so he's havin' a few people over. Oooh! You should come! Hop in. I'll give you a ride, my hot lil' city girlllll. . . ."

He had more of a buzz on than I had thought. Roadrunner was his partner in crime from second BCT. Together, they had been responsible for contributing heavily toward our squadron's *wing-wide* reputation.

"Ha-ha, Junior Jr. . . . Wait, you're not seriously driving, are you?"

"Oh, don't you worry your pretty lil' head, Popopololooo! I'm fine—seriously."

He grabbed his sports bottle full of—something—and squeezed until he had swallowed the last few drops.

"Not to worry—I have not had *nearly* enough to *au pair* me. Ha—didn't think I knew French, didja . . . ?"

"Umm . . . I don't think you're making as strong an argument as you think you are, buddy. . . . How 'bout just staying here for the night . . . ?"

I cajoled, already sensing who might win this battle. Junior Jr. was going whether I was there or not. It felt like I had stepped on a mouse-trap, and now it had my conscience ensnared. I probably should have about-faced and walked back to my own room.

But I didn't.

Before Junior Jr. got to his door, I yanked the set of car keys from his woozy hand and offered to drop all of them at their destination. It was force of habit, after having spent four sober years of high school behind the wheel, always the designated driver. Apparently, I was going to continue the tradition.

On a deeper note, however, I had always felt responsible for preventing tragedy. In high school I had lost several friends and a family member to car accidents, though my sister's death was undoubt-edly at the root of it. The day after her tenth birthday, Sary had come home from an assembly on drunk driving and immediately taken me up to our attic playroom. While there, she made me pinkie swear that I would never be drunk or drive drunk. My frame of reference for drunkenness at the age of seven was little more than an exaggerated Hollywood representation mixed with glassy-eyed relatives pinching my cheeks a bit too hard. I didn't have the weight of peer pressure, or the need for any coping mechanism yet, so I solemnly wrapped my tiny pinkie around hers and swore to avoid drunkenness. Sary then took two sugar cubes from a yellow Domino box that we had kept hidden, and placed one on each of our tongues to seal the promise.

She was killed five months later.

Intellectually, I knew that my sister would not have held me to an oath we had taken as small children. Emotionally, however, I had just tucked drinking away as something distracting from my life goal at the time, not to mention a mortal betrayal to her, so I had never even tasted alcohol. I just hadn't yet found a reason that was more profound than my promise.

———————————

Sunday throbbed like a vein about to burst. The arterial walls of our squadron pulsed with the rumor of C4C Roadrunner's wild party—an incident that rivaled the only other reputation-defiling episode in Jacks Valley. Every task I undertook, whether it was polishing, shining, ironing, Sta-Floing, rolling, vacuuming, dusting, pinning, reading, memorizing, computing, writing, reading, memorizing, reading, memorizing, reading, memorizing, added to the bulging membrane of impending doom. The pressure built. Taps precariously wrapped its soulful melody around our bloated fate.

"CADET FOURTH CLASS JUNIOR JR., GET YOUR LAZY ASS INTO MY OFFICE NOOOW!"

POP. The vein burst.

The baritone reverberation snapped me like a jackknife out of bed before reveille on Monday morning.

"CADET FOURTH CLASS THEODORE JINX, GET YOUR LAZY ASS INTO MY OFFICE NOOOW, FOUR-DEGREE!"

The ferocious tenor of the voice was familiar, but I was stumped as to its origin. *Two classmates down. How many to go?*

"CADET FOURTH CLASS POLO REO TATE, GET IN HERE *NOOOW*, GIRL! GET YOUR ASS IN HERE NOW, FOUR-DEGREE!!"

Fuck. FUCK.

"NOW!"

I jumped into the pants and the blouse that I had worn for the last two days and whacked my head on the faucet as I shoved it underneath in a futile attempt to tame my hair into regs. I took a swig of neon blue mouthwash.

"NOW, TATE!"

My stomach dropped with fear, causing a vacuum that made me choke on the antiseptic liquid that I had started to gargle. I gagged and vomited the rest up into the sink. The blue and burning backsplash sprayed all over my shirt. *Oh my God.* I ripped it off my body, popping three buttons in the process.

I buttoned, tucked, smoothed, and zipped my way to the door of my room. I fell in *hard,* then *sprinted* down the hallway to the office of our air officer commanding—our *head* Troll.

My squadron commander, C1C Wick, stood outside of our AOC'S office. I swallowed. He grimaced. I racked my brain for clues as to how to report in to an *officer.* C1C Wick, already aflame, extended his strong arm to point at me as if he were shooting a bow and arrow, and then snapped it back like an archer with his thumb pointing over his shoulder.

My heart was back in my room. My stomach was in my feet. I

picked up one heavy foot after another until I was toe to toe with the line separating the hallway from my AOC's office.

"ENTER!"

"SIR! CADET FOURTH CLASS TATE REPORTS AS ORDERED!"

Captain Troll, our AOC, the officer in charge of our entire squadron—who reported to the three-star general in charge of all of USAFA—brought his heavily cambered right hand up to the corner of his right eyebrow. Before he made it past his shoulder on the return trip, I whipped my stiff arm down the centerline of my body and beat his speed to the right-hand seam of my pants. The salute felt like the only thing that I had done correctly that day. And that included having woken up.

I could only assume that we had all been caught for Friday night. So I yanked my shoulders up, back, and down even harder. I stuck my chest out even farther. And I locked my knees for the sake of form, bracing myself for the velocity and ferocity of my AOC's voice.

"CADET TATE, I AM GOING TO ASK YOU ONE TIME WHERE YOU WERE ON FRIDAY NIGHT, AND YOU HAD BETTER BE AWARE THAT YOU ARE NOT ONLY UNDER THE HONOR CODE—BUT YOU ARE IN *MY* OFFICE! WHERE WERE YOU ON FRIDAY NIGHT?! I KNOW ABOUT THE WHOLE COCK-AND-BULL *PARTY* THAT YOU WERE *STUPID* ENOUGH TO ATTEND—WHAT I *WANT* TO KNOW ARE THE *DETAILS*! EXACTLY WHERE DID YOU GO, WHAT DID YOU SEE, WHAT DID YOU DO, AND WITH WHOM DID YOU DO IT?!"

"YES, SIR!!"

Shiiit.

The room started to spin. The consequential permutations of what I was being ordered to divulge swirled around me.

It took me thirty minutes to tell my version of the events of Friday night. It felt like three lifetimes. I gave the barest of bare-bones accounts, not wanting to betray my classmates but also not wanting to be caught withholding the truth.

Captain Troll ordered me to return to my room and type my confession on a form. I was to go nowhere, nor make contact with anyone until further ordered.

I walked sullenly back to my room. My muscles shook from the residual fight-or-flight chemicals. I sank into my desk chair and rolled until I could see Jinxy and Junior in their room across the hall. They slouched in their desk chairs as well, looking like deer caught in the headlights of a truck. This look would become very popular among the freshmen of the Tough Twenty Trolls in the days to come.

Cadets received what were called *hits* when they got caught screwing up. Like judicial sentences, these varied in intensity and number of *demerits*, *tours*, and *confinements* according to the severity of each crime. Guilty cadets could not go anywhere or do anything during their free time until their tours and confinements were completed. Varsity athletes or cadets with injuries were required to sit confinements, while other penalized cadets walked tours out on the terrazzo. A confinement consisted of sitting for two hours in full service dress uniform at your desk, feet squarely on the floor and hands on your desk, doing work. A cadet was allowed to sit as many as ten confinements in one weekend— and I would add that a case of bleacher butt from sitting through a major-league doubleheader could not even remotely compare to a full weekend of confinements. A tour was completed by walking for one hour in full service dress uniform, weapon in hand, back and forth between two posts above the terrazzo.

All of the Tough Twenty Trolls who had attended the party met in Junior Jr.'s room the night that our punishment was handed down. The aftermath had exploded like a grenade, raining hits down upon cadets all over the wing. Our squadron had come close to setting the record for the most freshmen from one squadron to get caught during one debaucherous event. Our prize was the opportunity to celebrate the memory of that night for twenty hours every weekend for the following three months.

I looked down at the carbon copy of my future, neatly typed in a series of boxes. I had received the *most* hits in our entire squadron— including Junior Jr. My coach was going to kill me. My team captain was going to kill me. My team was going to kill me. *Shit.* I had tarnished my record at USAFA. I had never even been grounded before in my civilian life, yet there I was. Confined.

16

THE ACADEMY

I was up early, chained to my desk on yet another Saturday morning to do my confinements before volleyball practice. My civilian friends would have laughed, but not until well after noon, of course, when they had woken up. I had only thirty-three more minutes to go until I could leave for practice. I could not wait to check off another confinement at the CQ desk. I could not wait to finish them all. I could not wait to return to having some sort of life, some sort of freedom. I looked down at my computer science homework. I had read the same sentence six times without taking in a single word of it.

Twenty-one minutes. A nagging thought bubbled to the surface once again, like toxic waste, along with an image of Tip in my red Polo hat.

I think I'm in trouble.

My eyes grazed over the same sentence for the seventh time as I tried to figure out how I had gotten into this mess.

I was waist deep, for lack of a better term. It was hard to explain. I mean, you didn't just wake up one morning automatically *in* something like—whatever this was. People didn't get waist deep in something without first being toe deep, then ankle deep, then mid-calf deep, then knee deep . . .

I remembered Tip giving me candy in the chapel during basic training. I remembered her taking me aside on the first day of practice and telling me how good I was and how much she had wanted me on her team. She had apparently played a significant role in my volleyball recruitment altogether. Naturally, I was flattered and excited to get better.

I replayed the ways that she had taken me under her wing and spoiled me. She would set me perfectly arching balls for hours while I hit them, solidly, to numbered zones she had called out. She, a high-ranking senior—a firstie—would stop by my room every so often to bring me hard-to-find vegan treats. My roommate was impressed. We would talk and joke and laugh.

Toe deep.

She picked me up in her car for practice. She brought me home from practice. She rarely offered this service to any other freshmen, unless I asked on their behalf. She was our team captain, our leader. I had thought that she was just mentoring me. She was the best and wanted to bring up the next-generation best. It was just as it had been in high school.

Ankle deep.

She started to come by more frequently and message me more frequently. Gabby asked if all teams were as close as ours, and I had shrugged. Tip began to ask me for advice on a regular basis, "because she considered me such a good friend." It was not in my nature to judge her; if anything, I sympathized with her struggles. I never wanted to see anyone I cared about in pain. We had all had friends that we doubted, relationships that we questioned, struggles to fit in and find who we were. But deep down, I knew that something was . . . off.

She picked out my team jersey for me. I had waited years to be able to pick my collegiate jersey, but she had already done it. She told me why she picked the number six for me, that together our numbers made a sixty-nine. She laughed herself sick at her joke. I skipped the laughter and just felt sick.

She said that she was just kidding and that I should lighten up—and then took me out for a slushy and a bag of jumbo jelly beans. She made me her seat buddy on the buses to away games. She made me her roommate in the hotels at our overnight games.

Calf deep.

She ordered me to massage her shoulders after practice and games, though she rarely offered to reciprocate. Whenever I questioned her, she had said that "tomorrow's leader had to be versatile enough to be able to thrive in any situation," so I should suck it up. So I sucked it up. Things were done differently here. She outranked everyone on the team as the only senior. She was best friends with the coaches, and assured them that she would "whip me into shape." Make me better. She shared things with me, made herself vulnerable around me—and I wanted to honor that. She had stopped drinking as much because of our friendship. And I wanted to be worthy of her trust. I understood what it felt like to feel pain, and I wanted to help alleviate hers.

Knee deep.

She started saying profane things to me, telling nasty jokes. She ordered me to say profane things back. She laughed at these exchanges. I cried. I was at a *service academy*. Training to be a *soldier*. And I *cried*. I couldn't help it. It just felt so . . . *off*. She told me to lighten up, that I wasn't new anymore. She told me that I was a really good friend, that she needed me, that she couldn't live without me. I said *yes, you can* and walked away. She ran after me and ordered me to stay. I couldn't leave. She made me stay.

I felt like a total fool.

Eventually, the pride that I had felt in being chosen as the next team hopeful soured into a rancid, sickening fear that I was some kind of twisted, chosen prey—and that I had no recourse. I realized much too late that her grooming was designed to shackle me to her and only her. The special and selective attention she had paid me had become predatory. She had created a sadistic emotional prison with one inmate.

Waist deep.

The water had risen gradually. It had lured me, seduced me. And now I was stranded—and that water was still rising.

———————

The bell ending confinement jolted me out of my contemplation. I stood up, checked myself off at the CQ desk, and changed into my USAFA tracksuit and tennis shoes. I grabbed my bag and left for practice. When I emerged from the stairwell, Tip was waiting with her car running.

Waist deep.

"Get in, smackie."

"Aww, no thanks, I need to seriously stretch my legs after this morning . . . but thank you." I was trying to be gentle, ever mindful of her temper. Ever mindful of her influence over volleyball, over much of my life at USAFA.

"Hey. Why are you pushing me away? I'm helping you."

She had pulled her car in front of me so that I could not get around her. Her stare held me prisoner. I could not look away or I would hurt her. I could not hurt her because I would pay for it. I wanted to look away. She held her stare. She pointed to the open shotgun seat of her car. I got in.

We drove to practice. We listened to music the whole way. We didn't talk. I felt like a captive in her beige, two-door universe.

When we walked into the locker room, I was overjoyed to see Mo-Mo, Quinner, and Linny. We had been seeing less of each other, and none of us liked it. But USAFA was rigorous, and everyone was always busy, so we celebrated when we did get to see each other. Our mutual affection clearly sent daggers into Tip's heart. I pretended not to notice. I tried not to care. But I didn't want to hurt her, either—I never wanted to hurt *anyone.*

We dressed and hit the court. Right then, volleyball felt like the only normal thing that I had left. Schoolwork was burying me, the trouble I had gotten into was confining me, my military duties were caging me, and Tip was slowly sinking me. Volleyball was my sanctuary.

We ran, we jumped, we passed, we set, we hit. I smacked the shit out of the ball and it felt great. Practice went much too quickly.

Back in the locker room, I laughed and talked with my friends. Tip came over, took my arm, and pulled me over to her locker. She sat down in front of me and put my hands on her shoulders.

"I guess you would like a massage," I said, not bothering to keep the annoyance out of my voice.

"Umm, duh."

I started to walk away.

"I'm sorry, I'm so sorry," she whined. "I just missed you. You are my best friend. I felt like you were laughing at me and I got sad. I'm so sorry. Please stay. You don't have to rub my shoulders." She changed tactics. "I mean . . . Coach wouldn't like to hear that her freshman phenom has an attitude problem, but I don't mind. . . ."

I had *never* been accused of having an *attitude problem* in my entire athletic career. A bad attitude to a team was like rust to a boat. Both were corrosive and poisonous. She knew that I would be crushed if Coach thought that I had a bad attitude. I came back and rubbed her shoulders. I rubbed them because I was goddamn waist deep.

Eventually, I changed back into my USAFA tracksuit, T-shirt, and tennis shoes—handbook regs for athletes going to and from the field house. I hoisted my bag and started to walk back to my room.

The pressure built as I walked. The trouble that I was in, the confinements that I sat, the schoolwork that was never ending, the military knowledge that I had not yet memorized. The pressure built. The squadron mates that I had not spent time with, the other friends that I had not seen. The pressure built. I was caged. My eyes were caged, my mind was caged, my heart was caged, I was caged.

I had never felt this all-encompassing type of emotional imprisonment before. It scared me. I feared I would explode if I couldn't get out, at least briefly.

I am drowning in a sea of blue, blue, BLUE. Please. Help. I. Am. Drowning.

"Come ON, lil' freshie!"

Tip was standing between her open car door and the driver's seat. Her car doors spread like wings when they were both open. I wanted that big, predatory bird to just fly away. She jumped up on the frame of her car door and steadied herself with one arm on the door and one on the hood.

"Come on, CUNT!"

My face contorted at that ugly word. I turned to walk away. I heard her feet hit the asphalt and pound the cement with increasing velocity until she grabbed my shoulders from behind.

"No, come on, Polo—I'm just fucking with you! Come with me! I'll give you the break you need—the escape you need—come with me!"

I kept my face blank, not wanting to give her anything. She stuck her open hand in front of my face threateningly.

"FINE! But a REAL friend would get that I fucking *need* her right now—that I am only bugging her because I'm hurting deep inside and can't just come out and say it. So now I'm coming out and saying it. Please? I just wanna talk. You're so good with advice. Don't worry about your chain of command—I'll clear everything—I really need you. Just come with me, okay?"

"Fine. Okay. Okay. I'll go."

Of course I would fucking go. Of course she made me think it was my choice to go, but it did not feel like a choice. I was drowning.

"C'MON! FORWARD AT THE DOUBLE TIME, *SMACK*!" she shouted, jumping and clapping in a mockery of the USAFA cheerleaders at our football games. The doors of her car were spread like wings, but I was the one who needed to fly away. I threw my bag in the back seat next to a pile of civilian clothes that I had left at Coach's house.

What was Tip doing with my clothes?

We pulled out of the field house parking lot and started down the winding scenic route toward the main gate of the academy.

"Wait, wait—I haven't signed out for this!" I said in a panic.

"Po, don't worry about it. I told you I would clear it with your chain, so *SHUT IT*, SMACKY!"

"No, Tip, wait, I don't feel good about thi—"

"Shut up!"

Goddamn. I had been sitting confinements for too long as it was—and yet I couldn't help but feel my intestines untangle upon leaving the gates. The sun shone a little brighter. The sky turned a little bluer. The wind howled a little louder. I breathed a little deeper. We had escaped the confines of USAFA.

I opened my window and let my fingers dance upon the dry desert air. The sun shone high against the Tiffany-blue sky of the early afternoon, unfiltered. My hand made shadows on the pavement that continued to disappear beneath us. I looked up to the mountains for guidance, and they seemed to extend a hand as if to bring me back.

But I was already too far out of reach.

Tip turned up her favorite Cranberries song and begged me to sing along. I did, preferring to hear the words of the song rather than her pleading. I did most things she asked because I preferred doing them over listening to her plead.

> And oh, my dreams
> It's never quite as it seems

She closed her eyes momentarily and breathed deeply. I closed mine, too. For a moment I was transported. My life, my heart, my soul were transported. My voice came from a place deeper than my lungs and climbed to a place far above our ears. Tip turned the volume down for the next verse, but I didn't notice. I just kept singing, transported.

I kept singing.

I am flying. I am not in the car, I am not a cadet, I am not stranded in the deep dark blue. I am free, I am free, I am free.

"Wanna go to the mall?" She broke the spell. "I have to pick up a new CD, and I wanna go to Ralph Lauren and check out their selection of baseball caps. Come ooonnn—it'll be like going back to the mother ship for you!"

Of *course* I wanted to go to the mall. I had felt so cooped up lately that I wanted to go to the mall like other people wanted to go to the bathroom.

"Ha. Ha. Very funny." *Totally not funny.*

I looked down at what I had on.

"Shit. I'm still in my tracksuit—I didn't know we were going to go off campus—I'm not even supposed to be here, let alone be out of service dress—"

Tip sneered at me as if I were some snotty-nosed kid whining, *Are we there yet?* while on a family road trip. She pulled into the parking lot of the mall and parked near the entrance to the movie theater.

"Here—"

She chucked the cuddly white cotton sweater bearing my navy-blue namesake at my face.

"Change into this so you don't look like a freshman and we'll be fine. These, too."

She plucked my jeans from the pile in her back seat and tossed them.

"No one will know that you're a cadet, let alone a smack. We'll be outta here in like an hour. It's no big deal!"

"No way. Absolutely not." I held the clothes up to the window, shielding my face from exposure. "I shouldn't even *be* here, wearing what I'm wearing. Seriously. I don't feel good about this—Just take me back, okay?" I was starting to get nervous.

"Listen," she purred, shoving my shoulder. "I know I give you shit . . . but that's what being a freshie is all about. You're my best friend here. I know I don't say it very much, but I don't know what I'd do without you sometimes. You're, like, the perfect sounding board—I don't—I can't say it right, but you know what I mean."

She held my eyes for a second and then shrugged off her moment of vulnerability, her moment of softness.

"I'm not driving back to USAFA yet. You can either nut up and come with me like my best friend would, or you can sit here and pout in the car like a fucking baby. No one's gonna look twice at you if you're in civvies walking around the mall. And if we do happen to see someone, who caaaares! My rank will set them straight."

My fingers kneaded the soft knit of my favorite sweater. I knew it was hard for her to reach out. She was socially awkward, had trouble reading people, and yet she'd managed to become our team leader and a high-ranking firstie. She seemed to have some shame that she held on to tightly. I suspected that it came from her wrestling with her sexuality, and also from a tempestuous relationship with her father. But I wasn't there to judge her, just to reflect her incredible attributes. Sometimes her insecurity got in the way, however. I had seen her pain, buried deep; I had seen her destruction from not liking herself, not thinking she was pretty enough or worthy of love from her father, or anyone, etc., and had immediately felt an overwhelming need to help soothe it. There she was, at the helm of something amazing—an NCAA team with infinite potential—and she possessed personal potential that she hadn't even tapped. I could see all of that potential. I had glimpsed her pain and felt pain of my own. If I could help her, I felt the responsibility and desire to do so. I didn't want to be a burden, I didn't want to disappoint. I just wanted to do the right thing.

I gripped the sweater in one hand and the denim in the other. Both felt so warm, so comforting—like the best vestiges of a former life, a former identity.

"Nobody will even SEE you! I promise—we'll walk in, around, then out—it'll be fine! Maybe we can find you a new baseball cap—Now get dressed. I outrank you and I'm giving you a direct order. DO IT."

This time I shoved *her* shoulder playfully. She caught my hand

and twisted it into a vise grip that would have broken my elbow with only seven more pounds of pressure. I couldn't tell if she was serious, but I also couldn't move. I didn't *think* she would break my arm, but I was honestly not sure. I tried to move, calling her bluff. She put three more pounds of pressure toward the break. I bit my cheek to keep from whimpering. My heart started beating faster. She held her grip. She was a combat-trained, petulant child who took her jokes way too goddamn far. This did not feel funny. I made a conscious effort to stop my body's chemistry from gearing up to fight her. She was my friend . . . right?

Suddenly, she released my arm, thrusting me hard against the passenger door.

"I knew you'd come around!" She laughed as I peeled myself off the window.

What the hell? If this was part of the initiation process, a test of endurance or perseverance, then I should just suck it up. It would not have been the first time that I had overridden an uneasy feeling in order to accomplish a task.

I slipped off the fabric constraints of the military and slid on the vestiges of civilian life. The fabric itself seemed to welcome me back.

"Good. Now get out."

I didn't move. My lip was bleeding from hitting the window, and I could taste the iron. As I held it, a perfectly clear vision flashed through my brain in an instant. I saw myself walk into a menacing bear trap equipped with steel-tipped daggers wired to snap upon my entry. I did not want to get out of the car. I did not want this vision to come true. I felt like I had swallowed a ball of lead.

"GET THE FUCK OUT NOW, CADET TATE."

"Tip . . ."

"NOW."

I opened the car door, got out, shut it behind me, and walked beside Tip to the mall entrance. The doors reminded me of that shiny bear trap, cocked and waiting. I opened one of them and she pranced through it with her nose held high, reeking of arrogant invincibility. I followed her past the line of people outside the cinema box office.

Two of the most vicious trainers in my squadron were staring straight at me, mouths agape. In. Utter. Disbelief.

SNAP went the trap.

I stopped, about-faced, and walked from the mall straight to Tip's car. I got in, utterly crushed.

Rumor of my idiocy had already traveled up the chain of command by the time we returned. My AOC, and head Troll in charge of our entire squadron, *who had come from home on a weekend*, was in his office waiting to deal with our *situation*. I could count on one hand the number of times that I had gotten in trouble over the course of my entire life. And, before USAFA, every one of them had been before the age of seven. I had been at the academy for less than a year and I had already *exponentially* multiplied that number.

Tip, who had assured me that her power would shield me from all consequences, was immediately dismissed by my AOC to return to her own squadron. With her out of the way, he turned his burgeoning fury onto me.

"HOLY CHRIST ON A SWEET GODDAMN CRUTCH! WHAT THE *HELL* WERE YOU THINKING WALKING INTO THE MOST *POPULAR* SHOPPING MALL IN COLORADO SPRINGS?! IN *CIVILIAN CLOTHES*? I MEAN, I DON'T EVEN *KNOW* WHAT TO DO WITH YOUR LEVEL OF STUPIDITY, TATE! YOU MAKE ME

SO GODDAMN SICK. A GODDAMN MOTHER-CHUCKING *SHOPPING MALL*? A SHOPPING MALL?"

WTF did I just do?

I had made a wretched decision in one moment and was now making my AOC *sick*. What happened to the Polo who loved people, who had inspired people, who had made the most out of every connection? I was now making someone *sick*? *WTF was happening?!*

Tip and I both received a fraternization hit—a frat hit, in military parlance. We were not of equal rank, so, technically, we shouldn't have been spending time together. The hit was supposed to prevent us from doing so until I became an upperclassman.

Frat hits were usually reserved for military personnel caught *dating* outside their rank, so it cast a strange pall over an already unsettling period for me. I was shamefully confused at the whole of my situation. I was dumbfounded that Tip had ordered me to do something so obviously stupid. But I was even *more* stunned that I'd done it. Her power of persuasion felt way more threatening than any peer pressure I had experienced prior, but I still blamed myself for having given in. I was responsible for my actions, and yet I was supposed to follow orders. Apparently, I didn't yet know which ones I was *really* supposed to follow . . . and it made me feel like even more of an idiot.

Upperclassmen, and others who have military authority over freshmen—so, *everyone*—wield a tremendous amount of power. After having the rug pulled out from under us in basic training, and getting in trouble for nearly every arbitrary thing—suddenly and overwhelmingly—praise not only felt like salve over a burn, but it became our guideline and barometer for right and wrong. For what we should do and how we should do it. That was one of the tenets set up for how we learned. Everything.

The entire freshman year is designed to build back up the whole of us that is destroyed in basic. Ideally building us back up into good, competent, and proficient soldiers, as well as leaders. However, if we were depleted of energy or sleep or had not nourished ourselves properly, the amount of blind following that we did by taking orders could get out of balance. If the person giving orders was not healthy, then following them was dangerous.

It was very, very dangerous.

It was a relief to know that I had—essentially—been ordered to reestablish my friendships with others. However, I did not yet believe that a stand-down order against her would stop Tip from somehow yanking the chains that bound me to her.

17

THE ACADEMY

I am deep underwater. Everything is blurry—vision, hearing, my sense of smell. All of the sounds are muffled and indiscernible. All I see is a fuzzy patch of light way above me and a fast-moving patch of light below me. I am afraid I won't be able to hold my breath until I crest the water's surface. I blink heavily, deliberately, trying to see clearly through the salt water. I am running out of air. I blink again, trying to see what is barreling toward my feet. I frantically kick toward the light and away from the danger at my heels. The light is too far away. I cannot hold my breath much longer. I look down at my feet, and I see a picket fence of sharp, jagged teeth. The teeth clamp down. . . .

My eyes flew open. I sucked in a huge gulp of air. For a moment I heard nothing but my heart pounding in my eardrums. I was lying in Coach's guest bedroom, drenched with sweat, still drowning. I felt someone else's heat. My body registered panic before my brain caught up.

Something is very wrong.

There are hands on me. They hurt. I am in the same position in which I fell asleep, facing the door. No one has come in, but there are hands on me. They hurt. I am in danger.

I try to turn my head, and instead, metal clamps down on my neck like an iron vampire.

Someone is biting me. Metal retainer. Tip. She is biting me, tearing into me, trapping me. She is pressed hard against my back, searching, squeezing, twisting me. It's Tip.

My breath spikes sharp and panicky. I wrestle with her hands to release them from my breasts, my stomach. Her legs and arms together feel like more than just four tentacles. They clamp down tightly around me. Suffocating me. Panic makes my head slow down, down, down. Adrenaline makes my heart speed up, up, up.

Her heel breaks open my legs with a swift kick. She replaces her fingers faster than I can remove them. She is panting. Hot and sweaty. I can't get any air; she's too heavy. Beat. Crash. My heart. She takes a break from biting my neck to pant. Her salty, sweaty arms are draped heavily over mine. Her salty, sweaty legs pry my legs apart with surprising strength.

My struggle is turning her on.

I feel one of her hands scurry between my legs. A surge of panic floods my eyes with tears. It blinds me. I let go of her right hand, which I've been trying to pry off of my right breast. But it binds me. I headbutt the monster behind me, but she maintains her grip. She's getting even more excited. I try to kick, to twist, to flip. Her fingers tear through the fabric of my pants in search of what they want.

Beat. Crash. My heart.

She tears more than fabric. I am bleeding. I elbow her chest once, twice, three times in quick succession. Beat. Her breathing changes. Crash. Her gasps turn from pleasure to pain. She struggles for air. My heart. I throw myself off the bed. I bounce, hard, on the floor. I bound, fast, out the door. My heart. Out of the bedroom into the bathroom across the hall. Beat. Crash. My. Heart.

I crossed the threshold of the tile floor, locked the door, and spun to face the toilet. I threw open the lid and heaved with a force that nearly took my feet out from under me. My head spun like the porcelain whirlpool beneath me. I vomited again. I could still feel her hands on me. I heaved. I could still smell her sweat, her breath, her pleasure on me. I heaved. The odor of her sank into my skin and turned to poisonous shame and disgust. It made me sick. She made me sick. I made me sick.

I blinked hard. Black droplets of salty mascara tears fell into the bowl of sick below. My vision cleared. I saw, clearly, a bowl of one person's sick and another person's sickness. *Desire and repulsion, sick and sickness.*

My skin throbbed where her hands had squeezed, pressed, and torn at me. The startling force of her actions made me twitch and spasm in delayed attempts to fight her off as I bent over the toilet.

I vomited again, expelling nothing but dry, empty heaves. My legs shook. They could not hold me anymore, so I crumpled to the cold tile floor, still clutching the toilet bowl. I checked to make sure that I had locked myself in. Two shadows appeared beneath the door like macabre shadow puppets. I stayed silent, motionless, hoping the beast from which I had escaped would leave me to disintegrate on the cold tile floor. My eyes were fixed on the lock. The doorknob turned. Panic started to rise in the back of my throat. The doorknob rattled but did not twist. Two palms hit the wooden door in exasperation. My body flinched, but my eyes stayed locked like missiles on the shiny silver lock in the center of the doorknob.

It rattled but did not twist.

It rattled but did not twist.

The shadows retreated.

I lay on the tile for the rest of the night, shaking violently. A thick and sticky fatigue settled over me once the current of adrenaline had finally stopped pulsing through my veins. The blue-gray light of dawn crept over the room from the small window behind the toilet. I tried to stand on my tingling limbs but couldn't. I wrapped my arms around myself instead, and waited for the first signs of morning life outside the bathroom door.

———————————

What the fuck just happened? What . . . I don't . . . how . . . what . . . ? What do I do now . . . ?

Mo-Mo, Quinner, Tip, and I had been talking on the bed in the guest room late, late into the night. I must have fallen asleep. I woke up to Tip hurting me. I must've fallen asleep. I was in the same physical place that I had been the night before, but everything had changed. Nothing was the same. Nothing was safe. It had *really* happened—I had not imagined it. She was not the same. She was not safe. I had the bloody, bruised proof stamped on my body. I was not the same. I was not safe. I should not have fallen asleep.

So . . . what . . . now? What do I do?

My coach's house, my soft place to fall, had hardened into a jagged, daggered booby trap overnight. I needed to think.

As I shivered on the cold tile floor, I forced my mind to follow a single train of thought. *Do I tell someone . . . ? If I do . . . will they believe me? Who is going to believe me, the dumbfuck four-degree, over the decorated firstie? Even I don't believe it. I don't believe that . . . that . . . horrible . . . actually . . .*

Was I going to put words to what happened? Make it more real? Launch it like a grenade in the middle of our team huddle, so it could blow us all apart upon detonation?

I don't want to be responsible for blowing apart our team, for blowing apart my life. I don't want to make this more real. I don't want to inflict this grenade—my truth—on my team, my life. I don't want to hurt my team with the shrapnel of something they had nothing to do with. The explosion would be my fault. The whole thing is my fault. And if it is my fault, then it is my responsibility to deal with.

But . . . is this my fault?

It feels like my fault.

I pulled myself up and over the rim of the toilet and heaved one last thick and sticky, dry and tired heave.

The clanking of pots and pans from the kitchen downstairs startled me out of my trance. It reverberated through the floor, making my joints ache and my muscles burn. As I tried to crawl, the lactic acid slowed my limbs. I did not feel safe. I stood up on shaky legs and peeked through a crack in the door. The door to the guest room, through which I'd fled, was still closed. I needed to get back to campus without having to be alone with Her. I needed to get back to campus without having to be alone.

Quinner shuffled past me, rubbing sleep out of her eyes, on her way downstairs. I didn't want to walk down alone. I did not want to face Her alone. So I ran, limping, to Quinner's side. She smiled at me through sleepy, squinted eyes and put her hand on my shoulder for balance. I shrank inward at her touch and folded my arms across my chest. I felt a draft through the hole that Tip had torn in my pajama pants, and it electrocuted me with a chill.

I had rinsed my pants, but the draft attached itself to the wetness and froze me to the core, and my skin still screamed along the path of her trespasses.

I felt alien within my own body, inhuman. My arms crossed my chest like an ammo belt. Quinner was touching me, and that fact was all I could think about. Without the tether of her hand tying me to the present, I might have drifted away into oblivion. I felt empty of what I knew and full of what I feared.

———————

Tip took her time coming downstairs. When she finally did, she held her head high and brushed past everyone to commune with Coach Wifey, who was griddling pancakes. She put her arm around Coach's shoulders. They exchanged pleasantries and an inside joke. Tip glared at me while she laughed. She glared at me. Her eyes brought my stomach back up. I swallowed hard, not wanting to leave my seat to go vomit up what was long gone. I scooted closer to Quinner.

Tip's glare quickly turned ice-cold and threatening. I scooted my chair even closer to Quinner, who was grateful for the attention, as always, and reached around my waist in appreciation. I shot out of my chair with a yelp as if her arm were a freshly juiced jumper cable. My cheeks flamed red at my own outburst. I felt exposed, naked—ashamed.

Tip inserted her chair into the space that I'd made when I moved closer to Quinn. *Checkmate.* I should've anticipated her fucking audacity. My face, my heart, my stomach, everything dropped.

Except my guard.

I did not touch my warm, home-cooked food. Instead, I sat on my hands, at a total loss as to what to do. I sat on my hands next to the person who had taken full advantage of me the night before, my team captain, my superior, my teammate, my friend. I felt her prickly attitude of betrayal throughout breakfast. *I had betrayed* her? I wanted to leave. I pinned myself to Quinner and Mo-Mo for the rest of the morning until it was time for each of us to ascend the stairs to our respective squadrons.

ACCEPTANCE.

One thick envelope.

Sitting on the dining room table.

One. Large. Thick. Manila. Envelope. Separated from the rest of the mail. With a return address label from the United States Air Force Academy in Colorado Springs, Colorado. Usually, if a senior in high school gets a *thick* enveloped response from college, it means they got in . . . otherwise, the school wouldn't waste money on postage to send more than a one-page rejection. However, USAFA had such a rigorous admissions process that the envelope could have just been them returning test scores, transcripts, my birth certificate, medical files, possible files from the FBI, NSA, CIA, and who knew what else. After all, it was too early to hear whether or not I had been accepted.

I grabbed the letter and ran up to my room. I opened the envelope, took out the leather sheath, and unfolded it to find what looked like a gorgeous, silver-embossed diploma. Inked in perfect calligraphy was my acceptance to USAFA. Peeking out from behind that was their official offer to play NCAA volleyball. My excitement soared. I had done it. Over two years of academic and athletic studying, testing, vetting, interviews, having to earn personal nominations and then appointments from senators and congressmen, psych tests and evals, medical tests and evals, social vetting. It was a long, intense, arduous, and challenging process in order to even *apply* to the service academy. Let alone get in. And on top of that, earn a scholarship to play NCAA athletics.

Every teacher, civilian, officer, and law enforcement official with whom I had spoken about the academy had raved about what an opportunity it was to attend. The butterflies in my stomach grew with the knowledge that every single person already at the academy, along with each freshman, had been chosen by the same standards that I had. And if that was the case, we were walking into an institution full of our nation's best and brightest. The perfect team.

I could not have been more excited to join this group of bright, strong, intelligent, athletic, trustworthy, well-spoken, and solid citizens. It sounded like the highest honor, the biggest challenge, and one that had the most payoff. I could not *wait* to go.

18

THE ACADEMY

I *am chest deep.*

I sat at my desk, staring at a Chinese vocabulary list, feeling irrevocably changed. I had crossed a threshold, been dragged by a riptide out past an invisible . . . something. How had that happened? How was I supposed to play volleyball with Her again, take orders from Her again . . . *see* Her again?

Clearly, Her Horrible Her had not said anything to anyone. Nor had I said a word. I had passed cadets, officers, civilians on the way back from beyond the threshold, and continued on. My life had been divided by a chasm—before the incident and after—while the world kept spinning, uninterrupted. In the eyes of others, nothing had happened. We'd had a normal team sleepover. The first person to speak of it would make it real. The first person to break the silence would drop the bomb . . . and that bomb was not the incident itself but the *disclosure* of the incident. This shifted the responsibility, the blame, the potential catastrophe over to me. It felt like everything depended on me. If I said anything, the consequences would all be my fault.

It was all my fault.

I stared at the Pinyin (the phonetic spelling of Chinese characters) typed neatly on my crib sheet. I kept hoping the words would stave off the roller-coaster sense of gravity that kept sending my stomach through the floor and then up into the back of my throat.

Her hands, her teeth . . . They are digging into my flesh again. Her legs, her feet are splitting mine apart again. Her fingers, her nails are penetrating my clothes, my body again.

The memories violated my mind, my heart, my spirit. They infiltrated every silence and flooded my stomach with acidic bile, which made me double over in discomfort. My homework stared blankly, futilely back at me. The black letters looked small and insignificant against the vast white paper.

I am somewhere dark and treacherous, looking back at myself before this weekend but unable to return. I can never return. I am stranded. I am chest deep in something so sinister.

Reveille shot its melody over the grounds and straight through me. I began to vibrate. My hands shook. My legs bounced. My jaw shivered. I could not stop shaking. My stomach, my mind, my heart shook at the advent of a new day. Gabby climbed down from her bed and stopped beside me. She squinted over the paper on my desk, then whacked me playfully on the head, her palm slapping me into the present.

"*Chinese?* All night for Chinese *vocab*??"

"Oh . . . I just thought I'd get a jump start on the day," I managed.

Gabby furrowed her brow with the effort of piecing something together. Her facial features were absent of guile so early in the morning.

"What's up with you, girl? You didn't sing while you shined your shoes last night, or crack *one* joke while we studied. . . . Maybe that volleyball team is sucking the fun outta you."

Her laugh bordered on a cackle. Gabby may not have been piecing things together as much as fitting them into her own agenda. She had grown increasingly resentful of my athletic obligations taking me away from the squadron, and bringing me accolades and perks that she couldn't share. I didn't have the energy to laugh off her comment this time, so I just stood up and walked over to my wardrobe.

"Shheeesh!" she said, miffed at my disengagement. "Aren't we a little *sensitivo* this morning!"

I shook my head slightly. "Nah. Just tired."

I put the finishing touches on my UOD, running my fingers over the soft, quilted AF adorning my athletic jacket. If only Gabby knew the price I was paying to play on this team.

I hoisted my book bag, left our room, and descended the squadron stairs. I felt like a banana shucked of its peel, stripped of my thick, protective skin, naked, soft, and bruisable. I ran the strips to the chapel. Perhaps an hour of quiet would force my brain and body back into symbiosis.

My feet pounded the marble of the strips. My mind meditated on their rhythm, foot to stone, foot to stone. I wondered how many miles I had traversed in boxy patterns along this alabaster perimeter, how many hours of entertainment we freshmen had provided the upperclassmen in the world's longest game of centipede.

Upperclassmen. Her Horrible Her.

The roller-coaster sense of gravity returned and I doubled over as my stomach dropped. I tripped and landed hard on the marble ground but hopped up quickly, hoping to avoid notice. *Ow.* I checked my uniform for holes, scratches, or untucking. It looked fine. I continued jogging. The strips blushed a brilliant shade of rose for me.

Blood was now seeping through my polyester uniform pants at the knee. I adjusted my flight cap and glanced at the sky. The sunrise was a Monet. I had become a character that blended, blurrily, into the impressionistic backdrop around me. I was colorful and happy from a distance. I was a mess of scattered dots and anxiety up close.

My eyes shifted from the sunrise to the mountains. They stood stoically, almost broodingly. I looked closer. They were blushing an even deeper shade of red than the strips. They were reflecting sorrow. I dropped my head in shame. I was such a disgrace that I had made the marble blush and the mountains mourn. Brilliant, blushing marble. Magnificent, mourning mountains.

I am sorry.

I walked up the steps to the main cathedral. The grand hall was as remarkable as ever. I slipped unobtrusively into the last pew. The cycles of acid and nausea persisted while the minister set everything up for his service. The shining silver-and-stained-glass ceiling reminded me that I was a mere character in the magnificent mosaic above me.

I scoped out the Monday-morning crowd, wanting to think about anything other than what was in my own head. The first familiar face I saw was a freshman member of the USAFA Christian Fellowship. She had introduced herself to me in our SAR—squadron assembly room—a month and a half ago, after her squadron had trounced ours in a weekly freshman trivia competition known as the Knowledge Bowl. I thought back about that brief encounter.

"Cadet Tate! I'm so glad I caught you!"

Caught me? We just spent the last two hours in the same room. . . .

"Congratulations on winning the Knowledge Bowl, by the way. And, please, you are welcome to call me Polo. . . ."

"Aw, that's sweet. Thank you for that."

Her robotic smile had made me want to check the base of her skull for a microchip.

"And I want to remind *you* that a tight-knit Christian community can offer you the support system that I sense you could use . . . you know, given today's morally corrupt waters. . . ."

You sensed I could use some help? From moral corruption . . . ?

The language of C4C Saint Mary's invitation had been totally incongruent with her saccharine tone. She might as well have handed me a beautifully wrapped gift certificate to a fat farm and signed it, *Thinking of you.*

"Oh, ah, okay," I had stammered, "thank you for thinking of me—I'm just . . . strapped for time."

I had just wanted to leave. Quickly. C4C Saint Mary had cocked her head to the side.

"Hmm . . . it's funny, our Lord and Savior Jesus Christ *always* makes time for *us.* . . . Maybe you will change your mind about making time for him! If you do, just give me a call."

She had extended her hand.

"Nice Knowledge Bowl. God Bless!"

She had sent a chill down my spine. I had given her hand a quick pump. She had not spoken to me in weeks.

I pivoted in my wooden pew. Across the aisle from C4C Saint Mary was a notorious four-degree couple. Dating was technically prohibited within five miles of academy grounds, especially for four-degrees, but these two had made little effort to hide their mutual infatuation. Many of us had spotted them groping each other on campus. They held hands, nuzzled, and spoke softly to each other in their own private pew.

I tore my eyes away from them and moved on to the three freshman boys seated in front of me. Their reason for having chosen chapel over formation this morning was evident in their disheveled uniforms. Their A-jackets and pants were wrinkled. Their gig lines were completely off. Their shoes were not just dull but actually *scuffed*. I wouldn't have shown up to morning formation that way, either. I could only *imagine* what kind of shitstorm these four-degrees were going to incite at lunchtime.

The only other churchgoer that day was a freshman boy who hardly looked up from his Bible. The minister was droning on with a story of how someone had suffered and how Jesus had soothed him. He peppered his recitation with encouraging looks over to the boy, who appeared to be very focused on the pages of his Bible. The boy mouthed something that could have passed for Scripture while the minister smiled like a proud papa bear.

I leaned forward to see what page I should turn to . . . but propped in between the pages of his Bible was a crib sheet for some sort of history class. I smiled and leaned back against the pew. Even a slight smile was an enormous relief from all that I had been feeling.

Her Horrible Her. Nausea.

Just the thought provoked a giant flume of acid to cascade inside of me like a waterslide. I needed to stand up. I shuffled out of the pew and headed to the bathroom at the back of the chapel.

I stepped inside and took a deep breath. It smelled like a bathroom at an amusement park and immediately sent my mind back to Her Horrible Her's outstretched, candy-filled hands the first time I had met her in this very room during beast. *Jesus.* She might as well have pulled up next to me in a windowless white van and asked if I wanted to see the "puppy" in the back. I should have known. *Should I have known?* She was my *teammate. My female teammate.* Although what happened . . . that . . . that had nothing to do with gender. And everything to do with power. *Should I have known? Couldn't an upperclassman be kind to a basic without harboring an ulterior motive?*

If this had happened to a friend of mine, would I have encouraged her to blame herself?

Of course not.

The very thought of making a friend take the blame—for *anything*—made me want to make snow angels in a pile of glass shards. It was a moot point, anyway. It had happened to *me*. Double standard or not, it was my situation to deal with, mine to handle, without dragging anyone else down. *Mine.*

I left the chapel and headed for Fairchild Hall. The sun's rays pummeled me, but I needed the distraction. Fear created a firestorm inside my stomach as I anticipated that afternoon's practice.

God, I wish the sun would just take off its gloves and beat me to the ground. It would at least ensure that my external pain kept pace with what I was feeling inside. The wind was fierce. It swept under, around, and through me as if I were a kite. It probably would have lifted me right off of the strips if my bag weren't so full of textbooks. I wanted to let it. I wanted to be swept up by the wind, pummeled by the sun, and crushed by the mountains . . . swept up, pummeled, crushed . . . into oblivion.

19

THE ACADEMY

I kept checking the clock in anticipation of the afternoon's practice. It was the first time I had split focus from my classwork, and it felt as if I were committing academic adultery.

English was my last class of the day. And while I loved this class, and my teacher, I was cheating on English with the clock. Every four-degree in the room was struggling to stay awake.

Roooooaarrr . . .

I put my hand over my stomach, hoping to muffle its cry for nourishment. I had skipped our team lunch because I couldn't bear the thought of looking at Her Horrible Her over hot turkey sandwiches.

"Sorry . . ." I whispered to the classmates at my four-top table.

Tick, tick, clickity-clack, bang, tick tick . . .

"God . . . sorry, guys . . . sorry!"

The battery acid that had caused my angry growl had also sent an electric current through my legs, which vibrated, bounced, against my chair, hitting the underside of my desk. *Rooooooaarrr . . . !*

I shifted in my seat again, embarrassed. Nobody had whispered a response, so I snuck a peek over at my neighbor. His eyes had rolled back, leaving nothing but the whites. All at once, his head gave way to gravity, falling back into a cartoonishly open-mouthed *snort*. . . .

This woke him just enough to yank his head upright but not enough to stop the full-throttle overcompensation that sent him face-first onto the Formica desk.

THWACK!

I jumped at the sound, even though I had watched it all unfold. Stares flew in from all corners of the room. C4C Forehead rubbed the growing red welt over his third eye.

"AHHemm . . ." said Major Grammar, our professor, who was a stickler for all things linguistic. He pointed to the back wall.

"Yes, sir," mumbled C4C Forehead, who stood up and slunk to the back of the room to join C4Cs Drool and Snore for the remainder of class.

I looked at the clock again. Four more minutes. Four minutes until practice. Four minutes until I had to face Her Horrible Her.

Three minutes and forty-nine seconds.

My belly twisted and burned in anticipation of seeing Her Horrible Her again. Practice had always been the highlight of my day, and I hoped, prayed, that my sport, my love, would still be my saving grace.

———————————

I jogged into the gym as quickly as I could, avoiding extensive locker room exposure. I had become an actress, trying my very best to appear as normal and undamaged as I could. The gym was empty. The net was already set up. I took a ball out of the royal-blue canvas cart and went over to the cinder-block wall. I threw the ball up and smacked it, its trajectory sending it first to the floor, then the wall, and finally back toward my right arm. I smacked it again. *Floor, wall, hand. Smack. Floor, wall, hand. Smack.* I got a rhythm going.

Betrayal, hurt, pain. Smack. Betrayal, hurt, pain. Smack. I switched hands, rocked back and forth, kept the rhythm going. *This is my sport, my catharsis, my saving grace. This is my sport and I love it. It has never violated me in the middle of the night; it has never dragged me underwater. It has been my unwavering, consistently available outlet for managing my inner turmoil for so much of my life. This sport is mine, and I love it. Smack.*

I kept the drill going until the air shifted and I mis-hit the ball for the first time. Her Horrible Her swooped into the gym, barking orders.

"Okay, guys, line up on the end line!"

I felt her icy stare locked onto me.

"Coach Wifey is running late. I'm running practice for now, so knees up! Start runnin', let's go!"

"Hey, number *six*!"

Her command stopped me immediately. I hated my number. I could not think of another person, place, or thing toward which I had ever, in my whole life, harbored *hatred*. She knew this. Calling me by the number that *she* had chosen for me cut instantly to the quick, and she knew it.

Choosing a jersey number was a sacred ritual for every athlete. I had looked forward to christening my college athletic career in this way for over a *decade*. Her Horrible Her might as well have lifted her leg and marked her territory when she threw me that giant royal-blue number six. Every time she had called us the "Sixty-Nine Twins," I had felt like a urine-soaked fire hydrant. The number six was *not* my number, it was *hers*. I stopped jogging halfway to the baseline. I turned and stared at her.

"I expect a lot out of you, number six!" She pointed at me and looked down her nose defiantly. "A LOT TODAY, YA HEAR ME?!"

I feared the contents of my stomach would edge out any possible words if I opened my mouth, so I nodded.

"You *better* nod!" She shoved the ball cart to center court. "Now getchyerfuckingass over there!"

SWAT!

She *drop-kicked* a ball into my lower back, and it made a loud *thud* that was overshadowed only by how much it stung. Everyone in the gym froze, wide-eyed.

"Ha—Tate's got some learning to do . . . so let's all show her, shall we?"

Her Horrible Her scoffed, wild-eyed, trying to temper what she had just done and justify what was coming.

The next two and a half hours reeked of vengeance. She sabotaged every single drill where she put me in the center, making the entire team run after every arbitrary imperfection in my performance. Eventually, the whole team was hurling dirty looks at me as we gathered on the baseline for the bazillionth time. Red and Flip even hissed.

"Look, whatever you did to piss her off—whatever you did to her—just apologize, okay? Just fuckin' apologize—you're killin' us," said Red in an evil whisper.

"Yeah, Po—you're fuckin' killin us!" echoed Flip.

Their words punched me in the gut. I bent over, hands on my knees, trying to catch my breath. The fact that my teammates—even unknowingly—were now stomping over the already-soiled trail of her violation broke my heart.

I wanted to scream, but I had no air.

Can't you see the gun to my head? I am not safe. Don't you see the danger swirling all around me?

But they couldn't. They couldn't see it.

All they could see was that I had gotten in trouble somehow and they were suffering the consequences. I was alone with my secret truth. From the outside, it looked like I was royally messing up. The most expedient way to deal with the situation was to take responsibility for all of it and limit the casualties to one. I knew that I could take a lot of shit. I had been silently taking it my whole life so that others wouldn't have to. Perhaps I should just apologize to those around me, suck it all up, put it away, away, away, and go back to being the phenomenal cadet that I had started out being.

I took the net down after practice so that I would be the only one of my team left by the time I dragged my worn-out, sweaty ass back to the locker room. The place was nearly empty, yet Her Horrible Her had managed to linger. Placed squarely on top of my running suit in my locker was a note addressed to me. I wanted to rip it up, burn it. I wanted to run from it—but I couldn't. I sat down on the bench instead, and read it. Even though I could barely see the words through my blurry tears, the sentiment burned itself into my memory:

> *God, I must be a monster to feel the way I do*
> *about you . . . only some sick freak of nature*
> *would fall for someone of the same sex. . . .*

Fall for someone? Her intention was egocentric. Her sentimentality was unapologetic. Her rationalization was unbelievable.

> *I swear to God I couldn't live if you told someone*
> *about this. . . . I would clear my medicine*
> *cabinet in the middle of the night or jump out*
> *my window. . . . I just can't imagine how you*
> *could hurt me so badly by telling someone. . . .*
> *Don't fucking tell, please. If you care about my*
> *life at all, please don't fucking tell. . . . I wouldn't*
> *be able to go on. You know what it feels like to*

not have been able to save your sister's life, and
you wouldn't want my *blood on your hands, too,*
would you? Would you?! Please . . .

The room started to spin. I sat on the bench in front of my locker and put my head between my knees.

She is using my sister?

I felt as if I were tied to a merry-go-round gathering speed. Round and round I spun, unable to stop my mind from flashing back eleven years to the day my sister was killed. That memory was like a lifelong game of boomerang. I kept pitching it away from me, but it always arced right back to my heart. Right back. To my heart.

HEARTBREAK.

The phone rings. It pierces the silence like a harpoon through a butterfly. I drop my oversized Sesame Street sign-language book onto the blue carpet of the bedroom that Sary and I share. I skid quickly downstairs on my bottom, knowing that my little legs can't move fast enough. Bump, bump, bump. I see Mommy drop the kitchen phone. She just drops it. It falls all that way down and bangs loudly on the linoleum floor.

BANG.

Something in me drops, too. She grabs my arm. Too hard. We run, run, run down the tiny cement path leading to the garage. I cannot catch my breath. We squeal out of the driveway. Something is stuck deep, deep down inside Mommy's tummy, and it must be hurting, because she is moaning from deep inside. I cannot catch my breath.

We speed down the four-lane road. I'm scared. Mommy says the same words over and over. "Our Father, who art in heaven. Our Father, who art in heaven." We turn and speed down a bumpy dirt road. Rocks spit, kick, and peck at the big glass windshield. We stop so fast that we scare the tires, too. They scream and screech. We are at the stables. We get out of the car and Mommy grabs my arm again. Too hard. We run, run, run. I cannot catch my breath. My legs cannot keep up. I'm too little. I try, I try. I am scared. I cannot tell if we are running from something that is chasing us or toward something that is calling us. Either way, I know the thing is bad.

I run, run, run faster. I smell horses and it reminds me that I was supposed to clean the stables today. I was supposed to be here working and riding today. I should have been here already. I am supposed to be here. We run into and through and out of the stables. Bruce Springsteen's "Dancing in the Dark" blares from a tinny FM stereo hanging next to where I last put the bridles. I love this song. I know all of the words. I love it. It is playing loudly. We go out the back door of the stables toward the field. We run, run, run. Faster.

I'm scared. Mommy has no more words left. Mommy moans. I squeeze her hand as hard as I can. I can't, I won't, I don't want to let go. I'm scared. I squeeze Mommy's hand, but she still can't find her words. We finally see Sary. We stop running, but Mommy is still moaning. We reach Sary. We reach Sary. We finally reach Sary. She looks like she stopped in the middle of making a snow angel. Why did she stop? She looks like an angel. Why did she stop?

The two men from the ambulance are kneeling over her. Mommy is squeezing me. Too hard. I can't breathe. Mommy squeezes me and rocks me and moans. I'm scared. Something deep down inside of Mommy is hurt and dying and it moans and howls and we rock and hold on to each other. We moan and rock and hold on and try to ease its pain, but it is dying. Sary looks like a snow angel. Why did she stop? Mommy? Why did she stop? Mommy . . . I'm scared.

20

THE ACADEMY

I concentrated on my breath. There was not enough air in this locker room. Over a decade had passed since the day Sary died and I still hadn't caught my breath.

I cannot believe she used my sister's memory.

I had told her that I was supposed to be at the stables the day my sister was killed. I had told that to her in *confidence*, not to be loaded like a bullet into the gun she held to my head.

She described what she did as having *fallen for me*?

I plunged my head deeper between my knees. I felt dirty, stupid, tricked, sick, and—now that she had threatened to commit suicide—responsible. I could not let her kill herself. I didn't know if she was bluffing or not, but she was right about one thing: I would never let someone else die on my watch again.

I forced myself to stand, and fought the serpentine current of dark blue water all the way back to my room.

I didn't know what to do.

I didn't want her to hurt herself.

This is so fucked up.

Part of me knew that it was *hurt people who hurt people* . . . and Tip was hurt people. Like all of us, she carried past pain. Some of it came from fighting with family and friends and feelings of inadequacy. And if she struggled with her homosexuality, then I had tremendous sympathy for her. I was not gay, but I certainly understood the feeling of isolation. I had felt alone in a room full of people for much of my life. It didn't matter from what circumstance it germinated, pain was pain. And I knew pain.

The other part of me was screaming that what Her Horrible Her had done at Coach's house had *nothing to do with homosexuality* and *everything to do with power, violence, brutality.* She needed to master me. Period.

But I could not let her die.

So I wrote her a letter back.

I gave her just enough reassurance that I cared about her life. That being gay was not the same thing as being a monster. That she should not hurt herself. I said not a word about her violating my body, my soul, my spirit. I said not a word about her having hurt me irreparably. I treaded the deep water because I could not let her die.

Thinking about that day's practice, the note, I understood that I would not be able to run from her or from what she'd done. The compartment in which I had tried to stuff it was bursting at the seams, capable of exploding at any moment. Her Horrible Her was always going to lord her position over me. My mind, my body would not let me forget what she had done.

I am in deep.

I could feel the water swirling around me, pushing me, pulling me, drawing me further out into a murky abyss. Something started to rise in the back of my throat, lighter than vomit but far more sinister. It tickled and burned as if I had swallowed fiberglass insulation. It rose from my core, forcing me to acknowledge it. It was *panic.* And it was rising.

21

THE ACADEMY

The blue-gray filter of dawn fell over the morning like a cashmere blanket. I wanted to wrap myself in the safety and comfort of daylight, where everything could be seen and nothing could sneak up on me.

Wrap me in your warmth, sun. Pummel me with your rays. Come on.

I climbed out from under my desk, where I had finally felt safe enough to sleep after Gabby went to bed. I could barely move. It took nearly a full minute to unfold my extremities and stand up. I grabbed a can of diet jet fuel from behind my computer while I assembled my uniform. I had bought a surplus yesterday so that I would be able to stay vertical between sunrises. Since Tip's ambush, I no longer trusted what lay hidden behind the darkness of the night.

I put on my uniform from the day before, having barely enough energy to fall in and walk down the hall to use the restroom, let alone prep a new uni.

Reveille blared over the loudspeaker as I walked back to the room, startling me so much that I whacked my knee on the hardwood door frame and woke Gabby out of her usual coma.

"Jesus. You're all dressed? What's the occasion? Am I late? Jesus."

"No, no, no, honey. You're fine. I just couldn't sleep. Sorry."

"Well, maybe you shoulda been here last night for the training of a lifetime from Cadet Renfroe. That would've made you tired enough to sleep! That's epic training sesh number THREE that you've missed because of '*practice*'—in case you're wondering."

Her snarky comeback cut through whatever softness the morning had brought. I did feel guilty for missing training sessions with the rest of my squadron. Gabby, of course, had no idea of the tradeoff.

I became an absolute shit magnet as soon as we got out into the hallway. There were so many cadre descending on me—and Gabby by default—that the boys across the hall actually fell out of attention, folded their arms and legs, and leaned against the wall to talk to one another while we got reamed. Apparently, some of my compatriots shared Gabby's resentment and decided to take the opportunity to let fly their stockpiled munitions.

"WHERE WERE YOU YESTERDAY BEFORE MORNING FORMATION, TATE?!"

The cadre tag-teamed their rapid-fire questions before I could even answer the first one.

"WHERE WERE YOU AFTER CLASS YESTERDAY?!"

In another kind of hell.

"DON'T YOU THINK YOU OWE YOUR CLASSMATES AN EXPLANATION AS TO WHERE THE FUCK YOU'VE BEEN THIS WHOLE YEAR, TATE?"

I could always tell what resentments each upperclassman trainer held over from being a smack, because it always spewed forth from them the loudest. Oftentimes, if you spot it, you got it. And these guys were unforgiving when it came to athletic commitments. They were not varsity athletes, and some of the things they screamed while training sounded like they would've been the first to join the male equivalent of Gabby's bitter "volleyball widow" club, had it existed when they were four-degrees.

"WHOTHEHELLDOYOUTHINKYOUAREANYWAYYOUPA THETICEXCUSEFORACADET?"

The flaming continued throughout formation and all the way into Mitchell Hall. Apparently, my squadron mates had forgotten our requisite procedure of running immediately over to stand beside a fellow peon while she was getting trained. Not *one* other freshman came over to lend their support for me while I was getting flamed—even Gabby retreated. Neither did *one* cadre member do anything to rectify it.

So much for "leave no man behind."

I desperately needed to regroup. I asked the upperclassmen if I could use the restroom and, shockingly, they granted me permission. They probably just needed a break from screaming at me so that they could eat their *own* food.

I hustled to the restroom near the entrance of Mitch's—the cadet nickname for Mitchell Hall—still at attention. I sat down inside one of the stalls and made a game plan. It was time for me to make some changes. I abhorred getting in trouble, and I felt especially wretched about getting other people in trouble. It was time for me to climb back up to the top of the performance ladder, to make my room and uniform perfect—in military parlance: shit-hot, to study and memorize all of my academic and military knowledge, and to once again offer help to my squadron mates.

In other words, it was time for me to get over what had transpired and just suck it up so that I could perform as well as I had before that unspeakable weekend. I just needed to get through the rest of this day before I started my regeneration.

I collected myself, energized, and left the restroom. Unfortunately, in my haste to get back to the Tough Twenty Trolls, I collided with a firstie, our shoulders meeting with a force that knocked the wind out of me, and spun me 360 degrees. The cadet appeared unscathed. I rubbed my throbbing shoulder, straightened my uniform, and apologized as best I could while falling back into attention. She made no attempt to reciprocate the sentiment. Instead, she penetrated my psyche with a look that could have turned the Easter Bunny to stone. I fell in even harder. She held her stone-cold stare without even blinking. I had seen her before but could not remember where. She leaned in until her nose was an inch from mine.

"Get back to your table, Tate."

Stone. Hard, gray, ice-cold, scary, and unmoving. I about-faced and ran back to my table, rattled.

Fairchild Hall was my sanctuary all morning long, and I was reluctant to leave its safe and relaxed atmosphere, but everyone was required to assemble for noontime formation. I should have skipped it, as it turned out, because we actually had a surprise ORI (open ranks inspection) where I managed to bring the term *shit magnet* to a whole new level. As if that morning's training session hadn't been wretched enough.

I had been through a gauntlet by the time I reached our volleyball team table for lunch. I fell into my chair, exasperated but relieved to be at *rest*. Her Horrible Her was at the head of the table. I could feel her eyes on me as she spoke.

"Who's gonna go get the food and serve it?"

Tam-Tam, one of only two three-degrees on the team, stood up to grab the cart.

"Sit down, Tam."

Her Horrible Her sat with her elbows on the table, hands clasped under her chin, glaring at me.

"Tate's gonna do it. She's a SMACK. Do it, smack. Do it."

"Dude, she's just kidding," said Tam, waving her hand at me and starting to get up.

"TAM-TAM. SIT DOWN. Let her do it."

She did not, once, take her eyes off of me.

"Do it, SMACK. *NOW!*"

My chin dropped, too embarrassed to look at anyone. I stood and walked at attention over to the steel cart that held the food. Quinner shot up from her seat to help, but Tip put the immediate kibosh on it.

"Quinn. SIT."

Goddamn.

I placed the appropriate serving utensils into their respective dishes and passed them to the highest-ranking cadet at the table—Her Horrible Her. The rest of the team averted their eyes and talked amongst themselves. Other varsity athletes from neighboring tables pointed and laughed at what I was doing, no doubt thinking that it was an initiation joke. This was no joke. It was another reminder that I was in deep and drowning.

Afternoon classes went too quickly, and before I knew it, I was at practice and, once again, dragged into Her Horrible Her's murky undertow. She robbed me of every opportunity to touch the ball. It was ridiculous.

One of my favorite things about the game of volleyball—much like the military, actually—was that it was the consummate *team* sport. In volleyball, it was exceptionally difficult to showboat and virtually impossible to ball-hog. Two opposing teams of six stay on their respective sides of the net, and each has only three hits to send the ball to the other side. Individual players may not touch the ball more than once in a row. These tenets prevent play from becoming selfish and contact from becoming dirty—to play successfully, you have to play as a team. *Together.* Volleyball is a beautifully strategic, intellectually and physically challenging, perfectly rigorous *team* sport.

On that day, however, I witnessed the closest thing to ball hogging that I had ever seen. Our team captain flew in from all corners of the court to intercept every single ball that I called. I would have been totally impressed with her hustle if her motive hadn't been so utterly malicious. Her zeal to keep me under her thumb was so distracting that both Coach Hubby *and* Coach Wifey ordered her to ease up. If only their orders could extend to areas off of the court.

During our final water break, I ran into the locker room and left the letter I'd written on top of her gym bag. After practice, I took down the net and waited until the coast was clear before grabbing my bag and walking back to my room. I didn't go to dinner with the other freshmen. I didn't go to Her Horrible Her's car. I walked. Alone. As I had felt for days. I looked up at the mountains on my way back to Vandy—Vandenberg Hall—and they seemed to be pointing at my bootstraps and telling me to yank.

I know. I need to get myself together. When I am organized, I can weather anything. Lock it up, Tate, and get it together. I can weather anything.

That night, I spent three hours making my room and uniform shit-hot. Every piece of metal sparkled and shined. Every piece of fabric was wrinkle-free with crisp, clean creases. The next day, I could tell that the upperclassmen noticed the effort and, though they did not compliment me on it, they also did not yell. *Progress.*

Things were calm until I went to leave Mitchell Hall after breakfast. I was stopped by a firstie before I reached the exit doors. She waved off my squadron mates, who had stopped with me in a show of renewed solidarity, in order to tear into me. She ripped apart my uniform, my bearing, my posture, and my etiquette at the top of her lungs. Nothing that I could eke out in response was sufficient for her. Her explosion felt both premeditated and arbitrary. I felt like a basic all over again.

Who is this girl?

It took *seven* full minutes for her to let everyone in Mitchell Hall know that she thought I was the worst cadet at the United States Air Force Academy. She bellowed until she started to lose her voice. I started to lose my voice. Even cadets six tables away eventually stopped to watch her over-the-top flame session. I stole a glimpse of her face and her name tag when she glanced around to make sure that there were witnesses to my incompetence. She was the *same* firstie I'd run into the day before. Upon *seven* minutes of reflection, I realized it was actually *she* who had run into *me*. C1C Medusa. She leaned so close to my ear after her tirade, that her spit nicked my vibrating earlobe as she hissed, "Keep your fucking mouth shut about volleyball team secrets, Tate. *Fucking. Shut.*"

I knew who she was.

My head dropped; my stomach dropped; things deep, deep down dropped.

Except my guard.

C1C Medusa. She was Her Horrible Her's only other close friend at USAFA. Her Horrible Her had regaled me with countless stories about their drunken shenanigans, said that she couldn't wait until I was an upperclassman so that I could finally hang out with Medusa and see how much fun she was, blah, blah, blah.

Oh yeah. She's a riot. Remind me to look her up when I get recognized as an upperclassman so we can party together.

C1C Medusa had apparently spewed enough.

"Get your fat fucking ass outta my face, Tate, you pathetic piece of shit."

I put my head down and ran, ran, ran all the way to Fairchild Hall. My mind reeled.

Keep my mouth shut about volleyball team secrets? WTF?! Her Horrible Her told Medusa what happened?

I wanted to blow right past Fairchild and just keep on running until my legs gave out, but I didn't. Instead, I grabbed myself by the bootstraps, and I yanked.

My classes went well. I loved aviation, calculus, all of our sciences. And my teachers were great. I participated in noontime formation; the cadre noticed. Lunch was quiet. I floated back up to a positive, buoyant headspace until I realized that it was a bit *too* quiet around our team table. Everyone was talking amongst themselves. They did not talk to me. Everyone seemed colder, more awkward. Flip, one of the only other team members who was friendly with Her Horrible Her off the court, leaned over to me and whispered harshly.

"Look, Po, just right whatever wrong you did to Tip, okay? It's so not cool for you to just pull something like that and then not apologize for it. Tell her you're sorry so we can all just move on!"

Her words socked me in the stomach, and I doubled over, my head spinning.

"Wha—Did she say what I'm supposed to apologize for?"

"Yeah, like you don't know," Flip sneered.

I kept my mouth shut, fearing that if I uttered one word the tears welling up in my eyes would spill over. How was I supposed to refute or placate lies that had clearly come from Her Horrible Her when I didn't even know what they were? I looked over at her, and her eyes seared into mine. She was pleading for reconnection, for me to allow her to pull on the chains that bound me to her.

I left before lunch was served.

All day, I concentrated on keeping my thoughts buoyant.

By the time reveille played, I had ironed, shined, folded, pinned, memorized, and prepared everything I could. My room and my uniform were perfect. Shit-hot. My mind, however, was not.

The next morning, I participated out in the hallway, I sounded off during formation, and I marched like the honor guard on the way to breakfast. The cadre complimented me on my effort. *Progress.* I socialized with other freshmen in the library between classes. We laughed and swapped stories. It felt great—until Her Horrible Her walked past. She stole a glance at our table, attempting to cop a cavalier attitude—but she was anything but suave. I knew her too well to fall for this alleged coincidence.

On my way to practice, I was stopped by another firstie, a guy. For a moment, I wondered what firstie had *time* to stop and train a four-degree. First-degrees were supposed to mirror air force officers. Their positions were managerial; they were chiefly responsible for the squadron and staff logistics. The dirty work of day-to-day training was usually relegated to two- and three-degrees. Rarely did a firstie step in to train a four-degree smack, unless said smack had committed a grievous error. Apparently, this firstie guy thought that my mere *presence* was a grievous error. And then I saw his squadron patch. It was the same as Her Horrible Her's.

He put me in the mother position (a straight-arm plank) . . . forever . . . and ordered me to do flutter kicks, grasshoppers, and drill maneuvers without my weapon. When classmates from other squadrons joined me on the terrazzo, he pulled them up off of the ground and pushed them on their way. He yelled, screamed, and pointed at me as I did sit-ups and push-ups, and sounded off. When only a small patch of my shirt remained undrenched with sweat, he let me go.

"Keep your fucking mouth shut, Tate."

What? It was startling enough to be stopped out of the blue and trained. But it was petrifying to feel like I had been specifically targeted. *What did I have to do to stop this hit man parade?*

My attempts at improving my performance and being more sociable within my squadron seemed inversely proportional to the severity of flame sessions inflicted on me by Her Horrible Her's henchmen. I was afraid her intimidation tactics would poison the water all around me and sabotage my attempts to redeem myself as the prodigal—and previously stellar—cadet.

I went to bed each night with a growing feeling of dread.

22

THE ACADEMY

I am crawling on a six-inch-wide wooden board 150 feet above the middle of the ocean. My destination is ten yards away. The plank is narrow and bowing from my body weight. The breeze is making it sway, and it is hard for me to hold on. I gasp; my hands slip with sweat. I look down even though I don't want to look down. The end of the plank is still so far away. These last ten yards feel like a mile. The wood bows and sways. I am crawling, but I'm not making any progress. Fear escalates to panic. Panic escalates to terror. I want to make it to the other side more than anything in the world. I keep scooting along the narrow plank. A sudden gust of wind sweeps me off the plank, and now I am hanging on to the board from below. I can barely see the white caps of the water hundreds of feet below me. My hands are sweaty. They slip. I fall.

I jackknifed out of my bed unit and immediately felt a sharp pain shoot through my chest. Before my stomach flipped, it flopped, it dropped. Sweat rolled down my face and beaded at the tip of my nose. I had been sleeping for less than an hour, which was apparently more than enough time to have had an eviscerating nightmare. I jumped down from my bunk and reached behind my computer for a cool can of diet jet fuel, which I held under each eye for thirty seconds. It did little to reduce the huge, puffy bags. I showered quickly, and when reveille started to blow, I was already dressed and putting on mascara. I finished all of my homework—academic and military. I cleaned my room and did my squadron chores. I organized my cadet life.

I am sick of feeling like a bad cadet.

Gabby hadn't gotten out of bed yet, and I did not want to wake her. It had taken precious energy to apologize to her for my performance, and to pull more than my weight around our room and our squadron until things between us got back to where they were before. Gabby knew that I would never intentionally cause her pain. But my own shitstorm had unintentional consequences that blew my shit her way. Just by virtue of us being roommates, Gabby was required to stand next to me out in the hallway when we were getting trained. During SAMI inspections and room inspections, my trouble had brought more foot traffic of uppers and officers into our room to keep tabs on me and train me—and Gabby by proxy. When I wasn't in our room, it fell on her shoulders to clean and prep more as well. In the grand scheme of things, my subpar performance and volleyball commitments did not impinge too greatly onto Gabby. However, she took my life outside of the squadron—and thus *her*—extremely personally, which thereby severely affected our camaraderie. It was this that I had recently been trying to mend.

After our frat hit, Gabby had started to ask more about Tip and our team, but had then changed the subject before I had time to answer. Not that I would've divulged anything anyway. But it was an interesting trend that I had increasingly seen and experienced at USAFA. Even roomies or besties would sometimes pull the emotional ejection handle inside the cockpit of your friendship if the subject matter started to infringe upon their own time and duties. It was a self-preservation mechanism that had abruptly shot her out of the range of learning something that would take brain space or time from her life and responsibilities. And I understood. Cadets were busy all day, every day. I didn't want to burden anyone else with shit that wasn't theirs to deal with, either, especially Gabby, having just rekindled our roomie-hood.

I wanted to let her sleep.

I sat on the flat, rectangular table at the foot of our bed units, folded my legs up underneath me, and closed my eyes to meditate and regroup. It was time for me to take back the shiny, perfect cadet that I had been when the school year started. I knew I could be that again.

Perhaps I was meant to go through the incident in order to humble myself. Perhaps it was supposed to serve as a reminder that I should be forever grateful for the gifts with which I had been innately blessed and those that I had been recently given. Grateful for the opportunity to attend USAFA, to play my favorite sport here, to have my university *paid* for, to be trained in so many things, to learn to *fly*. Grateful for second chances.

I sucked in a rib cage full of air and let it out like a slow-leaking balloon. I had an opportunity right here, right now, to take the lesson of humility from the incident and keep my head down, work hard. No excuses.

Work hard. No excuses.

It was time for a fresh start.

Bring it on, USAFA.

————————————

The week went by quickly, and Friday morning arrived like an unexpected present in the mail; I was sticking to my plan of making a fresh start. Today was merely one in a series of good-feeling days. At breakfast, I volunteered to sit in the load master position and was able to remember every upperclassman's order. I paid attention in all of my classes, crushed two pop quizzes. I sounded off during every formation, put my fist out to answer questions, and even ran back to my squadron after class to get trained before practice. I felt productive. I didn't flash back into wretchedness once.

I ran, hit, dove, and served harder than I ever had at practice. I did not let Her Horrible Her take my joy. *No one can take my joy.* It felt great, and I was utterly grateful. I focused on the premonition that I would survive here. *Survive her.*

She hated that I pulled away, but I pulled away anyway. I refused to be at the mercy of my memory anymore. I had cleaned the slate, and for the first time in a long time, I felt as if I could do anything that I set my mind to.

After practice, I walked with Mo-Mo, Quinner, and Linny to get touch-and-go from the dining hall. Tam-Tam and Lassy escorted us. I put together a salad and walked back to my squadron. It was quiet throughout the deserted halls.

A civilian university on a Friday night probably felt the same way—empty—but peace and quiet was rare in the Tough Twenty Trolls squadron, and it felt good. In fact, everything today had felt good. I had turned a corner, been reborn in positivity, awareness, and appreciation. Cheesy as it may have sounded, it was the truth. It felt *good.*

Gabby had taken a weekend pass, so I had our room to myself. I was not going to go anywhere for the rest of the night. I had too many things that I needed to catch up on, including sleep.

The salad was the first thing that had tasted good since the incident. I wrapped my headphones around my ears and grabbed my artist markers from the desk drawer so that I could start drawing

Mo-Mo's birthday card. I concentrated on my contoured lines, heavy and black, curvaceous and fluid. *Perfect.* I vibed and sang along to TLC in a throwback attempt, letting their voices wash over, around, and through me. I moved on to coloring between the contoured lines calmly, carefully. As I took off the cap of the eggshell-colored marker, I caught a whiff of something new, something fruity, peppery . . . and getting stronger. I followed my nose upward toward the smell, and saw—A FACE.

I recoiled at the sight of C3C K-bar bending over me, his face much too close to mine. *Too close.* I knew who C3C K-bar was. He had never talked to me directly, but I had seen him visit friends in my squadron before. He was a quiet three-degree who played first string for one of the Fighting Falcons varsity athletic teams. He was staring at me coldly, intensely. *Too close.* I whipped my headphones off and shot out of my chair at attention.

"ROOM TENCH-HUT!" I called out, per regulations.

He put his giant hand up in front of my mouth.

"SHUT THE FUCK UP. Shut the fuck up."

My eyes struggled to focus beyond his huge hand, which was blistered and calloused from hours of practicing his sport. I uncrossed my eyes and swept the back wall of my room. The door was closed. It was against the rules for freshmen to close their doors before taps, so I had kept it open, and now it was closed. The rule was enforced expressly so that freshmen would not be alone with the opposite sex, especially upperclassmen.

I looked at my door again. Closed. An alarm sounded and started to crescendo in the back of my mind, and my heart took an adrenaline shot. My door was not just closed; it was *locked.*

The hairs on the back of my neck shot to attention. My heart started to pound in both of my ears. My door was *locked.* I started to move toward it, muttering how I was uncomfortable breaking the rules, and before I blinked twice, he had effortlessly moved four feet to stand in my way. He ordered me to fall back in at attention, reminding me that he had not given me permission to fall out in the first place. I fell back in.

He was huge. His six-foot-two frame blocked my view of the door completely, blocked my view of everything except him. All I could see were his tanned muscles bulging out of his USAFA T-shirt. All I could see were his muscles and his crazy eyes, and I was claustrophobic.

"I understand there has been some dissension within the ranks of your volleyball team, smack. . . ."

His voice and face were cold, devoid of affect. His mouth was the only thing that moved when he spoke. His full lips moved. His uneven teeth moved. Everything else stayed still.

Dissension within the ranks?

"Umm . . . yes, sir?"

"Um . . . Um . . . Did your superiors teach you to reply to an officer using the word *um*?"

Officer? Where was the officer?

If this was a joke, this guy was good. He was so stract that it was freaking me out. I fell in harder.

"No, sir!"

"SHHH! Shut the fuck UP, SMACK!"

Whoa, wait. There was an unspoken bond between varsity athletes at the academy, so none of this made any sense. *What the fuck is he doing here? Did Tip put him up to this? Am I just paranoid?*

I needed to get him out of my room. If I could do that, then we could just go back to acknowledging each other from afar. I started to reason with him.

"Sir, I apologize—"

This triggered his trip wire. He exploded.

"I DON'T WANT YOUR FUCKING APOLOGY, BITCH!"

The back of his hand meets my cheek with such force that it knocks me off of my feet. Oh my God. Oh my God, he just hit me. *I scramble to get up. I scramble, but he is already on top of me. This time he opens his hand and hits me full force against my other cheek. I hear my neck crack loudly. I feel my nose start to bleed. I throw my arms up into his face. I scratch, poke, gouge at any soft tissue I can find.*

"What the fuck you gonna do, bitch, huh?! You're gonna keep your mouth shut, that's what you're gonna do—keep your motherfucking mouth shut unless you wanna make this worse—got it?! GOT IT?"

He straddles me. He kneels on my arms. He covers my mouth. He presses up against me, and I can feel the violence turning him on. Oh God no. Oh holy God. No. No. No. *He strikes my other cheek with the back of his hand again. Blood from my nose spatters underneath my desk and onto my bed unit. I know some unarmed combat from basic training, and I attempt every maneuver that pops into my head. C3C K-bar has undergone extensive field training. He has undergone athletic training, strength training, modified special-ops training, and endurance conditioning. I am no match for his muscle and agility. I am close to six feet tall, but I am no match.* Oh my God, I can't stop him. *I feel pressure up against my stomach. He is fully aroused by this. In one painful maneuver, he traps both of my arms in one of his hands. With his free hand, he pulls his pants down.* Oh my God . . . please, no. *I hear my thoughts start to come out of my mouth.*

"Oh my God, no . . . please, NO!"

"SHUT UP!"

He shouts his whisper up against my face. His breath is hot. Blood is already coursing through my cheeks and dripping down my face. His breath compounds the additional bloody heat, and it is unbearable.

I start to see spots. Something is being shoved into my mouth. I snap back to consciousness. I cannot breathe. My mouth is too full. I cannot breathe, I cannot bite, I cannot move. It is too full. I start to vomit. I gag, I choke, I start to vomit. He pulls out of the way. I gasp for air. I gasp, gasp, gasp. I choke, I gag, and I start to vomit as I struggle to breathe.

"You dirty, disgusting fucking whore! You fucking make me sick, you nasty bitch! Swallow that shit comin' outchyour mouth! Nasty cunt! Dirty, sick, nasty bitch!"

I gasp for air. This turns him on even more. I cannot die here like this. I will not die here like this. He pulls my pants down as I fight to pull in air through my wounded mouth. I see spots and splotches again. My exposed skin is cold. I am being split in half. Searing, searing pain. I fade in and out. Searing pain. Searing pain. I feel the blood below my waist. It feels like he's shoving shards of glass deep, deep, deep into me. I fade in and out. In and out. Searing pain. Searing pain. In and out. Bloody, piercing, splitting, searing pain.

After he finishes, he forces me to my feet. I bend at the waist like a marionette suddenly given slack. I hold my stomach. Tears drip down. My tongue wipes their salty tracks from my cheeks and metallic blood from my lips. He grabs me by the shirt and yanks my shoulders upright. My feet come off the ground. I bite my tongue when I land. I bend over, clutching my stomach again.

"FALL IN, FOUR-DEGREE. NOW."

He is panting. He is panting as if he won the gold medal in the fucking Olympic one-hundred-yard dash. His voice is stone-cold. It sends a violent shiver through me.

"I AM NOT LEAVING THIS ROOM UNTIL YOU ARE CLEANED UP AND PULLED TOGETHER."

His words don't quite register. My eyes are blurry, and I cannot comprehend what he is saying. I silently plead with him to get out. Oh my God. Just fucking leave. I beg you to just fucking leave. *I stand up straight. I wipe the tears and the blood from my face onto my pants. I bite my lip and cage my eyes. I cage my eyes. I do everything in my power to lock myself up. I do everything in my power not to double over, vomit, cry, bleed, or make a fucking sound until this animal leaves my room.* Please just leave.

"Now, I KNOW you'll be quiet about this and ALL matters of a secret nature, right?!"

He is still breathing heavily. I can see his pulse in a vein next to one of his eyes. His evil eyes bulge with each beat. All other matters of a secret nature? What?

He wipes the sweat from his forehead with his shirt. On its way down, I notice a tiny crimson streak of blood amidst the moisture. My stomach flips, it flops, it drops, again. He is not wiping his sweat off of his face—he is wiping my sweat off his face. My tears. My blood. Mine.

I get lost in this horror just long enough to pass as pulled together. He puts his finger to his lips. He shushes me, then inhales through his nostrils. He sniffs his disgusting, awful, horrid fingers and closes his eyes, transported. I watch as he relives what just happened. I feel my blood staining my pants as my body shakes and tenses. I watch as he relives it. He looks in the mirror. He fixes his outfit, wipes his forehead, neck, and arms with my roommate's towel. He turns and walks out of my room in a thick swagger. He leaves the door wide open. He leaves me physically, emotionally wide open, eviscerated. As soon as he is out of my peripheral vision, I run to the door in a frantic and blotchy panic. I slam it. I lock every lock there is. I crumple to the floor. I am broken.

An hour passes. I lie on my side in the fetal position. I squeeze my hands between my legs, hoping to alleviate some of the pain. I force myself to

my feet. I feel like I am climbing Mount Everest. I cannot let my room-
mate come back and find me like this.

*I slowly, methodically take off each pant leg. I pull each arm out of
its sleeve. I put my clothes into a trash bag from the bottom of the trash
can and knot the top. The blood, the stench will never be washed out of
the fabric completely. It will never be washed out of me completely. It
will never, ever be washed out. Tomorrow morning I'll buy another
running suit.*

*I bend into my trash can and get sick. I heave harder than I ever
have. Old, hard chunks of vegetables spew out of me with great difficulty. The blood comes next. My jaw cannot stay open anymore, and
the vomit gets caught in between my teeth. I open just enough to spit
the last of everything I have inside of me into the dirty, rusty can in the
corner of our room. I am empty. My throat is now empty. It was too full
moments ago, but now it is empty. My stomach is now empty. It was
too full of what felt like shards of glass moments ago, but now it is empty.
Using tissues from the box behind the mirror, I wipe the blood that has
dripped down my legs. I wipe and wipe, trying to remove traces of the
nightmare that just happened. The adrenaline that fueled my fight has
moved out of my muscles, and lactic acid has settled in. I can barely lift
my legs to put them into the soft cotton sweatpants. Every move is work.
I put on a USAFA T-shirt. I pull my sweatshirt over my head. I hobble
over to the sink.*

*I look at my face in the mirror. It is red and tender. There is a car-
pet imprint over a red handprint on my cheek. I wet Gabby's towel. I
wipe the blood from my nose, mouth, and cheeks. Giant, bright red
hand marks on either side of my face remain, but I understand even
then that there is no permanent damage to my face. Still, it looks like I
was backhanded by every member of the offensive line. There are lay-
ers of red fingers.*

I finish my sponge bath so that I can lie down. There is no way that I am stepping foot out into the hallway. I have changed clothes. I have completely wiped my body down with soap and water. I have done all of this on autopilot, methodically, but I can still smell him on me, in me. I take out my bottle of perfume and drench myself in it. I put so much perfume on that my finger gets tired from squeezing the atomizer. I do not feel as nauseated with this new smell. I splash cold, cold water on my face to try and soothe the redness and burning. I fish down to the bottom of my footlocker, where I hid my contraband stuffed bunny rabbit. I take him by the arm, and I carefully climb atop my bed unit.

I feel like I am torn in half. I am torn. I know I will not sleep, but it hurts too much to sit at my desk. I am shivering. I am in the fetal position on top of my class-color-trimmed bedspread, holding a bunny against my stomach. My face is swollen, and blood is dripping down the back of my throat. I hurt inside and outside. I am shaking, shaking, shaking. I am moaning. I don't feel as if I am moaning, but I hear it, and no one else is in my room, so it must be me. I am in pain. I am curled around a stuffed bunny, and I am shaking.

My roommate does not return until Sunday. I am in the exact same position that I was in on Friday. Still shaking. Still moaning. Still torn in half.

PART THREE
DROWNING

23

THE ACADEMY

I am, officially, neck deep. I am on my tiptoes, in a sea of deep dark blue, trying not to drown. I am neck deep.

I sat on the floor of my room, in the corner where the two walls met, holding my knees, rocking back and forth, and trying not to panic.

I cannot . . . I cannot not think about him, about what he did, about what I'm supposed to do now. I cannot . . . What am I supposed to do now?

I sat in the corner and rocked, far from the door and all who might enter, far from my desk and all that I hadn't done, far from my bed and all the pain that had been inflicted there. I sat where the two walls met—they would support me; they would not let anyone sneak up on me. I needed them right now; they were the only stability I had.

It had been this way for several days. I had somehow walked to the Cadet Clinic the Monday morning after Him Horrible Him and procured a Form 38, which excused me from all duties due to illness. When they asked me about the bruise and swelling on the side of my face, I said that I had gotten dehydrated and fainted. And that I still felt nauseous.

Documentation that I was "under the weather" gave me temporary refuge from having to answer questions from my roommate, chain of command, teachers, or coaches. It gave me temporary refuge from having to leave my room. So I sat, rocked, shivered, shook, shivered, shook, moaned, and cried in the corner of my room. I only stood up to run to the bathroom and vomit. There was nothing else important enough to move me from my spot on the floor where the two walls met. I used all of my energy to reassure Gabby that I was just sick to my stomach and would try to stay out of her way until I felt better. She asked only once if I needed food, and then stayed away, fearing contagion.

It was my last night on bed rest. I would have to return to class, to my cadet life, the next day. An exhausting hypervigilance had set in, and I felt as if the marrow was being harvested from my bones with each twitching movement. I spent the night on the floor behind my bed unit, attempting to prep for class, for formation—for reentry into the world.

I woke up feeling frigid, naked, exposed in the neck-deep water that was still swirling around me. I dressed in the UOD and forced myself to join my classmates in the hallway. The polyester felt like sandpaper against my bruised and burning skin. Even the most familiar faces of my squadron mates overwhelmed my senses. I flinched at every aberrant noise, every sudden motion, anticipating harm from every angle.

When I managed to get myself out of our squadron, every face in the crowd of cadets looked like His Horrible His. Every touch on the shoulder felt like Hers Horrible Hers. Constant surges of adrenaline electrified me like a stun gun, then crashed my muscles like a tranq dart. I continued to feel frigid, naked, exposed. It took me until noontime formation to warm up. As I marched to Mitch's for our team lunch, my brain, my body, my heart protested. I didn't want to see Her Horrible Her. I didn't want to sit next to her and feel the cold steel chains of her manipulation tighten around me. In my mind, in my muscle memory, her chains, her hands, her instruments of manipulation were already clawing, grabbing, ripping, groping, scratching, beating, tearing, choking what they wanted from me. They had already taken what they wanted from me before my body even walked through the dining hall doors.

The heat from my shame warmed my body, finally, and brought with it a wave of salty tears. A lump rose in the back of my throat. I swallowed hard, but my sadness was stuck there. My disgust crept slowly up to meet it. I sprinted full tilt toward the restroom just inside the entrance and plowed through the door of the first stall just in time to donate the contents of my stomach to the toilet. Up came the water, vegetables, bile, mucus—and then the heaves that always came and came. The vegetables that I had forced past my lips midmorning plunked into the blue water like stones into a still pond. They kicked up droplets of toilet water that I did not have time to dodge. One landed high on my cheek, the thought of which made me heave again.

Since the incident with Him, every time my stomach had come close to feeling full my body had expelled everything I'd ingested. My legs were weak from having vomited so many times already that day. I had been stuffed full by Him Horrible Him that night, too full, and my body would not let that happen again. *Please don't ever let me feel that full again.*

My head spun as I stood up, so I braced myself against both walls of the bathroom stall. My tears, which had been dripping straight into the bowl, now tumbled down my cheeks. I stumbled over to the sink and spit into yet another shiny white porcelain bowl. I gargled with water from the tap. I looked down at my uniform to make sure that it hadn't been soiled. It looked fine. I did *not*. I pulled my head up from the sink and looked in the mirror. Someone else stared back at me. The bruising, the swelling had receded, but this girl had dark circles under her eyes and blood dripping from her nose. She looked tired, sad, and trashed. She was wet with tears and empty of sustenance. I wiped her cheeks, her neck, her forehead, her chin. I wiped her uniform. I wiped her gently, lovingly. She looked like she had not been handled with care.

The corner of the mirror was broken, and cracks radiated outward. I touched the glass. It was cold, hard, and fractured. Shard after shard radiated from the initial point of impact, like the web of a glass spider.

I am caught in a web. I am fractured into shards. I am cold, hard, and empty. I am broken.

I stepped back from the girl in the mirror and picked up my bag. I gathered my things, my senses, and ran all the way to my next class.

My chemistry lab partner was absent, and I was, too, mentally anyway. I would have been perfectly content to sit at my station and catch up on the assigned reading—I truly loved this class—but the teacher told me to shadow a neighboring pair. I had sat next to these two freshmen all semester, and had listened to them ping-pong catty comments back and forth to each other in their game of Hot Gossip: Cadet Edition.

Like they had been each class period, C4Cs Butt and Out were deep in their own conversational ping-pong match, and I didn't have the energy to interrupt them or engage in the experiment. I spent the majority of the period studying their hair products and grooming habits from my vantage point behind them. I had counted seventeen bobby pins holding their freshmen mullets into regs by the time that class had ended.

English was my last class, and I had not read any of the assigned material. Fortunately, nothing was due. Just showing up and paying attention in class was difficult enough without the added pressure of turning in homework. Major Grammar called on me to answer a question, and I had barely met his gaze before I started to break down. Taken aback, he immediately redirected his question to a comatose freshman on the opposite side of the room. I bowed my head in shame but was grateful for the reprieve.

Major Grammar took me aside after class. Before he spoke, I could feel him trying to warm up his usual stractness.

"Miss Tate, is there something going on that I should be made aware of?"

He called me *miss*, then reached over to take my book bag from my hand, most likely all out of chivalry. However, I nervously side-stepped the potential contact in a residual protective reflex that had been guarding my body, mind, and heart hypervigilantly. My duck and weave left a residue of awkwardness between us.

"Sir, I apologize!" I said, not even processing the question he'd just asked. "Please don't let me keep you! I know you must be terribly busy, and I would never want to interfere. . . ." I bumbled, while backing out of the room.

My rear end bumped into a chair, toppling it to the floor. I picked it up, still moving backward.

"Everything's fine, sir, totally fi—" I yelped. The handle of my bag had looped around the doorknob, yanking me back into his room. My lizard brain had thought for a moment that someone had grabbed me. I froze, then dropped my chin to my chest.

"I'm sorry, sir. I don't . . ." Tears rolled down my cheeks in spite of my effort to hold them back. "I—I have to go. But thank you, sir . . . for asking."

Major Grammar was not an effusive, warm-fuzzy man, but in that moment, he had a sad curiosity in his eyes that could have provoked a tear from a statue. The compassion emanating from him was more than I could even comprehend, let alone bear to witness, or receive. I about-faced as fast as I could, and faded from the door.

I ran from Fairchild Hall to the field house as soon as I finished my last class of the day. I did not stop by my squadron. I did not grab a snack. I did not walk, even though my body begged me to. I ran in full UOD to the locker room. I threw on my practice clothes, put on my headphones, and hid under the benches in front of some lockers to try and steal a half hour of sleep. I had hidden far away from Her Horrible Her's locker so she wouldn't see me if she came down early for practice. I set the alarm on my watch and backed my body up against the cement wall.

I am well hidden from the Horribles. I am barricaded from physical danger. I am safe here.

I had to keep reminding myself, *I am safe here.* I just needed thirty winks of sleep, sleep, sleep. I was so tired that my bones were sore.

I could have hollowed out a nook in NORAD and still have been vulnerable to my own memories of my recent past, however. The problem was not outside of my body; the problem was inside of my mind. It came to life when I closed my eyes. Silence was not silent anymore. Darkness was overwhelming and terrifying. I just needed thirty winks. One half hour of reprieve. I pulled the hood of my sweatshirt down over my twitching eyes for another layer of protection.

I am in no physical danger here. I am hidden. I am safe. I am so tired. My. Bones. Are. Sore. Sleep. I close my eyes, I plug my ears without plugging my ears, I retreat without retreating. I concentrate on my breath, inhale, exhale.

As usual, the darkness came to life. Hands started to grab, hit, rip. Pain started to puncture, sear, split. Fear gripped me again and held on. It wouldn't let go. *Please let me go. Please. Just. Let. Me. Go. Please. Let. Go. Please.* The squeal of the alarm around my wrist shot me back into the present. I peeled the hood off of my face, unplugged my ears, and came back from the depths. I opened up all of my senses to the locker room. I was tired but wired. I walked zombielike to the gym for practice.

AFTERLIFE.

"Popo . . . ?"

I watched, from under my school desk, as a run in the flesh-colored nylons of my second-grade teacher, Mrs. B, grew bigger.

"Popo, we're gonna need you to come out from under there, sweetie—your mom is here."

Only the bottom half of her legs were visible from my hiding place under the desk. And I watched as the run made its way down her shin, past the glob of clear nail polish that she had futilely used to stop it, and into the side of her sensible black pump. She knelt down to see me, and the run split wide open.

"Come on, Popo, let's go talk to your mommy."

She nodded in the direction of the classroom door, and I took her outstretched hand. We walked to the door together, past a line of my classmates who were staring at me, and my tearstained face, on their way in from recess.

We had lost my sister in the summer before this school year had started. And the transition was . . . difficult. For everyone. My mother had left that morning for a Junior League trip, and by "Reading Circle" midmorning, I was hyperventilating under my desk, terrified and hysterical.

"LOMMYYY!"

Her name came seemingly out of my *soul*, with so much force that it shook my little seven-year-old body as I sprinted down the hall toward my mother. Having just come off of a plane, she wore her smart trench coat, which was open and bouncing over her tailored business attire, and she had a tight, worried look on her face, while she moved toward us at a clip. I ran, jumped into her arms, and held on like a barnacle.

She hugged me so tightly. "Popo, honey, what's going on?"

"If you two would like to come this way, we can talk in here." Mrs. B ushered us into the school counselor's office, which felt color-fully contrived and trying too hard to be a "hangout spot," even at my age. "I asked Ms. C to join us, since it seemed pretty serious. Polo wouldn't talk, so I asked her to draw what she was feeling." Mrs. B pointed to a large picture on top of Ms. C's desk.

"It is very well done, I might add, but it is . . . *alarming*." Ms. C looked at my drawing, then at the two other adults.

The drawing showed a plane crash in vivid detail, and me, orphaned and alone, in the corner.

The choking panic I had felt, the fear in Mrs. B's eyes, the stares of my fellow second graders as I had stopped their school day, the look of concern from Ms. C, and the raw sorrow seeping out of my mother was all too much. It felt overwhelmingly big, awful, and scary. It didn't feel good.

It didn't feel good.

It didn't feel good.

Sary's death had made me feel that way. But *I* had made *them* feel that way *today*. I had pressed the pause and panic buttons on the world. Again. It's scary when the world stops. Each time I talked about what happened, the world stopped. It wasn't their fault that I got scared that my parents were going to die, too. But I got scared and they got sad, and talking about it more made the world come to a crashing halt. So I wouldn't talk about it anymore. I wouldn't bring sadness to anyone anymore. I'd bring smiles and laughter and love and fun and joy. That felt so good.

That felt so good.

That felt so good.

I could be sad, or even scared, but if I was the only one who knew, then the world would keep on turning. And as long as I focused on the good things, the world would keep on turning. As long as I acted normal, the world would keep on turning.

24

THE ACADEMY

I snuck out the back door of the field house. My stomach pitched and rolled. Practice had always been my sanity and my sanctuary.

Until now.

My lip quivered, and I could feel myself start to break down. I bit my thumb to stifle the tears.

I looked up at the rambling steps of the cement labyrinth that stood between me and Vandenberg Hall. For a moment, I doubted whether I could climb—but I had no choice. I lifted each foot robotically, one step at a time. The closer I got to the cadet area, the further into despair I sank. My spirits, the staircase, they were inversely proportional. The rhythm my footsteps made pulled a jody—one of those military marching jingles—word by word across my tired lips.

I see a sea of blue.
It is all I see, that hue.
I am lost, so lost,
Paid every cost,
Now I don't know what to do.

I was behind in my schoolwork. My roommate and squadron

mates hated me because volleyball took me away from responsibilities they had to endure. The volleyball team, to which I had joyfully cleaved in the past, was now the source of too much pain.

I am drowning and I don't know what to do.

Per usual, I entered my squadron during ac-call and made it to my room without incident. I unloaded my book bag and resumed my place in the corner of our room, where the two walls met. I stacked six thick textbooks, two homework packets, one workbook, eight notebooks full of assignments, and four folders on the floor in front of me like a child's fort. The amount of unfinished work hid me almost completely. My insomnia was finally going to pay off. I cracked open a fresh can of diet jet fuel, opened a textbook, and began to read.

My eyes skimmed the words while my mind skimmed what had transpired over the last few weeks. *Goddamnit.* My body started to shake, slowly at first, like the initial tremors of an earthquake.

Hands and blood and pain, searing pain. Him Horrible Him. Heat and pressure and choking, gasping, choking. I am full, too full. Shards of glass are being thrust up into me, too deep, too deep. I am being split in half. I am sick, dirty, full, unstable, split. I am disgusting, eviscerated.

In a moment of silent lucidity, I stood up and yanked my standard-issue robe from the hook inside my wardrobe so that I could change and take a shower—my third one of the day. My skin was dry and taut from too many scrubbings with industrial-strength soap. My face pulled tight when I moved my mouth. I put my robe on over my clothes before slowly, methodically taking off each article. I had redefined modesty to include fear. My room may have been empty, but my head was full of ghosts. I grabbed my towel, which was still wet from an earlier shower.

I ran to the bathroom and climbed into the last shower stall with my robe still on. I did not take it off or drop my towel until the water started to pour. I stood under the spout looking for some sort of twisted baptism.

Please wipe away the trespasses that have left their bruised and bloodied path on my body, their punching bag, my body.

I stood under the spout and turned the hot water up as high as it would go, until it scalded my skin bright red. It scalded the air as well, creating billowy clouds of steam. I scrubbed, I cleansed, I disinfected until my skin was bright red and raw, but still, I could not erase the tracks of what had been done to me. I could not scrub inside myself.

I am unclean, I am damaged.

I returned to my room and my roommate gave me a look that matched how I felt on the inside: disgusted, disappointed, disengaged. The few remaining pieces of my confetti'd heart threatened to break.

Instead of tonight's UOD, I would've loved to wrap my body in my hooded civilian sweats, the clothing equivalent of gauze bandages. I returned to my post behind my bed, a little cleaner . . . for the moment.

Pepe clicked his heels outside our door and squared his turn into our room. He and Gabby barely acknowledged each other as he headed straight for my corner and poked his head past my bed unit.

"Tater tot!"

Normalcy. A reprieve. Take me away from my mind, my memory.

"Pepe Le Pee-You!" I responded, grateful to see his friendly face. We high-fived. In a sea of growing resentment toward me on the part of my friends, teammates, and squadron mates, there were still a few buoys. Pepe, my marching partner and fellow jokester within our squadron since day one, was one of them. He must have telepathically sensed my need for some comic relief.

"Hey, you start the chem homework yet?" I asked, both of us ignoring the fact that we were having a conversation in something akin to a children's fort. He answered, unfazed, in his auctioneer-speed, staccato rhythm.

"Does a bear shit in the woods? Is the grass green? Should you always avoid yellow snow?"

It was just one of the reasons that I loved him.

"Oh, yay—so you have!" I responded, relieved that at least one of us was current.

"Nope."

"OMG, Pep!" I spat, palms up.

He giggled out a proposition. "You wanna get together later and work on it?"

I responded with a rhetorical question of my own. "Is a submarine filled with navy seamen?"

"Only if you rub it!"

"Eeewww! Pep, get outta here!"

I swatted him away from my perch. He laughed and danced his way out of our room. My pain was not his pain. It felt . . . foreign, but better to just be able to act *normal*. I wanted to stay in that headspace. To rent a room in Normal, Colorado. I went back to studying.

By the time taps taunted me with its lullaby, I had been writing outlines and illustrating crib sheets for hours. All of the information, however, was on a series circuit: in through my eyes, out through my hand. My brain was out of the loop. I started to shake again. I started to slip into that night again.

His Horrible His hands searching my skin.

No, no, no, please, I don't want to have to endure that night again, please don't let me slip, please?

It was late. Every light in our room was off except for my tiny desk lamp. Gabby was cuddled up in her blanket, fast asleep. Her snoring was my only tether to the present. I was trying not to return to that night, to an amalgamation of both nights, but I was slipping.

Please. Stop. Please.

When I opened my eyes, I was curled up on my side, hugging my knees to my chest. My tears had affixed my cheek to the carpeting. I was rocking, rocking back and forth. But I had resurfaced in the present, finally. I heard Gabby's snoring. I saw my tiny desk lamp.

I unfolded myself like a fawn fresh out of the womb, stiff, sticky, disoriented. My body ached and my limbs protested and my jaw clicked and my face was stained with salt. I was scared, but I was in the present again.

I picked myself up off the floor with the help of an unknown force. I walked down the hall to the study room with my books, paper, pens, and fear. The room was empty, the squadron asleep. I moved robotically toward the cinder-block wall. I cocked my arm back, way back, and I swung. *Hard.* I channeled the hurt, the pain, the rage, the fear, the fury, the horror, the horror, the horror of it all into a powerful punch. I punched, punched, punched until I could finally feel another kind of pain besides the pain inside my head, heart, and soul. The physical pain was faint at first, compared to the pain inside. It was a bizarre relief to feel another kind of agony. The pain in my hand paled in comparison to my emotional pain, but at least it registered. At least it was a distraction.

I looked down at my swollen, discolored hand. I concentrated on staying in the moment, on seeing the hurt limb and feeling the pain of it at the same time. This would surely have seemed bizarre to anyone who witnessed it—but the physical pain in my hand was acting as a life preserver, bringing me up from the dark, suffocating water of my memory into the breathable lightness of the present.

I am in the present. I am grateful.

Pepe entered shortly after that with his chemistry book in one hand and his notepad in the other. He looked at me, then down at my hand, then back up into my eyes. He cocked his head. It was the first time that I had ever seen him speechless. I was not registering an appropriate pain response, so Pepe didn't quite know how to react. Rather than try to explain, I grabbed my book with my good hand and asked what page he was on. I could feel him trying to decide how to best honor the situation at hand. How best to honor our friendship. I knew that he was contemplating taking me to the Cadet Clinic, but instead, he took my lead and opened his book and joined me. Just like Gabby not really wanting to know more about the frat hit I had received with Tip, this was just Pepe's way of bailing out emotionally for the sake of self-preservation. I had seen it and experienced it more in the high-pressure environment of USAFA than anywhere else, and in the dark of that night, I actually appreciated his choice to ignore the black-and-blue elephant in the room in favor of studying.

We researched, read, and calculated all night long. Occasionally, I followed his gaze to my hand, pulled a witty deflection out of my arsenal, and we moved on.

We broke an hour before reveille. Pepe hugged me and kissed my injured hand like he would a baby sister's boo-boo. I pulled it back self-consciously, knowing how crazy it must have seemed. I thanked him, my sweet friend. In the übercompetitive academy world, he was the first person who had responded to my vulnerability with unquestioning kindness . . . and that included myself.

I tiptoed past the rest of my squadron, safely snuggled in their beds, and returned to my room to prep my uniform and military knowledge for the day ahead. The pain in my hand had diminished to a dull and penetrating ache. My room was dark, and as I closed the door behind me, the darkness in my room caught up with the darkness in my head, sparking fear from the still-smoldering ember inside my belly. It quickly grew into a burning fire.

The next thing I knew I was on the floor, in the fetal position, rocking back and forth, back and forth. Dawn covered me like a lead blanket. The familiarity of the fear did not make it any lighter. I wanted to run. I wanted to hide. I could not go to breakfast and risk seeing Him Horrible Him. I could not go to lunch and sit across from Her Horrible Her.

I cannot leave this spot on the floor. I cannot move. I am scared.

Once reveille lurched me toward the light of day, I forced myself to my feet before Gabby awoke. I dressed in the UOD and ran to the Cadet Clinic. I had no idea what they would be able to do for me, but I could not stay in my squadron, and I didn't feel safe anywhere else.

25

THE ACADEMY

A nurse called my name and rank, and I followed her into a little room. I pushed my bangs away from my face, to stay in regs. She squealed at the sight of my hand.

"What do we have here? Looks like you broke your hand. We're gonna have to get some X-rays on that thing. You want the doc to look at anything else while you're here?"

I shrugged, appreciative that my hand had done the talking.

"Okay, sweetie, sit tight."

She picked up her clipboard and left the room. Her kindness made my eyes tear up. Five minutes later, another woman walked in, chomping on her gum like she was on a mission. She wielded her clipboard with authority, and my eyes followed it around the room like a sobriety test. As soon as I caught a glimpse of her rank, I slid off of the paper-padded table to stand at attention. This was clearly not a person who minced words or actions. She waved off my gesture and pointed me back on the table. The sterile white paper crinkled underneath me. I cocked my head. I recognized her. She read my mind.

"Yes, we met during orientation, lovey. Lieutenant Colonel Pats.

I briefed you on a number of things, including how to not take any *shit* from *anyone*."

She flashed a smile that neutralized her gruff manner of speech. I had spent a good part of my childhood visiting family in Boston, and recognized her Southie accent immediately. I considered their sports teams my own.

"Go, Sox . . ." I ventured weakly, but my sentiment was genuine. She flashed her fiery smile again and grabbed my hand.

"Sheesh! How'd the other guy make out?"

I winced and instinctively pulled away.

"So . . . how did this happen . . . ?" she asked quietly, ignoring the fact that I hadn't risen to her previous, baiting question. I could barely look her in the eye. I broke military etiquette and answered her question with a question.

"Ma'am, may I ask, where in Southie did you grow up?"

"You know Boston?" she replied, without looking up from my hand.

"Yes, ma'am, I have aunts and uncles in Boston . . ." I said, hoping to avoid—or at least delay—divulging the details of my injury. She looked me in the eye and softened, willing to take the conversational long way around.

"So, Cadet Tate . . . how many times have you sat behind the Green Monster?" I smiled, having been to Fenway Park and seen the Green Monster many times. "Cuz if you climb all the way to the top and stand on your tiptoes, you can just about see my old neighborhood." ˙

I was fine when talking about things outside myself. In fact, Lieutenant Colonel Pats and I connected easily and quickly found ourselves chatting about everything under the sun except the reason for my visit. Eventually, she tried again.

"I'm glad you came in today. And don't get me wrong, I don't say that about many people. But if you don't tell me what the hell is really goin' on, I'm gonna break your other hand!"

At that, a laugh bubbled up from my gut unexpectedly, like a sneeze.

"Well, ma'am . . . I . . . I can't seem to keep food down very well . . . and, well, I hurt my hand."

She pulled her glasses down to the end of her nose and looked at me over the frames for a beat.

"Yeah. No DUH!"

I smiled. My head dropped to my chest. I didn't have the energy to laugh anymore. She asked me about my stress level and diet before sending me to get X-rays. I returned to her office after they were taken.

"Well, kid, you're lucky. You only broke your hand in three places . . . not *four*!"

I furrowed my brow.

"I really *broke* it . . . ma'am?" *Shitballs.* ". . . What do I do now?"

She looked at me crookedly for my lack of emotion. But I was a neophyte at feeling things in real time.

"There's something you're not telling me, kid. But I'll wait. I'll wait until you decide you want to."

I smiled weakly. "Thank you, ma'am. It was so nice to meet you, ma'am. So nice."

She patted me on the shoulder and looked deep into my eyes.

"I'll wait for you to tell me," she said again firmly, then spun me around and pointed me toward the casting room.

The technician set my bones and wrapped me in a compression splint to take down the swelling.

"Come on back in a week, when the swelling's gone down a bit, and I'll cast you."

"Thank you, Sergeant." I smiled and nodded.

No goddamn way. Not before spring volleyball season is over.

On my way out, the exit nurse gave me a stack of forms and another set of explicit instructions. Lieutenant Colonel Pats had put me on bed rest and a liquid diet. She had *ordered* me to return to my room, get into my pajamas, climb up onto my bed unit, and close my eyes until I fell asleep. I was not to consume anything but the liquid-diet Box Nasties (the cadet term of endearment for different versions of portable boxed meals) that were going to be delivered to my room three times a day until I felt better. The exit nurse handed me a Form 38 to pin outside of my dorm room. She reiterated that I was not to be bothered, trained, questioned, or summoned while the form hung outside my door. Lieutenant Colonel Pats had ordered me to concentrate on getting well. I didn't even know what that meant or what it entailed, but I was so grateful that she wanted me to try.

How am I supposed to get well?

I walked out of the clinic like a turtle without its shell, naked, vulnerable, and moving slower than any potential predator. My tears spilled over. *What is wrong with me?* I had never cried so easily in my whole life. If I didn't grow a new shell soon, I was going to be gravely hurt. Again.

I don't want to be hurt again.

26

THE ACADEMY

My hand started to heal. My mind did not.

My body didn't suspend its healing process to whine and cry and reenact the injuries inflicted on it; it simply got better. Why couldn't my mind, my heart, my spirit do the same?

I fully understood the freakish implications of self-inflicted injury. I probably should have just taken up binge drinking or some other more socially acceptable form of self-flagellation. But, to me, this was a controllable form of self-discipline, distraction, release. I had always been able to conquer physical pain. The pain that held me prisoner was something different.

It was out of my control.

Hours, days, weeks passed. My body broke. It healed. It functioned, it did not function. It consumed, it purged. It laughed, it cried. But it did not—could not—forget.

I was huddled in the corner of my room again and the scenario was getting *really* old. I smelled familiar perfume. I resurfaced to the present momentarily to find my two-degree teammate and squadron mate Jetta in my room. I tried hard to stay in the now. But I slipped back in time. I rocked and shook and shivered. I tasted salty tears from my eyes and iron blood from my nose. I felt a hand, a hug. Jetta. She was sitting next to me.

Jetta had been excited about my volleyball prowess and sociability since I had arrived at USAFA. She was pleased when I was assigned to her squadron. Everything had been fine until the mall episode and my frat hit with Her Horrible Her. Jetta had distanced herself from me with each moment I spent with Tip and each blip in my performance. She was stract. She had aspirations of being both our squad commander and team captain. Her pulling away stung, but I didn't blame her. Clearly, she felt that she'd be better off avoiding me than having my behavior reflect poorly on her. And she was probably right. The others followed suit, each one afraid of catching residual flack from my shameful situation.

I am a shameful situation.

"Po, what's the deal, kid?" Jetta said quietly. "You were aces for so long. Why are you tanking? What the fuck is going on?" She was trying to soften her natural sternness, but there were only so many ways that you could tactfully call someone a shit show.

I cannot escape. Jetta, help me. . . .

"Why are you like this?" I heard her say. "Are you sick? How long have you been hiding in your room? Can you even hear me?"

"Look," she continued, "you are my teammate and my squadron mate and I am responsible for you, so you need to tell me what's going on . . . Po? What happened?"

I slipped in and out, looping back and forth. Then I heard a different voice—it was *my* voice. I heard words, *my* words, escaping.

"Tip . . . touched . . . hurt me . . . Coach's house . . . can't tell . . . suicide . . ."

Between loops, I heard my words.

"Tip . . . I can't escape . . . threatening . . . help . . . I'm stuck under her grip . . . I don't know what to do. . . . I am neck deep. . . ."

I knew that I should not be saying these things. My words had escaped. They were scary, they were sad when I heard them outside of my head.

I'm scared.

I saw Jetta's jaw slacken for a moment before I slipped away again. There were hands and mouths and legs and teeth. There were sour smells and suffocating heat and fear and fear and fear.

I resurfaced. *Oh God. I heard my words outside of my head.* I wanted to snatch them out of the air between us and run, far away. My words were true and now it was real. Now What Happened with Her Horrible Her was real.

I saw Jetta's mouth moving. I heard her voice. "Holy shit. Okay. Holy shit. God. Okay, well, she obviously can't be our team captain anymore. . . . I mean . . . holy shit." The wheels began to turn in her mind. The snippets that I heard gathered momentum, and the more her brain's wheel rotated, the more debris it kicked up from her own perspective of the situation. "Okay, it's okay, I can take over for her. God, what a fuckup. I *knew* she was a fuckup. I have to tell Coach. . . . Holy shit."

Her train of thought made my stomach drop, and I put my head between my knees to stave off the nausea. *What have I done?* Deep down in my heart, I knew that Jetta was concerned for my well-being, but her words . . . her words were scaring the shit out of me. I heard my voice for the second time.

"Jetta, please, please, please don't take my words out of this room . . . please. I don't know what I'm going to do. Leave them in here when you go . . . please? Jetta? I'm scared." I swallowed hard, forcing the creeping vomit to about-face back to my stomach. I tried to breathe.

"Oh God, Popo, no, no, you're okay. You're okay. This was *her*. She is a sick fuck." I felt Jetta's hand. It was cool and soft and strong. It was not searching, scratching, ripping, or restraining. It was innocent, stroking, soothing. Her wheels started to turn again. "I fucking *knew* there was something off about her. God. She gets away with everything . . . but she can't get away with this."

"Jetta . . . please . . ." But I could not finish my sentence. One more word and I would have thrown up right in her lap. Everything was spinning: my stomach, the entire room, my entire world. I wanted to take my words back.

I am sorry, I am sorry, I am sorry. I heard my words outside of my mouth and I am so, so sorry.

27

THE ACADEMY

Shortly after reveille the following morning, while Gabby was in the shower, Jetta popped her head into our room.

She had done it.

She informed me that she'd felt she *had* to tell our squad commander.

The squad commander then felt he had to tell our AOC. Our AOC had to tell his chain of command. Jetta said we would hear something soon.

I heard something right then. I'd pulled the pin out of the grenade of truth and in the quiet of the morning, I heard the tinkling of that pin hitting the floor.

Jetta left the doorway for a split second, then came back to let me know that she had told our coaches as well.

And just like that, the truth exploded in the middle of my squadron, my team, and my life at USAFA.

BOOM.

The grenade detonated and shrapnel rained down upon me.

Her Horrible Her bombarded my computer with messages saying that she had popped the cap on every pill bottle in her medicine cabinet and was sitting on her window ledge ready to swallow the pills and then jump. She said she had already written her suicide note telling everyone that I had broken her heart and forced her to jump.

The team was told some . . . version of what had happened. I was not sure who knew what. Beyond our coaches' orders not to talk about it, none of them knew how, exactly, to respond to me. *I* didn't even know how to respond to me. I tried to interact as normally as I could with my teammates. Some responded; some shut down.

My squadron was told that . . . something official . . . was going on. The only change I noticed was the slightly intimidated and/or disgusted looks on their faces as they sidestepped the mess of me.

I received a certified e-mail from a JAG (judge advocate general, aka legal counsel) officer in the USAFA legal department, officially summoning me to their offices. And just like that, the grenade had exploded and left me lonely, confused, frightened, and heartbroken. I was scared of what would transpire with Captain Jag. I was scared that Him Horrible Him would hear about my words escaping and come back to shove, stuff, and choke them back inside me, to keep them from ever coming out again. I was scared of people knowing what had happened in the darkness, my darkness. I was scared of not being able to control the information, the situation, the devastation. I was scared I wouldn't be able to spare my actual friends, my squadron mates, my other teammates, my family.

Please . . . let me take my words back. Help me put this grenade back together again.

28

THE ACADEMY

On the morning of my summons, I shined, pinned, ironed, and Sta-Floed the shit out of my uniform. I had not slept, so I had plenty of time. My stomach dipped and whirled in anticipation of having to give my words, my sick, disgusting, private words away . . . again. I could feel my cheeks aflame with the fire of my *embarrassment*. How was I going to give my words to another person. To a *lawyer?*

I kept picturing Captain Jag as a towering, imposing, rotund man with a set of fleshy lips under a wild mustache that he twirled as I recounted the titillating "girl-on-girl action" of his fantasies and my own personal hell. Maybe instead of a sworn affidavit, he would have me sign his favorite issue of *Jugs* magazine.

I stopped in the bathroom twice on my way to the office and heaved out my guilt, my pain, my fear in acidic streams of foamy bile. By the second stop, I felt totally empty.

I am empty.

I sat in Captain Jag's office, waiting for our meeting to begin, my chin resting on my chest because I was too spent to hold it up. My bangs had given way to gravity as well, and they covered my eyes. So, by childhood hide-and-seek rules, I was invisible to the outside world.

I was about to run to the lavatory one more time when I saw legs enter the room. I shot to attention and was immediately put at rest and ordered to sit back down again. Through my bangs—my cloak of invisibility—I peered over the desk at the officer now sitting across from me.

Captain Jag was a *woman*.

She met my gaze. She looked me over. I was ashamed that she was meeting me in such a ridiculously screwed-up state. I sighed and ventured a small, exasperated smile. She smiled back—a warm, wide smile. *No red flags.* A spark passed between us. Captain Jag's energy seemed honest, safe. Our connection was instant, intrinsic. The circumstances surrounding our meeting were toxic, but I liked her immediately.

We made small talk for a bit, but it did not feel small to me. Captain Jag looked at me as though she could see the water in which I was drowning, as though she could see the real me beneath my wrecked façade. She excused herself from the room for a moment, and I bit my knuckle, hard, to stop myself from crumpling to the floor and sobbing in gratitude.

She returned thirty seconds later with a frosty can of diet jet fuel. *Holy shitballs . . . Was that in my dossier?* We talked easily, we smiled honestly. We sparked.

And then she asked for my words.

Damn, damn, damn, damn, damn. I don't want to say my words. They are disgusting, and I don't want to say them or hear them or clean up the aftermath. Please, no.

She asked me for them on behalf of the inspector general.

I gave her my words. I had to.

She took notes as I spoke, at one point leaning back in her chair with her hand over her mouth.

"Okay . . . okay . . . okay." Her hand dropped from her mouth. "Okay, this is more than just an admission of homosexuality—"

Wait . . . what? Admission of homosexuality . . . ? Is that why I was called here? To substantiate a claim that Her Horrible Her is . . . gay?

"We've dipped into criminal territory here. This is more than just an admission. Okay, wow."

She scribbled on her legal pad. My head spun. So . . . what I had told Jetta had filtered through the chain of command and been distilled down to a rumor that Her Horrible Her—Cadet Tip Attila, who had hijacked my very sense of self—was a *homosexual*? That's not even a *crime*. That's eye color, or right- vs. left-handedness.

What?

"I will need to talk to Cadet Attila. I will be in touch with you shortly, okay, Cadet Tate? Hang in there."

I nodded because it was all I could do. She had my words. And not even *all* of them—only the first half of everything that had transpired—and still I felt duped, confused, mortified. At the time, I hadn't known why I had stopped talking to Jetta before telling her about Him Horrible Him. I hadn't thought about whether to reveal one incident and not the other. I was so shocked that I had let *any* of my truth escape—let alone all. And if the truth about Her Horrible Her had detonated a *grenade* . . . I could not even *imagine* the unfathomable fallout from the *nuclear bomb* I was still harboring inside of me. Her Horrible Her had threatened to take her own life. Him Horrible Him had threatened to take mine. Would it be possible to survive this? All I could do was hope.

29

THE ACADEMY

I jumped at the sound of reveille, though I had been awake since taps the night before, trying to quell the desperate, stabbing pains in my abdomen. I turned over in my bed so that I was facing the wall. It left me vulnerable and exposed to the room behind me, but it was worth it to avoid Gabby's scrutiny. I was on bed rest for the third morning that week, and I knew she resented it. She made that abundantly, noisily clear, as she banged and clanked and hit and bumped and rattled around, readying herself for the day. She turned on all of the lights. She stopped in front of my bed unit on the way out of the room, and I swear I could *hear* her looking at me.

"Tsssk!"

For the love of God, Gabby, I get it.

She slammed the door on her way out just to drive the point home. My heart rate was jacked. I flipped over again, pulled my stuffed bunny to my chest. I forced my eyes to stay open, not wanting to give my memories any more power. I thought about the blue carbon-copied Form 38 pinned outside my door and wondered if "shit show" was considered an official ailment. I could hear my classmates calling minutes out in the hallway all together.

"TROLLLLS! THERE ARE FIF-TEEN MINUTES. FIF-TEEN MINUTES AND COUNTING UNTIL THE TOUGH TWENTY TROLLS MUST BE IN THE MORNING FORMATION! THE UNIFORM OF THE DAY INCLUDES: AIR FORCE DRESS BLUE UNIFORMS, ATHLETIC JACKETS WITH FLIGHT CAPS, BLACK LEATHER GLOVES! THIS MORNING'S MEAL INCLUDES: FRENCH TOAST WITH GLAZED PEACHES, A SIDE OF HAM, YOGURT, MILK, AND ORANGE JUICE! THERE ARE T-MINUS FIF-TEEN MINUTES AND COUNTING!"

We had acted as the upperclassmen's alarm clock every morning, including a snooze feature in which we had just given five more minutes of silence before yelling again. As conflicted as I was about not being out in the hall to support my classmates, I was glad to be out of the line of fire. I pulled my bunny closer, hoping to spread the silence like 2nd Skin over my wounds. The more I tried to embrace the quiet, the more familiar I became with the sound growing beneath the scuttle out in the hallway. The calm was giving way to a storm rolling in . . . and I could already hear thunderclouds clapping.

"CADET SMALLTOWN, WHERE IS YOUR GOOD-FOR-NOTHING ROOMMATE, CADET TATE?!"

The storm.

My stomach sank. I fixed my eyes on the doorknob, half expecting it to turn and the door to burst open. Gabby's voice resonated through the heavy wood of the door.

"Sir, may I make a statement?"

No one was supposed to sound off outside a door with a Form 38 attached to it, but the storm had come, as if the form were a lightning rod.

"YOU'D BETTER, SMALLTOWN!"

My gut tightened. I rose up on my haunches to peer through the grate above our door. Cadet Crow was standing in front of Gabby and pointing at our door with a white-gloved hand. He resembled his namesake, with spiky black hair, beady eyes, and a long, pointy nose. His jaw protruded when he yelled, forcing his nose up and down in a pecking motion. It was uncanny. He also seemed to take pleasure in picking fear off the bones of a fresh, four-degree carcass.

"Sir! She is sick in bed!"

The volume of Cadet Crow's questions had startled every class-mate in the vicinity. They rushed to take their obligatory positions at Gabby's side.

I should be down there.

He flicked the flimsy Form 38 with his angry finger, totally ignoring the fine print that ensured the patient a *silent*, restful recuperation.

My classmates should not have to suffer because my dumb ass can't seem to get it together.

C3C Crow wasted no time in escalating the matter to a full-blown training session.

"HOW DO YOU ALL FEEL ABOUT THIS? HOW DO YOU FEEL, CADET SMALLTOWN? HOW DO YOU FEEL ABOUT YOUR ROOMMATE *ABANDONING YOU* WHILE YOU STAND OUT HERE AND GET TRAINED, HUH?!"

I held my breath. Gabby ordered à la carte from our seven basic responses.

"Sir, I do not know!"

"WHAT DO YOU MEAN, YOU DON'T KNOW?! THIS IS NOT THE FIRST TIME THAT THIS HAS HAPPENED, SMALLTOWN. DO YOU *LIKE* BEING PIMPED OVER BY YOUR ROOMMATE?!"

They all answered in unison, without skipping a beat.

"NO, SIR!"

Crow pecked wildly.

"DON'T YOU THINK THAT IT IS *UNFAIR* FOR CADET TATE TO *SKIP* BEING TRAINED WITH THE REST OF YOU?!"

Shit. He was breaking the rules by leading this training session right outside our room, and that hurt. But infinitely more scarring was my classmates' immediate response.

"YES, SIR!"

I had tried to function on all cylinders. I had tried to muster as much of my excited, fun, jovial self as I could during daylight hours . . . before the darkness came and I dissolved into a frightened, quiet, dissociative wreck. The vacillation back and forth was surely confusing to those around me—but couldn't they see that I had fallen down on the battlefield? I was listening to my squadron choose to leave me behind.

I could feel the vomit start to rise from my belly. I climbed down from my bunk, sank to the floor, and wrapped my arms around my trash can, hoping to stave off sickness until everyone left for formation.

God. How did I get here?

Once all of the cadets had scattered in a stampede, I pulled myself up, wrapped my robe around my exhausted body, and hobbled at attention to the restroom. My knees squeezed both sides of the industrial-strength toilet. I assembled the wavy pieces of my fractured face in the small pool of water, as yet undisturbed by my regurgitated waste. I had been logging too much time bent over porcelain basins. My legs started to shake. I leaned against the stall door to steady myself, propping my hands above my knees to support my upper body. I looked down at the open wounds above the second knuckle on each hand. The dark burgundy blood seeping through the gouges was my only proof that I was alive. The wounds were from the repeated irritation of my teeth when I stuck my fingers down my throat. I had done this so often that I had open *wounds* on top of *scars*.

I am so fucking disgusting.

After Her Horrible Her and Him Horrible Him, the mere thought of something going into my mouth or triggering the least sense of fullness caused my stomach to heave. But now my body was fighting to retain nourishment. It was hungry. My body was hungry, but my brain remembered the pain associated with sickening fullness. My brain sent my fingers chasing after anything that might contribute to my fullness.

No more fullness.

When the deed was done, my legs were shaky and wobbly. My head felt light and high. My body was empty and my mind was soothed. The dichotomy between my physical and emotional states was momentarily bridged by the wretched expulsion of everything from inside of me.

I brushed my teeth, splashed water on my face, and patted my cheeks dry with a coarse paper towel before entering the hallway. I floated back to my room. As soon as I squared my turn to walk through the door, the aftermath of the morning's training session reached out and slapped me across the face.

LIAR

It was scrawled in thick black pen across the Form 38 pinned to my door.

My stomach dropped as I stared at the word. At another school, this might have been just an unclever insult. But here, it was an indictment, the implications of which had the power to launch a full-scale honor code investigation. I ripped the epithet out of the form, leaving a gaping hole in its place. It matched the hole in my heart.

I closed my door and paused with my back to it. At that moment, the thick, mahogany-stained slab felt like the only thing in my squadron that I could lean on. I looked at my loft bed and the desk underneath it. I flashed back to a hard slap across my face, the feeling of hitting the floor. . . .

I don't want to die. I can't breathe, I can't move, please stop.

I was a malfunctioning time machine, straddling worlds. I started kicking the Formica. I kicked the fucking Formica. I kicked at the memory of Him then and the pain of me now. I kicked and kicked and did not stop until I saw my blood splatter. My past and present overlapped and I regained consciousness.

My foot was bloody, bruised, tripling in size. I stared at it. The pain did not register. The pain between my legs, down my throat, in my obliterated heart was still far more overwhelming.

I watched the blood flowing freely from the brand-new gashes in my foot. I watched the swelling as it expanded. The pain finally registered. It finally surpassed my threshold. It started to scream with fury, overtaking the deeper pain.

I hoisted myself up onto my bed unit, blood, bruises, brutality, and all. I pulled my dream box out from under my pillow and wrapped my arm around it. My dream box. My very personal item that I'd kept, I'd hidden since basic. My tiny contraband incubator of hopes and dreams, my tiny repository of goals in their purest state. I clung to the smooth, supple leather. I clung to the rounded wholeness. Inside were all of my pledges.

I had gotten the box from my maternal grandfather. Inside were a tiny pad of paper and a tiny pen. I wrote my dreams, my goals, my desires in present tense—as if they had already come true—so that I could keep my eye on the ball and attract the exact outcome I wanted. Once I had manifested each desire, I would lift the secret false bottom and place the manifestations inside. Like perpetually burning-hot coals, they would incubate the ones that had yet to actualize.

I had pledged before I started at USAFA that I was going to be a stellar cadet. I had pledged to stand out from the sea of air force blue like Polaris. I had pledged to make the most of my time at the academy. I had written these pledges on heavy-duty, handmade paper and put them inside my dream box. It was thereby decreed.

I opened the lid of my dream box slightly, so that none of the dark energy around me, swirling and scary, would slip into its pristine sanctuary. I grabbed the first piece of paper on the pad attached to its lid. I found the tiny pen attached to the pad. I wrote a new goal on the piece of paper, half pledge, half plea. I folded it, dropped it in the box, and quickly closed the lid. I wished that I could climb in next to my paper pledge and close the lid on this nightmare.

I put my dream box back under my pillow, hoping that its healing powers would soothe my heavy head.

30

THE ACADEMY

Over the next few weeks, the pendulum swung: functioning, non-functioning. Because of the inspector general's investigation into Tip, we were prohibited from having any contact. This allowed me some physical breathing room, but my inner turmoil persisted. Spring volleyball season had begun, and I participated as often as my grades and various injuries and broken bones would allow. Athletics had been my lifelong refuge, so it broke my heart that volleyball had played a role in my unquantifiable pain.

My grades were atrocious. I had had a nearly perfect grade point average coming out of high school. Anything less had always been totally unacceptable to me. It was considerably less right now. *Considerably.* I had been put on ac-pro (academic probation) after my first semester. Ac-pro curtailed much of my extracurricular activity and *all* of my social activity—which set me further adrift in my sea of isolation.

I was mortified to be struggling in arenas where I'd always excelled. I didn't know how to be a below-average student or athlete. I didn't know how to be a troublemaker. Yet, on paper, that's exactly what I was.

The great rapport I had established with all of my teachers made little difference in my GPA. I was failing. It was time to make a change.

———————————

I met Pepe in the study lounge so that we could prepare for a major test the following day. "How are you doing in aviation right now, Pep?" I asked in an effort to determine which of us should lead the study session.

He disintegrated into laughter. Pepe was on ac-pro as well. His GPA at the semester break started *after* the decimal point. He was on the varsity track-and-field team but was currently unable to compete due to his grades. We commiserated.

"Okay," I said, trying another approach. "Well, how far along are you in the textbook?" I had missed a considerable number of classes, so I had planned on picking up where he had left off.

"Umm, well, since you have probably missed more class than I have," he began, "we should probably start where *you* left off the last time you were in class. It's totally cool. I can go back to where you are—I mean, hey, I could use the review, right!"

I didn't want to admit to the last page that I had read in our book.

"Hmm," I said, "how about we *both* open to the last page we've read on the count of three . . . ? Ready, one . . . two . . . three!"

We opened our books simultaneously. We looked at each other's books. We looked at each other. We read in unison.

"*'Welcome to the wonderful world of aviation. . . .'*"

Oh my God. Neither one of us had read a goddamn thing. Pepe was doubled over on the floor, laughing uncontrollably. He got me laughing, too, and I welcomed it, even if the laughter was at our own expense.

We studied from taps until reveille, frantically cramming nearly an entire textbook into our brains in eight hours. Our grades were dependent upon this test. We high-fived and hugged each other before parting ways to get dressed.

I winked at Pep when the teacher passed out the test and did not look up again until the bell rang. The rest of the day passed in a fatigued haze.

By the time I got to my desk in aviation the next day, Pepe was already there. He was looking at his test with glassy eyes. I turned mine over before speaking. The big red *A–* at the top of the page might as well have leapt up and kissed me on the nose. *Thank God!* I looked over at Pep, hoping his was the same. He held his test up to me. Beneath the first question he had written, "Welcome to the wonderful world of avia . . ." His pencil had then trailed off into an illegible squiggle. The rest of the page was blank. He had fallen asleep.

He was laughing, but his eyes were sad. I put my paper facedown, crestfallen, and reached over to hug him. I suggested that he ask to retake the test. Major Glider, our professor, was stract, but very amenable to effort. I told him to ask.

My spirits rose a fraction. My body felt better. The test grade had reminded me what I was capable of and restored my faith that I might survive the year. *Buoy.* I had gotten an e-mail from Captain Jag, so I stopped by her office. She had finished up her part of the investigation and just wanted to check in on me. We spoke for a little while. *Buoy.*

I returned to our squadron after dinner with hope still in my heart. Perhaps this would be the turning point for me. It was surely time.

I ascended the five flights of stairs with a bounce in my step, squared my turn to enter my room, and—stopped short. There was a picture hanging on my door.

The undertow. It yanked.

It was me. Under a bloodred bull's-eye.

I pulled the paper down, crumpled it furiously, and threw it into the trash can just inside our room. I blinked back tears as I thought about the image and the message. I sprinted to the bathroom. I barely reached the stall in time to bow, forcefully, to the toilet below.

Stop. Please just stop.

I gagged and heaved and gagged and heaved. It burned. *I am so disgusting.* I closed my eyes. I smelled the dregs. I tasted iron. I opened my eyes to the rainbow of colors floating in the muck below. A brilliant crimson streaked the sides of the bowl. I blinked my eyes, hard. *Fuck, fuck, fuck.*

Cold water did little to neutralize the burning in my mouth. I wobbled on shaky legs back to my room. I stood in front of the sink, locking my knees so that I would not crumble. I brushed my teeth, which did little to quell the fire. I needed to clean myself up. Perhaps if I cleaned up my exterior, my interior would follow suit. Perhaps.

I inspected myself closely, obsessively, in the mirror for the spatter of crusty vomit or drops of bloody bile. I wiped blood off of my neck and cheek. My eyes were swollen, puffy, sad. Gravity had slid fluid-filled pillows beneath my eyes in hopes that I would take the hint and get some sleep. Perhaps it would happen tonight. Perhaps.

I pressed my fingers into the eye pillows and looked closer. I saw something I had seen before. Once. But not on me. Only once. But not on me.

The skin around my eyes was riddled with little red dots. The concentration was higher above and below my tear ducts, like a macabre stippling. *Oh my God. I know what this is.* It was petechial hemorrhaging. The trauma of my violent heaves had broken my capillaries.

Oh my God. I had seen the same red dots around my sister's eyes while she lay motionless in the field behind the stables. I had seen it when the EMTs were trying to revive her. I had seen this before. I had seen it once before. Sary had these around her eyes from the force of her fall. And now I had them, too.

She fell. I should have been there to break her fall. Oh God. I know what these are. I know what I've done. I should have been there to break her fall. I should have been there, and now it is my turn. I am already dying. How long will it take? Am I going to die? How long will it take? I am so sorry, Mommy. I am so sorry, Daddy. I am so sorry, Sary.

I tried to rub them off like I had the dried blood. I sat down in front of my sink and waited for it to come. I had seen them only once. They come only once, and then you're gone. Once and then . . . I'm gone.

———————

Dawn came before death did. I had a chance, a tiny window to move, to get help. I rose up off of my floor in a blotchy, exhausted sleepwalk, and I took my chance. The moment I walked through the door of the Cadet Clinic, I collapsed.

I am sorry, Mommy. I am sorry, Daddy. I am sorry, Sary.
I'm so sorry.
I passed out.

31

THE ACADEMY

I woke up on a gurney with an IV in my arm. Lieutenant Colonel Pats was standing over me.

"All right, deary, what the *hell* is going on?"

She demanded the answer like she was trying to defuse a ticking time bomb. Her concern seeped through her gruff exterior. My tears welled and then spilled. She spoke for me.

"All right. Okay. Now's the time. It's time we talk about this."

She rolled her stool over and sat beside me, putting her clipboard down in her lap so that she could gesticulate.

"You can't go on like this, Miss Polo." Hearing her use my first name made me, again, emotional. "This has got to end before that asshole"—she thumbed the air aggressively over her shoulder—"*wins* and *you* end up in the *ground*."

Her words hung in the sterile air between us. Lieutenant Colonel Pats did not even know the whole story—no one did. No one but me and Him. All she had to go by were my symptoms, my actions, and what few words I had given her. I could feel her deep intuition picking at my internal lockbox, and I knew that she had had experience with sexual assault victims. She had a hunch about at least some of what I had been hiding, but I couldn't, wouldn't speak about Her Horrible Her out loud to one more soul, lest there be more consequences. And the way things were already going, I didn't dare mention a single word about Him Horrible Him.

Her Horrible Her had threatened to take her own life. Him Horrible Him had threatened to take mine. And then there was what my life had become since the knowledge—only half—had come out into the world. The only viable option I saw was to try to gain control over the only thing that I *could* control . . . *myself.* I did not ever want my words to escape again. Not ever.

Emotions collided in my brain like weather patterns as Lieutenant Colonel Pats spoke. On one hand, I had managed to develop some friends here and an assortment of amazing memories. *For them, I am so appreciative.* On the other hand, the destructive gale-force winds of violence had caused me massive fear and pain.

I looked up at Lieutenant Colonel Pats through my conflict and sorrow.

I am scared. Help me, I am scared.

Lieutenant Colonel Pats put her soft, strong, and capable hand on my forehead. I became a child again in an instant. I felt my mother's healing hand on my forehead as I had lain sick in bed a lifetime ago. On the rare occasion that I had stayed home sick from school, she would monitor my fever with her big, cool mama hand just like this.

My mother—even with a full-time job—had traveled out to several weekend volleyball matches during the fall season, to both watch me play and ease the empty nest, I had suspected. She would always pass along any updates to my father if he was unable to travel due to work. However, once things had started to go downhill after the incidents, I had strongly discouraged her from coming out, using whatever strength I had to reassure her that things were fine-just-fine. And anything that wasn't would sort itself out. The last thing that I wanted to do was cause my parents—my two most avid supporters— any more pain or worry them in any way. However, the energy that I had used to try to convince them that I was handling my life at USAFA was . . . dwindling. To say the least. And as much as I wanted to keep any negative information from them, I could feel the rabid mama-bear instincts of my mother on the verge of breaching any wall of privacy I had tried to maintain. Especially given this latest Cadet Clinic visit.

I felt the cool mama-hand again as I closed my eyes tightly, and the memory merged with the present. I clung to both, grateful to have a vacation from my usual demons. My tears spilled through my tightly closed lids. Lieutenant Colonel Pats was gone by the time I opened them again.

Shortly after that, Pep poked his head through the curtain. I would have been embarrassed if it were any other squadron mate, but I knew that Pep would never judge me—I was glad to see him. His hug lingered. *Something's wrong.* Soon, his head was resting on my shoulder.

". . . Pep?"

He pulled away and turned his head to the side, not wanting to look me in the eye. He had been asked to leave USAFA. Captain Troll had called him into his office to tell him that his grades had not shown significant enough improvement for him to be able to remain a cadet. He would be gone in two days. He had come to say good-bye. And I was so sorry to see him go.

The IV filled me drop by drop. Searching, scratching, squeezing hands inflicted pain, pain, pain each time I closed my eyes, so I kept my eyes open. When Captain Jag walked in, I bathed in the warmth of her energy.

"Hey, you," she said, eyeing the needle in my arm. "I brought you some nourishment."

She pulled a *Cosmopolitan* magazine, a bottle of ice-cold diet jet fuel, and a bag of fruity Jujubes out of her plastic bag. My eyes filled with tears at her generosity.

Jesus. I'm such a fucking pussy right now.

It was as if the IV had finally hydrated me, and a lifetime of tears could finally shed.

"Oh my gosh, ma'am, I didn't get you anything! May I offer you a drink, at least?!"

I held out my arm with the IV needle as if it was cocktail. "Electrolyte-tini?"

She just smiled and wagged her head from side to side.

"But seriously, ma'am, thank you. That is incredibly thoughtful . . . and exactly the sustenance I need. Thank you."

I felt bad that she had to witness me in an even more pronounced state of decline. She had yet to see me functioning on all cylinders. In fact, I was shocked every time she wanted to see me again.

Since Captain Jag had finished her part of Her Horrible Her's investigation, she had popped in on me a few times, just to chat. It was nice to have dialogue beyond interrogation and disclosure. Captain Jag was not only a buoy in my unending sea of blue, she was also a *lighthouse*. I desperately wanted to only stay on the "normal" side with her, but she had met me on the sad side. The scary side. She had seen both sides of me. And she understood it.

She sensed my need to entertain, distract, and deflect, and she put her hand up in front of me softly but strongly. "Wait, Polo. Just listen for a moment. . . . Just relax and listen for a moment, okay?"

I nodded.

"There might be a way that you can make it through this

situation better than you are now—and let's face it, it needs to be better or we're in trouble."

I nodded, ashamed.

"I've been doing some research, and I think there might be a way for you to take some time off while the case against Tip proceeds."

The color drained from my face in order to surround my heart, which had just shattered into a zillion little pieces.

So it has come to this. She was telling me that I had to leave. That I had to quit.

Captain Jag sensed what I was thinking, along with my fierce and rising panic. She waved her open hand back and forth in front of my face.

"Not *permanently.*"

She presented her proposition very carefully, knowing how sensitive I was. She chose her words deliberately and enunciated clearly.

"Polo . . . It would just be until the trial is over. Just for these next few weeks of the school year. . . . Then you could return for SERE"—survival evasion resistance escape, pronounced *see-ree*, super difficult and required for all soldiers—"in the summer and continue on through your three-degree year and so forth. . . ."

She wrapped her hand around her thermal coffee mug and nestled it against her shoulder.

"Polo."

I leaned in. She had never called me by my first name before, and now she'd done it twice in the span of two minutes.

"You need to think about *you* for a moment. I mean, how long can this go on?"

The truth in her words sucker punched me, and I rolled onto my side.

I could not quit. I didn't even know how. I could not leave. I had nowhere to go. *I don't want to go back and search for pieces of my broken family.* Though I know that they would only want my safety, my parents, newly divorced, would be devastated . . . beyond disappointed. My squadron would hate me.

I brought my knees to my chest and fought the urge to hyperventilate.

Captain Jag broke the silence in between my labored breaths.

"You'll be back in a couple of months."

I started to shake.

"This does NOT mean that you are a failure—it means that your body needs a break from this entire mess . . . time to heal, to regroup, to come back."

The gurney rattled with my vibration. Captain Jag put her hand on my shoulder.

"I told Colonel Noble what had transpired between you and Cadet Attila, and he wants to meet you. Hopefully, after meeting you, he will support your 'stop out,' taking a temporary leave of absence. This situation, this offer, it is unprecedented."

Her touch was warm. It slowed my heartbeat. I started to hear less of the silence between her words and more of the words themselves. I breathed a little slower. I agreed to meet with Colonel Noble, who was the full-bird colonel in charge of USAFA legal affairs. Obviously, if he was summoning me, I was going to show up. With bells on. But I still felt unwilling to quit. I had never quit anything in my entire life.

32

THE ACADEMY

As soon as I could stand up and walk out of the Cadet Clinic, I reported to Colonel Noble's office. He put me at rest, and both of us sat down on the couch in his office. He, a full-bird colonel, and I, a smack, sat on the same couch to have a conversation based on a foundation of mutual respect.

His warmth and candor defused the situation, which was certainly an unusual one. I was awash in appreciation. He struck me as even-tempered and curious, powerful and fair. He seemed to wield his rank humbly and justly. I felt comfortable looking into his eyes.

Every once in a while, he would look at me sideways while we spoke, the same look that Captain Jag had given to me during her investigative interviews. He was sizing me up—but for some reason, it didn't make me nervous. I somehow knew that we were speaking on a level playing field, away from status, rank, and rumor. There was no reason to feel intimidated, just eager for discovery.

"May I be frank with you, Miss Tate?"

"Yes, sir, of course."

He shifted in his seat and broke eye contact for the first time. "I feel compelled to tell you this, having spoken to you a little bit now. Frankly, Miss Tate, if you were going to try and press criminal charges of sexual assault against Cadet Attila in a civilian court, there is a good chance that you would lose. If it came down to your word against hers, you might very well . . . lose. And it may behoove you to ask yourself what would be gained by dragging your name and the academy's name through the mud in the process."

He stopped talking with his mouth, but continued with his eyes. I understood. Before he put his cards on the table, he wanted to make sure that I wasn't going to show my hand to the rest of the world. He had to determine how much of a risk I was.

"Sir, I understand what you are saying . . . and all that it implies. And, if I may be frank with you, sir, I hadn't even thought about that. I just want to go to school."

I just wanted to learn, work, and train. I wanted to play volleyball and make friends and fly, fly, fly. I barely had the energy to get through the *day* without intravenous nourishment. . . . I had not even *fathomed* going through a civilian criminal trial.

I felt a hit of sympathetic sadness, and saw the same in his eyes as he nodded. Whether he regretted his disclaimer or feared that it would somehow now corrupt my honest, forthright desire to speak with him was unclear. But his emotion—understated as it was—was magnified exponentially in me, and threatened to spill down my face in a wash of tears.

Lock it up, Tate, come on. I bit my lip to prevent the cascade.

Maintaining eye contact, Colonel Noble settled back into a conversational tone. "Captain Jag and I have been discussing your options. Considering your position academically, militarily, athletically, physically, and emotionally—"

"Sir," I interjected, feeling waves of shame over my performance in every one of those areas, "I don't even know what to say. Never in my life . . . ever . . . have I struggled to perform. . . . Never have I performed less than stellarly. . . . I am just . . . so . . . ashamed. I truly apologize."

"You need a rest, Miss Tate."

"Sir, I'm not even sure what that means. The very language of your suggestion frightens me."

"Oh, no, no. This is a *positive* thing. Try not to be afraid. The leave of absence will last only a matter of weeks, and then you can return to USAFA. We hope it will give you just enough time to regroup, gather strength, and gear up for the third summer session, which, for you, will be SERE."

I didn't want to go back to Michigan. I didn't want to have to explain . . . anything. I didn't want to have to admit failure, defeat, defilement. I tried to keep listening to his words.

". . . Of course, leaving now and not coming back until summer session means you will miss recognition. . . ."

Recognition weekend was the crowning achievement of every cadet's four-degree year, a school-wide celebration of the freshmen becoming upperclassmen. It was preceded by a week full of hellish hazing festivities leading up to a ceremonial rite of passage where every four-degree was pinned with a set of "prop and wings." Upperclassmen that had spent all year socially avoiding and training the smacks would finally get to ask out those they had been eyeing, or hang out with those they had wanted to get to know as friends. It was very important and very cathartic for all involved. And I was going to miss it.

". . . I have been spoken to by the higher powers—"

God?

"—among them, the commandant, General Stoic—"

Ahh . . . USAFA gods.

"—and you will be able to return for SERE as a fully recognized three-degree. You can weave all of your makeup classes into the fabric of your sophomore and junior years, and if you work hard, you will be able to graduate with your class."

I digested his proposition silently.

"This has never been offered before, Miss Tate."

"Yes, sir, I understand. . . . I am just sorry that it even *has* to be offered. . . ."

As I sat on his couch, it suddenly struck me how exhausted I was. My cells felt literally like they started to slump, one by one. My cells settled the question. They answered his proposition while I was sitting on the couch trying to think. He reached over and touched my shoulder, captivating every bit of my attention.

"Now that we have met," he continued a little more warmly, "I can see why this generous option was offered to you. I am honestly very much looking forward to seeing your contribution to the world, Cadet Tate, to seeing how you fly and where you land. Best of luck to you. Truly."

We shook hands.

"Sir, it was a pleasure to meet you. I am exceptionally grateful to be given a second chance to flourish here. Thank you for wanting to meet with me. I appreciate you, sir. Thank you."

So . . . it was done. I would take a temporary medical leave of absence and return for the summer. I was failing, flailing, not functioning. I was bruised, battered, barely coherent. I needed to get away from here for a while. I still felt like a quitter. *But I cannot let myself die. And that trumps all.*

The paperwork for my medical leave of absence was set in motion. *It is settled, and I am grateful.*

33

THE ACADEMY

My leave of absence was being processed at an extra-slow pace, and things were becoming incendiary in the interim. My AOC was the first to ignite.

I was standing in Captain Troll's office. He puffed his robust chest up to capacity, like a loaded bellows aimed at the sleepy coals of a fire, and let fly.

"CADET TATE, DO YOU REALLY THINK QUITTING— *ABANDONING* YOUR RESPONSIBILITIES AS A CADET—IS THE ANSWER?! DO YOU REALLY THINK *FAILURE* IS THE WAY TO IMPRESS YOUR CHAIN?"

To which chain is he referring? My chain of command . . . or the one around my legs, my waist, and my neck?

"DON'T YOU FEEL *GUILTY* FOR PIMPING OVER YOUR CLASSMATES AND TAKING A *BLOW* FOR TWO MONTHS WHILE THEY WORK THEIR ASSES OFF TO MAKE UP FOR YOUR ABSENCE??"

YES, goddamnit. Guilty AF. Of course I did. I had sworn to do my duty, no matter what, and now I felt as if I was going back on my word because I couldn't seem to get my shit together, so YES. *Yes.* I felt enormous guilt for the whole thing.

Captain Troll inched closer to my face with every spewed word. His breath seemed to be curdling as it hit my cheek and rolled down my face like solid chunks of salivacious cottage cheese. His sweaty brow hovered over his tiny pupils. I was grateful that my eyes were caged. I drew prudent breaths as I prepared to sound off, but the phone perched on the corner of his desk jangled loudly before I could. The moment his face left my personal bubble, I sucked in oxygen as if I were about to dive underwater.

During his brief phone conversation, he shot several glances at me. *It's about me.*

"Yes, sir."

Whoa. I had never heard him defer to a more authoritative figure before. The elementary school poster of five fish—in order from largest to smallest and each being eaten by the bigger one behind it—popped instantly into my head. I guess we were all smacks to someone. He turned around so that his back was toward me.

"Yes, *SIR*," he fired again, like a bullet, into the receiver. Then he slammed it down, turned, and aimed his verbal ammunition at me.

"GET OOOUUUT!"

"ShhYESSSIRR!"

His redirection had startled me, and I turned to leave before I had finished speaking, my legs practically pinwheeling up a cloud of animated dust.

Unfortunately, the AOC's spark of disgust caught like a brushfire among my squadron mates. I put up a firewall that further isolated me, but I managed to get burned anyway. Gabby's complete silent treatment felt like a third-degree burn. We had been through so much side by side with each other, and I considered her a close friend.

Part of me understood—I didn't know what she had heard or what pressures she was under—which made it even more painful. I struggled with conflicting feelings: wanting to get out of the line of fire and not wanting to leave my teammates and friends.

Colonel Noble and Captain Jag had provided me a temporary solution *to* the academy with my temporary dissolution *from* the academy. I lost the rest of the spring season of volleyball—but at least I had been able to play part of my first NCAA season. Though I had received miserable marks, I had been given an academic mulligan for the classes I was failing. I would miss the gauntlet of recognition but had been given permission to advance militarily and return as an upperclassman. Objectively, the positives outweighed the negatives, but the tremors of what I'd experienced still coursed through my body, still reduced me to emotional rubble.

Captain Jag generously provided me with a kind of halfway house between the rigorously structured life of USAFA and the unrestrictive civilian world. She invited me into her home and acted as my surrogate sponsor and physical and emotional bodyguard. I stayed with her and her husband for ten days before going back to Michigan, gradually letting go of all that I had clung to in order to survive.

PART FOUR
DRY LAND

34

THE ACADEMY

I had been in Michigan for less than three weeks before I was ordered back to USAFA, summoned to appear as a key witness in the case of "Alleged Homosexuality Against Cadet First Class Tip Attila."

The academy had sent me home to heal without realizing that the "home" to which I returned was different from the one I had left months before. And despite my parents' attempts at taping together the picture of our family that had been ripped apart while I was gone, the time we spent together was forced, awkward, and painful. A new portrait would have to be taken. As strong as my yearning was for the familiar—albeit dysfunctional—family milieu I had come to know, I could no sooner be the perfect child than I had been the perfect cadet over the past few months. Nor did I have the energy to provide the family's emotional and comic relief, as I had always done. Everything was ass-backward.

I was still losing time to the crippling video montage of my memory. I was still straddling worlds, past and present. I was still vomiting, sometimes without provocation, sometimes deliberately purging to avoid feeling full. I was still trying to hold myself together by any means necessary. Part of me wanted to open the emotional floodgates, to let go completely and allow myself to feel, to grieve . . . whatever that meant. But the rest of me kept track of time and space. The rest of me understood that I was sharing the roof that my mother had kept in my parents' very recent divorce while remaining in close proximity to my uprooted father. My mother—ever the mama bear—had called Captain Jag to get a sitrep (situation report) on what the hell was happening out in Colorado. Captain Jag had given her a rough outline. I had not shared much of anything with my parents, except to reassure them that I would be—not to worry— returning to USAFA forthwith. I wanted to protect them both from any more disappointment, hurt, and pain. I knew that I had mere weeks before I had to return to school, and that was an impossibly short amount of time to turn our whole situation around—mine and theirs.

My entire existence was in conflict. I did not know how to be a failure, and yet I was failing. I felt incapable of being a cadet, yet I was no longer a civilian. I was no longer a perfect daughter, but I didn't know how to play any other role. I wanted to move past everything that had happened, but I was stuck in the endless loop of it.

There was one positive aspect to my return to Michigan. It had given me personal space and distance from immediate physical peril. I was no longer experiencing the relentless surges of adrenaline and acidic fear that had coursed through my body every time I climbed down from my bed unit, stepped out of my room, or left my squadron. I didn't face the imminent threat of seeing Her Horrible Her or Him Horrible Him. The 2,000-mile buffer gave my body a distinct— if temporary—reprieve, and I took advantage of it. I exercised as much as I could and tried to distract myself from harmful thoughts. I made small strides. I gained a modicum of strength.

Until I received the trial summons in the mail.

Trying to pack for the trip back to USAFA felt like trying to pack for my own kidnapping. I opened my suitcase and stared into the empty, rectangular void, conflicted about what I had gotten myself into. I was being ordered to testify against the person with whom I had spent the most time during my first year at USAFA . . . but she had also been the most toxic and abusive. I was being ordered to betray her completely and ruin her career—*not* because of her crime against me, but because she was *gay*. I would be the instrument of her punishment for a characteristic that, in my view, was akin to being born with green eyes.

But the result would be just. The result would be the same as if she were being prosecuted for her real crime. She would not be able to inflict pain on anyone else at the academy. She would not be able to inflict any more pain on *me*.

I sat down on my bed and closed my eyes without closing them. I closed my ears without closing them. I retreated without retreating. I breathed, breathed, breathed. In the midst of the rarefied silence, an insight materialized. I was just . . . being asked to *tell the truth*. No more and no less. In fact, I was being *ordered* to tell the truth, and wear my uniform when I did so. I opened my eyes, opened my ears, came back to the present. I packed my suitcase.

———————

I disembarked from the plane into the unsettling familiarity of Colorado Springs and drove to the VOQ (visiting officers' quarters). My mom had offered to accompany me on the trip, but I wouldn't have it.

My mom knew little more than the very bare bones of what was going on. And while it may have been much more than what my father—my poor father, whom I had never wanted to hurt, either—was privy to, and probably more than what my squadron mates knew, it paled in comparison to what would be brought out at trial. I had put my parents through enough by being sent home. There was *no way* I was going to subject them to the gory details of my downward spiral.

My stomach dropped as I passed the SPs (security policemen) guarding the front gates of the academy. It felt as if I had come home.

To a haunted house.

I checked into the VOQ and called Mo-Mo, who was on campus for jump training. We had kept in touch since I'd left.

Mo-Mo bounded into my room like a Superball you can buy from a vending machine outside a supermarket. She was barely five feet tall, and her shiny black hair had grown out of its beast haircut so that it now hung below her jawline in a bouncy bob. We hugged, high-fived, and performed our secret handshake, which was now up to a full minute long. I let the moment wash over me. I tried my best to feel comfortable with her hello hug, though I had been shying away from physical contact.

For a few minutes, I forgot why I was in town—and then Mo-Mo popped open the can of worms as if they were macadamia nuts from the minibar.

"Tell me, Mami. . . . Tell me your demons, and we can tame them together," she said, cocking her head so that her shiny bob bounced on her shoulder. I dropped my head. *Shit.* We had never talked about that night at Coach's house. However ridiculous my wish, I had hoped that we never would.

"I . . . I . . ."

I didn't know what to say.

I didn't know what to do, either.

"I . . . I'm so sorry. I'm not supposed to talk about anything until after the trial."

Mo-Mo nodded slowly, hurt that I wouldn't let her further into my emotional inner circle. We went back to talking about our squadrons and the boy that she was dating, but it wasn't the same. She left early for her summer class. I didn't know how to undo the hurt I had caused, so I let her.

I was alone and lonely. Again.

A little while later, the USAFA prosecutor called me to review my testimony for the following day.

"Miss Tate, nice to meet you. Please come into my office."

Captain Policy shook my hand efficiently as he spoke. He was a tall, slender, fastidiously groomed man who walked with a gliding gait, probably to cut down on wind resistance. I followed him swiftly from the building entrance to his office.

"What I would like to do, Cadet Tate, is go through each question that I am going to ask you tomorrow."

His demeanor and his gestures were equally meticulous. He pointed to a chair opposite his desk, and I sat. As he took his own chair, he pulled out a bound stack of papers the size of a phone book, grabbed his pen, and was ready to start writing by the time my ass landed on the seat cushion.

"Now, when did you and Cadet Attila meet for the first time?"

Blech.

He went through our entire chronology, pausing only to elicit more exposition from me or fact-check my answers against those I had given to Captain Jag during her IG, inspector general, investigation. The ream of paper was her investigative brief, though it was anything but. It was over *two hundred pages.*

Any relationship that takes that many billable hours to explain cannot be healthy.

After a long while, he finally ceased firing his questions about everything leading up to and through the attack. It felt as if I'd been through a painful gynecological exam.

"Very well, Cadet Tate," he said without looking up as he finished jotting down the last of his notes.

My teeth began to chatter. I was starting to get nervous about the trial and about seeing Her Horrible Her. I could feel deeper tremors coming.

"Sir, would you be willing to review the protocol for tomorrow, please?"

Captain Policy paused for a moment and looked up from the obsessively arranged accoutrements on his desktop.

"Essentially, Miss Tate, the information compiled in Captain Jag's report has proven substantial enough to warrant a hearing on the allegations that Tip Attila has admitted to being a homosexual. If the allegations are found to be true, she will be in violation of the military's Don't Ask, Don't Tell policy. She will, therefore, become a candidate for expulsion from both USAFA and the United States Air Force."

My teeth chattered. I sat on my hands, trying not to overthink the situation. Hearing the charge brought against Her Horrible Her again—homosexuality—was like hearing that a tiger had been put on trial for having stripes. Never mind that the beast was savage.

"The Board of Inquiry hearing will proceed much like a typical court case. I will ask you my set of questions and then the defense attorney for Miss Attila will cross-examine you."

A beat. His face contorted around his puckered mouth like he was sucking on a lemon wedge. My stomach tightened.

"I need to tell you, Miss Tate, that . . . you should be prepared for an . . . *animated* . . . defense."

Whaaat . . . does that *mean?*

"Sir?"

He lowered his voice an octave, dipped his chin, and locked his eyes onto mine.

"Well . . . Miss Attila has . . . well . . . she has turned this around on *you*, Miss Tate."

More puckering.

"She has made a serious attempt to paint *you* as the homosexual and the perpetrator of inappropriate actions toward *her*."

He steepled his hands and tap-tap-tapped his index fingers against his bottom lip. Behind his clinical gaze, he was observing and gauging my response.

"She is claiming that *you* are obsessed with *her*, that you want to be like her in every way, and that . . . well . . . you are in *love* with her."

His words socked me in the stomach. Thirty seconds passed as the chattering of my teeth reverberated around the claustrophobic office as I tried to pick my world up off of the floor.

Captain Policy dropped his eyes, his cheeks flushed, and he worked at straightening the already meticulously aligned calendar, stapler, and paperweight on his desk. He could not look at me.

"I realize it may sound ridiculous to you, but you . . . you should be prepared for . . . well . . . some downright nasty character assassinations. Miss Attila's defense attorney knows nothing about you except what she has told him and what is documented in your academy disciplinary file—"

Greeaaat.

"So I would strongly suggest that you mentally conjure up the *worst* things that you know her to have said either *about* you or *to* you in order to prepare yourself for tomorrow."

CHATTER, CHATTER, BANG, BANG, BANG.

All I had been doing since that night, since that wretched fucking night at Coach's house, was try to *erase* it all from my memory. Now the prosecuting attorney for the United States Air Force was encouraging me, *ordering* me to go back and riffle through every single conversation I'd had with Her Horrible Her. All so that I could try to anticipate what she could possibly use against me. Based on the lies she'd already told, I knew that it would be nearly impossible to try to anticipate what she was going to hurl at me—which rope, poison, pill, pipe, knife, crossbow, gun, missile, or nuke she was going to use to obliterate me.

Even though she knew the fucking truth.

The truth was difficult and painful enough to have to put into words in front of a room full of people. I did not want to imagine more or—worse—hear it.

Captain Policy barely looked up. "Well, I think that just about covers everything," he said, pointlessly picking imaginary specks of dust off of his spotless desktop. The room's silence had clearly become unendurable for him, and he desperately wanted me gone.

"Try to look only at the person asking you questions, keep your responses short, and tell the truth. Do you have your service dress uniform ready for tomorrow's appearance?"

He stood up and walked around his desk, barely interested in my answer to his question.

Wait . . . hold on . . . I'm . . .

"If you need anything, please feel free to give me a call tomorrow morning. I'm afraid I won't be available until then . . . but have a good night, get some sleep. Remember to shine your shoes and not to wear a lot of makeup."

He put his hand gently under my elbow, hustling me to a standing position.

"Okay, then. We'll see you tomorrow at Harmon Hall. Take care."

Wait . . . wait . . . I . . . ahh . . . wai—

He held the door to his office open for me.

"Sir, I—"

"Try not to worry, Polo. Tomorrow will be fine."

As I left his office, a female JAG captain hurried over to meet us. Captain Policy literally held out my elbow to her as if it were a hot potato and she was "it."

"This is Captain Wrangle," he said in machine-gun staccato. "She will be sitting with you in witness holding tomorrow and ushering you into the courtroom. Okay. Take care."

"Wait, sir—"

Captain Policy was speaking too fast, and I was hearing too slowly—but he had already closed his office door.

Captain Wrangle took my elbow and led me toward the foyer. "Now, Polo," she began in a soft, feminine Southern drawl that contrasted starkly with what had come before her. I finally looked over at her.

Where am I? What is happening?

"Make sure you get some sleep tonight, eat well, and drink lots of water. The altitude can do funny things, especially if you haven't been up this high in a while. So be sure to watch for warning signs—"

Wait, warning signs? Like . . . confusion? Complete emotional instability? Nausea? An overwhelming feeling of impending doom? Check, check, and double CHECK.

She handed me a bottle of spring water, spun me around toward the front door of the building, and practically shoved me out of it.

"Remember—water, Polo. Drink!"

I stumbled over the threshold with my papers and notebook in one hand, borrowed car keys and bottled water in the other. I was totally confused, paddling around in circles like a sad, one-footed duck. I barely got the car door open before collapsing onto the front seat scared, alone, and feeling completely unprepared for the next day's events.

I drove back to my room at the VOQ, curled up on top of the king-sized bed, and shook. The frame of the bed knocked against the wall. I got up and forced myself to drink a glass of Captain Wrangle's magical water. I needed to find my calm.

I pulled my dream box out of my carry-on bag and returned to the bed with it. I crossed my shaking legs and nestled it in their nook. The box was soft, supple, round, complete. It was the center around which I wrapped my limbs and life.

Eventually, the tremors eased up enough for me to rest my hands, palms up, on my knees. My attempts at deep breathing were short-circuited by my quaking diaphragm, but I persisted in drawing one breath after another until finally my heart rate slowed. Everything slowed. I closed my eyes without closing my eyes. I plugged my ears without plugging my ears. I retreated without retreating.

I pictured myself in the courtroom, answering the defense lawyer truthfully and smoothly, squarely and simply. I saw the judge behind his big desk and the brass in their big chairs. I envisioned the hearing, and I saw myself survive it. I opened my eyes without opening them. I unplugged my ears without unplugging them. I returned without ever having left.

I swept my dream box underneath my pillow and laid out my uniform for the next day. I shined my shoes and my brass, washed my face, brushed and flossed my teeth. I painted my nails and set everything out in the order in which I'd need it. I set my alarm and then set another one for four minutes later. I locked every lock on the door . . . three times. The night passed in a string of anticipatory, insomniac jitters.

35

THE ACADEMY

The first alarm propelled me out of bed like a tiddlywink, straight into the bathroom. I walked back over to the nightstand and turned it off, as well as the second one I'd set just in case. I had never pushed a snooze button in my life—when I got up, I was up. And I had been up since 0332. I began my pregame ritual, modified for the day's duties.

I showered, smoothed on lotion, and sprayed myself with my perfume, my home. I put on my underwear, socks, pants, shirt, and service dress. I applied what little makeup I had brought, mindful of academy etiquette. I swept my hair out of my face, off of my collar, and into regulations.

I took my dog tags out of my dream box, where they slept, imbued with the same energy they'd always had, and kissed them before wrapping the chain around my ankle and shoving them into my black sock. I walked over to the full-length mirror and methodically looked over every single inch of myself. My shoes were shined, my uniform was Sta-Floed, my name tags had fresh cardboard behind them, and my pins were shiny. My hair was out of my eyes, though I desperately wanted to hide behind it. My nails were freshly clipped, manicured, and painted. My jewelry was subtle enough to conform to academy and air force regulations. I was ready—externally, anyway.

A wave of nausea threw me back onto the edge of the bed. I put my head between my knees.

I will NOT be sick.

I breathed, in and out, in and out. I drank two bottles of diet jet fuel back-to-back. I breathed.

I took a moment to send good karma out to everyone involved in what was coming—even to Her Horrible Her. I pooled all of the energy I could muster to put forth the intention of a swift, smooth resolution.

I gathered my purse. I gathered my words. I breathed in and out, in and out. I tried to center myself. I bent down and touched my dog tags and walked out the door.

I entered Harmon Hall and checked in with a lieutenant sitting among a bullpen of desks that seemed to be guarding a set of dark and imposing wooden doors. He directed me to take a seat in witness holding, which consisted of a cluster of four chairs segregated from a matching set by a dilapidated fern. The plant seemed to have heaved itself over the side of its pot as if trying to get away from all it had seen.

A few minutes later, a large man with a shock of white-blond hair walked in with a service-dressed cadet in tow. I hadn't realized other witnesses had been called in, so I peeked through the fern to try and identify the cadet—but her head was turned away from me. All I could see was her closely cropped, product-free hair. When she turned her makeup-free face toward mine, the shock of recognition plunged my stomach through the floor.

Her Horrible Her.

I watched her attorney lead her into the courtroom, grateful I wouldn't have to enter until they called for my testimony. I treaded water until Captain Wrangle arrived to sit with me. She sat delicately, every bit the Southern lady, but her eyes and bizarre smirk hinted that she might be anticipating the freak show to come. It was unsettling, but at least I wasn't alone. Captain Policy came out of the courtroom and crossed the bullpen in four swift steps.

"Cadet Tate, hello." He shook my hand, then nodded at Captain Wrangle. "We're going to get started here; I will call for you when I am ready. Just walk straight to the witness box and try not to look over at the defendant or anyone in the gallery. And don't *ever* wear that nail polish when you are in uniform again, *especially* in a courtroom."

OMG. Fuck. I looked down at my nails, which sported a new coat of Bordeaux Symphony. *Wait—did I just ruin everything before it began?*

"Sir, what should I do? Shou—"

He shook his head and exhaled. "No, no, it's too late. Just . . . for the future."

For the—did he think this was a goddamn *hobby* of mine? I prayed I would never, *ever* have to repeat this experience. A flutter of panic rose in my throat.

With one more exasperated sigh, Captain Policy turned on his heels and walked back into the courtroom.

Wait! Sir—?! Holy fu—okay. Okay. Rein it in, Popo; rein it TF in.

I could not sit still. I stood, I paced, I bounced as I waited to be called. An eternity passed before a white-gloved hand waved me through the big doors. I felt myself stand and walk somehow, as if pulled by an invisible force. I zeroed in on the witness box, which seemed very far away. Her Horrible Her's mother, father, and sister were sitting in the front row of the gallery, their faces contorted into diabolical party masks.

The young, white-gloved NCO holding the door looked over at

the judge, but he was shuffling papers. Not being able to catch anyone's eye, he looked at them, at me, then away, uncomfortably, as Her Horrible Her's family glared. I affixed my gaze to the witness stand and tried not to hyperventilate. I managed to settle myself into the stiff wooden chair, sitting on my hands to hide the nail polish. A *full panel* of brass sat against the back wall of the courtroom, their collective shoulder boards reflecting the harsh overhead light. I wondered who was running the country.

"Please state your name for the record, Cadet Tate."

"Yes, sir. Sir, my name is Cadet Fourth Class Polo Reo Tate."

I took a deep breath and felt myself relax slightly. Silently attempting to repeat the meditation I'd gone through in my room the previous night, I reached out of manic-panic mode and pulled myself into ready-steady. The judge looked down at me from his bench. It had begun.

Captain Policy stood up and walked around the prosecution table, moving toward me until I could see nothing but his tall, lean form. *Thank you.* My focus narrowed.

Just tell the truth. No more, no less. Just truth.

He began his litany of questions, and I answered instinctively, reaching down for my deepest truth. He asked about the friendship between Her and me, about her confessions, about the content of our deepest talks, about her grooming me, coaching me, coaxing me—and eventually about her controlling me, gutting me, threatening me.

I did not hear my answers through my ears but through my heart, making sure each one resonated. Captain Policy asked, posited, and riposted. He summoned my words, and I gave them to him. He asked about my letter to Tip, heading off any pass made by the defense attorney. I told him it was in direct response to her letter, purely to prevent her from taking her own life. The energy in the courtroom ebbed and flowed. My answers, my heart, they beat as one. He finished and swiftly sat down.

Her Horrible Her's civilian defense attorney, Mr. Bicker, arduously pressed himself into a standing position and waddled over to the witness stand. His crown of bleach-blond hair contrasted with his beady, deep-set eyes. His tongue moved quickly back and forth over his lips, winding his verbal engine. A slick, unsettling energy oozed out of him. I took a deep breath and searched for the humanity in his eyes. I tried to find the place—the very basest, most primitive place—at which we were both one. He had no desire to reciprocate.

His questions, his accusations, his trickery, they came.

"Cadet Tate, isn't it true that you harbor obsessive feelings—lustful feelings—toward my client, Cadet Attila? And that you brought forth these baseless allegations to cover up for your academic and military failings?"

Holy shit. Here we go.

"No, sir. That is not true."

"You told Captain Policy a few minutes ago that your unsanctioned off-campus trip with Cadet Attila to the Chapel Hills Mall was her idea, not yours—"

"Yes, sir—" I started to reply, but before I could finish, Mr. Bicker threw a pudgy hand up in front of my face, then devoured the abrupt pause like a bucket of greasy fried chicken.

"But that's not true, is it, Cadet Tate? The truth is that you *begged* my client to take you off grounds. You were so sick of sitting confinements for yet *another* one of your infractions, you *forced* Cadet Attila into taking you to the mall."

His fleshy lips were wet with saliva, some of which had been pushed off the corner of his mouth by his short bursts of labored breath as he became riled. Each sentence was like a punch. I kept praying for an objection to the lies, but alas, as much as it resembled one, we were not in a civilian court of law. We were at a military hearing, and I was merely a witness. I held my head steady with all the strength I could muster as he continued swinging.

"It was *you* who had romantic feelings for Cadet Attila. Not the other way around, wasn't it, Cadet Tate?"

My heart took the impact like a shock absorber and—miraculously—gave back a smooth and steady truth.

"No, sir. That is not true. Cadet Attila insisted on giving me a ride home from practice that day. I had no idea we were going to travel off grounds, no idea we were going to go to the mall. I was neither driving the car nor in control of its destination."

"From what my client describes, it sounds to me like you emotionally blackmailed her into breaking the rules. . . ."

"Sir," I said, surprising myself with my own firmness, "Cadet Attila is a firstie. She is my team captain. She holds a squadron *staff* position. She is my superior in every way. I have *no* leverage with her. If she gives me an order, I am required to follow it. Sir, those are the rules. If my superior was driving the car, in control of where we were going, and yet had no feelings for me as you say, then how could I have emotionally blackmailed her into going somewhere that she did not want to go? I have no power—"

"That's enough, Cadet Tate. It's not your job to ask the questions."

He put his hands on either side of the microphone perched in front of me. The scent of his cologne mingled with the perspiration soaking his suit fouled the airspace between us.

"Let's move to the weekend spent at your coaches' house."

He asked some preliminary questions about our team gathering and walked me through conversations that had taken place and clearly been contorted by Her Horrible Her. I answered instinctively, honestly, emotionally . . . never disrespectfully. I heard the fabrication, the dishonesty, the deceit. I heard the insults and responded with the truth.

"Cadet Tate. What were you doing prior to the incident in question? How did the night begin?" Bicker put his fingers together and arrogantly rocked back on his heels. His hands were clasped over his protruding stomach so that he looked as if he were smuggling a beach ball. Each time he rocked backward, the face of Her Horrible Her popped into view. I saw her pale face, her angry, squinting skin surrounding her dead doll eyes, and my stomach dropped. I quickly put my hands on my knees to stop my head from lurching forward to whack the microphone. I steadied myself and pulled my hands off of my knees. My stomach may have been churning, but my hands? My hands were *rock steady*.

"Sir, after a long practice and a late dinner, several of us went into our coaches' guest bedroom to talk. Four of us, including Cadet Attila and me, fell asleep after talking well into the night. When I woke up in the middle of the night, I only saw Cadet Attila. She was on top of me, restraining me, hurting me."

I continued, letting the entire courtroom in on the horror of that night, before Mr. Bicker cut me off.

"Let's be honest, Cadet Tate—"

My body braced for impact, but my mind, my hands, my voice were all on autopilot; they were all rock steady.

"If what you claim is true, and Cadet Attila was the one to initiate physical contact between you two on the night in question, then why not say anything that same night or the next morning? Why not turn her in immediately? In fact, if you wanted to sink her career, why not just turn her in after the first time she allegedly admitted to having had adolescent homosexual feelings for someone in her past? Cadet Tate?"

"Cadet Attila is my team captain, my team*mate*. I was led to believe, and I *did* believe, that we were friends. I take the bonds of friendship seriously. Cadet Attila may have struggled with personal thoughts and issues, but as her teammate, as her confidante, as her *friend*, I only wanted to help her. I had no desire to share her confidences with anyone else. I had no desire to sink her career—"

"Miss Tate, Cadet Attila has stated that it was, in fact, *you* who made sexual advances on *her*. Why wait all this time to come forward with these far-out allegations now? You say that you take friendship seriously, yet here you are, willing to tear it asunder just to save your collapsing academic, military, and athletic career."

Smiling smugly, he spread his fingers wide and swept one hand, palm up, toward the judge as if he was Vanna White revealing the grand prize on *Wheel of Fortune*. I dove headfirst into the lull.

"I *do* care about her. That's what makes this all so *sick*. Even after everything that has happened, I still care about what happens to her. I protected the bonds of our friendship until that night when she violated them—violated *me*—so profoundly, so devastatingly that all I had left to hold on to was the gaping wound she had thrashed open in . . . my soul. In answer to your question, I said nothing because, for the better part of a year, she had groomed me to be her volleyball partner, her best friend, her legacy, responsible for her happiness, her stability, at times her sanity. She threatened to hurt herself, to *kill* herself, if I told anyone what she felt, what she had done. I kept my mouth shut because I did not want her to *die*."

For a moment, it flashed through my mind to just tell it all—everything—including Him Horrible Him. I paused. I continued.

"Sir, what happened that night eventually became so corrosive, so toxic that I could barely function. Eventually, one of my teammates asked me point-blank what happened and I told her the truth. In spite of myself, I told her the truth."

Suddenly, my ears opened to the room in front of me, as if I had surfaced from the deep water for the first time in hours. I heard the next nine words, raw and gritty, come out of my mouth.

"Tip Attila raped my body. She raped my mind."

Everything stopped at the moment of verbal impact. The lawyers, the judge, the brass, Her Horrible Her's family . . . everyone was silent. It was the first time that I had ever used the r-word. But I had sworn to tell my truth, and in that moment, I did.

Mr. Bicker wrapped up his line of questioning immediately, and I was hurriedly ushered down from the box and out of the courtroom. My duty was done.

Captain Policy called me just as I was about to get on the plane for Michigan.

"Cadet Tate, I just wanted to tell you that your testimony on the stand yesterday was riveting."

I could not read his tone. "Is that a good thing?"

After a beat, "Well, not if you are Miss Attila. . . ."

"Sir . . . what happens now?"

"Well, the brass determined that Miss Attila was guilty of breaking the Don't Ask, Don't Tell policy of the military. She'll be dismissed from the academy without a degree and immediately discharged from the air force without a commission."

I didn't know what to say. I didn't know how to feel.

"Cadet Tate?"

"Yes, sir. I'm sorry. . . ."

"Miss Tate, you have to know that your testimony was what directed the verdict. Your honesty and believability."

I knew he was trying to make me feel good about the outcome—but in that moment, it kept creeping into my head that *my* actions had gotten Her kicked out. Not hers. *Mine.* And that was the last thing in which I could take pleasure.

I could barely squeak out a "Hm . . . mmm," to break the silence.

"Well, look at it this way. At least you won't have to run into her when you get back to the academy. Best of luck to you, Cadet Tate. Great job, once again, and congratulations."

"Yes, sir. Thank you, sir . . ." I managed, but he had already hung up.

I boarded the plane in a confused haze, the captain's words running on a loop through my brain.

"*. . . you won't have to run into her when you get back to the academy.*"

I took my seat and rested my throbbing temple on the plastic window shade. My body was exhausted, but my brain was hosting a giant game of dodgeball. It suddenly dawned on me how much Captain Jag had done for me. She had pursued the truth with her investigation. She had made available that truth in her brief, and by doing so had made way for Tip's dismissal. She had stood up for me by doing her job. Thoroughly and brilliantly. I had been set free after nearly a year of being physically abused, socially isolated, and held emotionally hostage by Her Horrible Her. For a moment, I sat quiet in my appreciation for Caption Jag, in my appreciation for the hearing, the vehicle that quelled the anguish that Tip's presence in my life had caused. It was true: I would not have to run into her when I got back to the academy. . . . That was a relief.

Though I had no proof, I had a faint but gnawing suspicion that Her Horrible Her had sent Him Horrible Him to silence me from talking about her. Whether the viciousness of his actions was his idea or a plot hatched between them, I didn't know and I never would. The grim truth was this: While the person who had had the most overarching influence on my life at USAFA had just been removed, the one who posed the most acute physical threat was still there.

I felt as out of control in that moment as I had felt the night Tip assaulted me.

I pulled my head off of the jet's window and let it fall back again. And again. And again. Rap, rap, rap, my head hit the plastic shade. I stopped before drawing too much attention, but my thoughts thumped on.

The warning Colonel Noble had given me about dragging the matter into civilian court rose up in my mind, followed by his emphasis on my "once-in-a-lifetime opportunity" to return to the academy. I was being offered a chance to get back on track, heal, turn my life around, move on—and all I had to do was . . . nothing.

I had used my mulligan. I had used it on Her Horrible Her. Maybe . . . just maybe, this would be the end of it. Maybe I'd never see Him Horrible Him again.

I rapped my head on the window again. I couldn't let it rest.

God. I'm exhausted.

I had to conserve my energy if I wanted to get stronger. I had to turn my focus inward if I wanted to survive.

I want to survive.

I woke up as the plane touched down in Michigan, having slept deeply for the first time in months.

By the time I got back to my mother's house, I had just begun to scratch the surface of all that had happened on my short but deep dip back into academy waters. I was trying to reconcile everything that I had just borne witness to and been a witness in: the culmination of almost a *year's* worth of tumult, torment, and torture.

But I wouldn't have time to process any of it. In a matter of *days,* I was on another plane, flying back to the academy to start my three-degree, sophomore, year at USAFA.

36

THE ACADEMY

I was sitting in the wizard's office looking out over the cadet version of Oz. Across a giant desk from me was General Stoic, superintendent of the United States Air Force Academy.

It was my first stop upon resuming my cadethood at USAFA. The floor-to-ceiling windows behind his desk perfectly overlooked the terrazzo and cadet inner sanctum. Looking out the windows was like peering onto the Hollywood backlot set of *USAFA: The Movie*. I could see the chapel, the flagpole, every dormitory, every squadron's formation, every blade of grass on the freshly manicured lawn, and every alabaster pebble on the terrazzo. It was a perfect perch for the wizard.

It had been only days since I had been sequestered in the VOQ for the trial. While I was holed up, I had found out that Him Horrible Him would be out of town for the last summer session, not expected back on campus until transition week training camp. That meant that neither of the wicked witches—neither Her Horrible Her, nor Him Horrible Him—was lurking anywhere in the landscape below us. Being back felt like a fresh start, the beginning of something very different.

The superintendent had been only a name and rank written in tiny letters on the inside of my *Contrails* (our pocket reference guide to all things military) until now, a distant link in the chain of command. It was surreal to be looking at him over his broad desk. He was tall and imposing, with thick black hair and dark eyes. His voice was deep and heavy, much like his medal-laden uniform. He had called me into his office to set the ground rules for my second chance at USAFA life. He had my full attention.

"Ca-det Tate," he intoned, elongating the two syllables of my rank as if he had finally caught the first on the list of America's Ten Most Wanted. His voice reverberated through my sternum. "You are a fully recognized three-degree cadet, even though you missed recognition."

He paused.

"Yes, sir."

"We have advanced you militarily, even though you missed all of the training sessions, spirit missions, and renowned traditions of recognition weekend. This is unprecedented."

"Yes, s—" *Whoop, no pause, okay . . .*

"THIS is quite an opportunity you have been given."

Now, me . . . ?

"Yes, sir." I nodded, feeling the weight of the entire cadet world balanced on my head.

He nodded, seemingly satisfied with my understanding of the gravity of his decision. "The responsibility is yours, Miss Tate, to make the most of your new start here."

In other words, YOU'D BETTER NOT FUCK THIS UP.

I nodded vigorously.

He raised his eyebrows expectantly.

Oh, shit, that's my cue again—

"Sir, I want you to know that I understand what an unusual

opportunity I have been given, and it is my honor to take advantage of this second chance to fulfill my duty. Sir, I am so appreciative to be here. Thank you, sir, for letting me stay with my class and for entrusting me with this gift of time to prove myself."

I truly was appreciative to be an upperclassman. I loved the thought of being able to walk and talk freely, wear civvies at the end of duty day, leave grounds a bit more frequently, and be an equal to older cadets. I wanted more than to redeem myself. I wanted to experience USAFA on my terms. I wanted to experience the place that I had worked so hard to attend as the stellar cadet I knew myself to be. It was time to do well again.

General Stoic spoke. "I'm sure some of what you were going through at the end of last year was . . . *uncomfortable—*"

I could think of . . . other adjectives.

"—but the members of your class—and squadron especially—will most likely resent the fact that you didn't go through *their* . . . discomfort. We would like to make your reentry into USAFA as peaceful for your classmates as possible. I know that it is customary for cadets to stay in their first squadron for two years, but out of concern for your well-being, I have taken the liberty of moving you to a new squadron."

Hmm . . .

"Yes, sir."

. . . It was a small price to pay.

"You will be starting SERE in a few days, Cadet Tate, and I *strongly* suggest that you make this summer session an excellent segue into your three-degree year here. Fulfilling this summer session requirement will start you on your three-year journey to make up for your—how shall we put it—*less-than-proficient* academic four-degree year."

I could think of . . . other adjectives.

"Cadet Tate, I know I have already said this, but there has not been another opportunity like this one, nor will there be. I have made this happen for only you, so do not make me regret it. Are we clear, Cadet Tate?"

We are crystal fucking clear.

"Yes, sir."

"ARE WE CLEAR, TATE?"

I shot to attention, caged my eyes. "YES, SIR!"

I brought my eyes back to his. "Sir, thank you. For everything."

He stood and I followed. As he shook my hand, a strange bolt of energy passed between us, and a small part of me wondered what would happen if I clicked my heels together three times. Instead, I took one step back and raised my hand in a salute. He returned it. I beat his hand down as trained, then about-faced.

Off we go, into the wild blue . . . take two.

37

THE ACADEMY

Within the hour, I was moved into my temporary summer squadron, unpacked and sitting next to Quinner on the grassy quad, watching members of the boys' volleyball team play modified doubles. Their shirts were off, their dog tags slung backward around their necks. Best friends Mickey and Hopper, both firsties now, were *spanking* two of their two-degree teammates in the game and match, working together on the court, supporting each other, showing total reverence for our sport without a hint of drama.

God bless this Top Gun *moment.*

Mickey spotted me and veered off course on his way back to the serving line, high-fived me, then bent down and kissed me on the cheek and whispered, "By the way, Popo, Hopper's the one who was asking about you. . . ."

OMG. Could he really be finishing the conversation we had started down in the field house a lifetime ago? I worked hard to underreact as he bounced back into the game and jump-served.

I am safe here.

Quinner poked me in the side. "What was *that* about?" she asked playfully.

My stomach bubbled. It was the first time in an eternity that the wince-inducing rush of battery acid had given way to something infinitely . . . sweeter. I fell silent. I let myself feel it.

"Popo! Don't leave me *hangin'* . . . !"

I had liked Hopper from the moment I'd laid eyes on him. He was gorgeous, goofy, athletic, artistic, charming, and hilarious. I was a wounded, dysfunctional tornado of a smack in a vortex of pain and chaos. Let's just say the timing wasn't great. I had forced him out of my head because there was no room for anything beyond survival. And now Mickey had dropped the bomb that there might be a sliver of potential. I had no idea how to navigate any sort of relationship after all that had happened.

God . . . how do I be . . . undamaged?

"Remember the way, way back? When you asked me about Mickey and I asked you about Hopper?"

"DUH! You were way sweet on him!" Quinner squealed.

Aware that we were dangerously close to the boys about whom we were talking, I said, "Oh my God, Quinner! Shh!"

"Yeah, sooooo . . ." she prodded, this time in a whisper.

"Well, so . . . turns out he had been asking about me, too!"

Holy shitballs, it felt good to be . . . *giddy* about something. *Light* about something. It felt like an antidote to the toxic *poison* that had been coursing through my body for months. Quinner put her smiling face two inches from mine.

"This is SOOO good for you, Popo. Sooo good."

Quinner knew what had happened with Tip from talking to Jetta. And she had stayed an open, honest, loving, chill friend of mine. She had thought that Tip was troubled, but, like the rest of my team, couldn't do much to stop it from happening. What she had done was invaluable, however, and that was just to be my friend. I was ecstatic to get to spend the summer session with her.

Without thinking, I took a flying leap outside of my comfort zone—and back to my true self—and hugged her. She screamed and reciprocated, overjoyed. We made a total scene on the sidelines, but I didn't give a flying fucknut. This day had already trumped every one of the summer days leading up to it . . . combined.

Quinner and I laughed and talked and played and won and lost volleyball games against the boys. We made up for *a lot* of lost time. The entire afternoon passed in supreme bliss.

Even though I did not sleep a wink the first night back on campus, I spent most of it eagerly looking forward to the next day.

Quinner and I spent time over the next few days with Mickey and Hopper and sometimes a few others. We played ball, got in shape, had picnic lunches, laughed and talked and laughed some more. It all felt safe, consistent, healing, and empowering. Although it was frightening to be back in the setting where I'd experienced so much personal pain, I was able to focus on the present. The brass and the wizard had done all they could to wipe the slate clean for me, and with the help of my sweet buoys, I was beginning to feel excited about starting over.

One evening, as the sun receded behind the Rockies, we decided to go out to dinner together. Quinner called shotgun on our way over to Mickey's coupe, so Hopper and I climbed into the back seat while Mickey went around and opened the passenger door for Quinner—who immediately began riffling through Mickey's CDs to find a suitable summer-night soundtrack. And he *let* her. Hopper and I exchanged a surprised look. Mickey must've *like* liked Quinner—*a lot*—if he was letting her DJ on their first night out. Hopper and I dissolved into laughter—and we remained in sync all evening.

It was uncanny. We joked in the same way, both used weird voices, challenged each other, stimulated each other. Our airy banter came easily, and we sang along with the songs on the radio. We sang *without* songs on the radio. We played air volleyball in the back seat all the way to the restaurant. I felt myself falling for him, and it felt so good.

Dinner passed in a cloud of conversation, jokes, and laughter. Right before the check came, Hopper reached over and took the last of the food I'd left on my plate, devouring half of it and giving the rest to Mickey. He *finished my food*. And it felt so good to have that familiarity with a boy again. With *friends* again. I had officially fallen. Hard.

I excused myself to use the lavatory before our check came back, and once I'd snapped the stall door behind me, I sat down and put my hands on my head. I had fallen for Hopper and now I was scared. It felt way too risky to allow someone past the Fort Knox security I had put up around my heart.

I held my head and breathed slowly. I felt that I could trust the three people sitting at that table a few feet away. I had known them for a year and never experienced any reason to doubt their goodness. Hopper felt safe. He had to be safe.

I balled up my fear and threw it from me as hard and as far as I could. I rejoined the table and let myself revel in the laughter, the conversation, and the fun. I wrapped that feeling of safety tightly around myself like a cocoon. And it felt good. It felt so good.

38

THE ACADEMY

The classroom portion of our summer session had begun, and we four quickly settled into a relaxed yet conscientious routine. We became a modern nuclear family, sharing breakfast together and kissing one another good-bye as we went off to fulfill our respective duties. After long, intense days, we planned evenings of sun, fun, and volleyball, or field trips off campus for dinner. Without any basic cadets around for whom we were supposed to set an example, the academy atmosphere was more relaxed and tranquil. We could leave campus more often and were not required to eat in Mitchell Hall. Over long restaurant meals, Mickey, Quinner, Hopper, and I shared our thoughts, feelings, and whimsies. Her Horrible Her's name came up only twice, and it was only to say that the boys had never cared for her. She apparently had been mean to them. That was that. I never told any more and they didn't ask. It wasn't part of the present moment. It didn't have to be. We talked about every other thing that we could. It felt so unbelievably, amazingly good.

For several weeks, I lived in a whirlwind of appreciation for having been given this delicious second chance—for being able to experience cadet friendship and academy life in the supportive, team-oriented way that I'd originally anticipated.

The morning before I left for the field portion of SERE, I woke Mickey and Hopper with kisses on their cheeks and their favorite bagels from the best shop in Colorado Springs.

Mickey pushed my nose like it was his snooze button, then closed his eyes and fell back to sleep. Hopper took my hand, then my arm, then all of me, and pulled me up into bed with him. At first my nerves started to instinctively protest, but I had built up such a safe rapport with these boys that I allowed myself to relax into his arms. I actually felt physically protected and safer there than I had on my own, and my nerves abated. I let him touch me, pull me up, hold me. I had wanted to be there, right there, nestled in his warm and cuddly nook, since the day that I had met him.

He hugged me tightly, his legs lined up with mine in perfect tandem. He covered us both with his blanket and we lay there, big spoon and little spoon, as I let my fear drift away. Our chests rose and fell together.

I am not afraid.

I closed my eyes, safely nestled in Hopper's arms. I put my nose up against his hand, which was still wrapped around my wrist. His skin was soft and smelled like boy. I closed my eyes, and I took the moment in through each of my senses, remaining aware of every point of contact between us. I opened my ears to the sound of his breathing, heard him draw me in and then exhale me. He smelled like freedom, like laughter, like life, like love. I felt him behind me, around me, with me. His touch was a good touch.

I lay against him in the quiet of the morning and let myself be wrapped in the rapture of the moment. I wanted to stay in this spot forever. I kept my eyes closed and felt his wrist, thick, bony, and strong. I felt the skin on the inside of it, soft as a sun-ripened peach. I let my lips fall open just a bit. I let the tip of my tongue reach out and wet the inside of his wrist. I breathed in the air over his wet skin. I touched his wrist lightly again with my tongue, and it was freezing. I breathed him in. I breathed in all of the humanness he possessed. I heard him, I felt him, I inhaled him. I slowly, smoothly nuzzled the inside of his hand until my cheek rested perfectly in it. He drew in a deep breath with his entire body, pressed his chest against my back, and pulled me in tighter. I let myself be pulled in tighter. He was so warm, so strong. I wanted to be there, in the present.

From outside of our warm, dark, sweet-smelling world I heard plastic on wood. Something was being fumbled. Fumbling, bumbling was interrupting this perfect moment. I didn't want to open my eyes. I heard buttons being pressed and music start to play, but I didn't want to open my eyes to anything besides the beautiful calm of this moment. Noise, obnoxious noise, invaded the space around our spoon cocoon. Hopper was kissing, tickling the nape of my neck. He was breathing in my skin, my hair, my perfume. I started to giggle. Music played and Mickey stirred and I started to giggle. It became contagious and Hopper started to giggle, too. Whatever this was, right here, right now, felt so good. *Please, God, let this last forever.*

RRROOAAARRR!!

Mickey's big, openmouthed, lion-roaring, dimpled face was suddenly two inches from mine. His fingers—like claws—playfully squeezed the blanket, and then me.

"Ahh!" I yelped so loud. "OhmyGod!"

He leaned in and planted a big, fat kiss on my forehead, then walked over to the bagel bag and dove in. Thank God I had suppressed my reflex to punch "the disturbance" in the face.

Hopper turned my face toward his.

In one movement, he swooped his arms completely around me, whipped my shirt up to my belly button, and face-planted a huge zoober on my stomach. His scruff tickled and his vibrating lips itched and I was laughing too hard to be self-conscious. I was exactly where I wanted to be.

39

THE ACADEMY

After a little over three weeks of SERE training and a quick transition week, summer session was over. Mickey and Hopper moved back to their respective school-year squadrons; Quinner moved back to hers; and I returned from the field and moved into a brand-new squadron—my brand-new opportunity. The school year had officially begun.

SERE had been one of the most challenging, rigorous, hard-core experiences I had ever gone through. I had passed with flying colors and positive recognition from my superiors. Just making it through had baptized me in an excited glow and reaffirmed my faith in my ability to start fresh and succeed at the institution that had pushed me, challenged me, and, at times, disemboweled me. (It had also sworn me to secrecy about the details of SERE training.)

I arrived at my new dorm room with fear on the back burner and hope in my heart.

"HI! Oh my gosh, hiiii!"

My new roommate—C3C Apple Pie—as all-American as possible—waved to me with a matched set of perky jazz hands even though we were two feet away from each other. *OMG. Awesome.*

"How do you do? I'm Polo! It's nice to meet you. . . ."

I started to wave back, but instinct took over and I put my hand out to shake. She grabbed it with both of hers and proceeded to skip me in a circle around our new room as if we were six and I had come over for a playdate. Her energy, her vibe, it felt good. If her quirky behavior was genuine, it was adorable. I sincerely hoped that she wasn't overcompensating based on rumors she might have heard about my . . . fragile mental state or something.

"So this is *our* room. Put your stuff anywhere you want, as long as it's in regs . . . I mean, duh!" She rolled her eyes. She made me laugh.

"Duh!"

"So, I heard you play volleyball . . . ?" she said, sounding excited at the prospect. "I cheer." She pointed to her pom-poms. "It is, like, soooo much fun. I'm so glad I did it. I mean, I was worried at first, that being on the varsity cheer squad would be too much, but it is sooo worth it. . . ."

I peeped her corkboard out of the corner of my eye.

"Oh! Yeah—I have a lot of pictures!"

She hopped over to point out the collage of pictures featuring one particular guy.

"This is my boyfriend! You'll meet him a little later when he picks me up for dinner. He's so great. . . ."

I bent over to get a closer look at the photo montage, in which Boyfriend was holding a cutout heart with "Wish you were here" written on it in black magic marker. There were literally over a dozen selfies taken at various places around the academy grounds and on what looked like academy field trips. It was as if a trip to the *lavatory* was too much to bear without his beloved. Hilarious and amazing.

"He certainly seems . . . devoted," I said, straightening back up.

"Oh, he is! Mama Janice—that's what I call his mom—has already reserved the chapel for after graduation weekend. Mummy and Daddy flew out on homecoming weekend last year with Mama Janice and Papa Ray to hold the date. . . . It was sooo sweet. Ah! I am sooo excited!"

That last part, she didn't need to tell me. "Oh, wow . . . *congratulations*. It sounds like you guys have something very special."

She relaxed her entire petite frame in an instant and let her freckle-nosed, fresh-faced head fall gently to the side. She was genuinely touched.

"Awwoooh! Thank you."

OMG. I'm rooming with Elle Woods. And then she put her hands to her heart and twirled—yes, *twirled*—in a full pirouette of unconditional love for her beau.

"Now, come on, I'll show you the rest of the squadron!"

And with that, she bounced out of our room. This couldn't be an act: Her energy was way too pure. I had never met such a squeaky-clean, innocently naive soul. She was a giant bag of candy at the end of a strenuous workout—a total gift. It was awesome.

I had been moved across the terrazzo from Vandenberg Hall to squadron thirty-five in Sijan Hall. I paid close attention to the differences in layout and décor, to the names Apple Pie attached to faces, and to the new patch that had been painted on the window of our SAR as she took me on the grand tour. Apparently, squadron thirty-five worshipped some sort of burrowing animal. This former Troll was now a Wild Weasel. *Should I take this change personally?* I smiled at the logo.

After our tour, Apple Pie got ready for bed, gave me a good-night hug, and climbed atop her bed unit. Shortly thereafter, I looked over at her, fast asleep, cuddling a stuffed bear with a heart embroidered on its belly that said, I LOVE YOU. I hoped that my stuffed bunny was not going to corrupt her teddy bear with the things it had seen. I hoped *I* would not corrupt Apple Pie with the things that *I* had seen, done, and been through. I wanted to contribute only good vibes to this idyllic new beginning.

As I unpacked my suitcases, I packed away my new-squadron jitters and the pangs of separation from my summer surrogate family. Overorganization had served me well in the past, so I carefully unpacked and organized my belongings in the hope that my emotional keepsakes, too, would remain in their assigned places. I arranged well into the night.

Taps reminded me that I wanted to start this new year off well rested, and for once, my body complied. I took my round, buttery leather dream box out from its place beneath my pillow and rubbed the lid to coax the good juju out like a genie. I felt the weight of my dreams resting firmly inside. I had a second chance at life here: a new squadron, a new family, a new rank, new responsibilities. I had kicked ass in my summer session, and it was time to kick ass in my academic semester.

I opened the lid of the little box and looked in at the folded pieces of paper, each one curled as if in the fetal position. Curled up in fear, as I had been for so long? *No.* I knew my dreams were free of fear. Fear is a human construct. Dreams were free.

I unfolded one piece of thick, homemade paper placed inside the box what felt like a lifetime ago but was only mere months. The words on it were neatly printed in the center of the small square, full of promise and potential. I read them softly to myself.

> *I am so happy and excited that I am an upper-*
> *classman. I wield this new responsibility with*
> *the gravity and precision that it deserves and*

*I respect, fully, those who I am in the position
to teach and lead.*

I read it again. This dream had technically come true. I *had* made it to upperclassman status, albeit unconventionally. However, I kept this intention in the belly of the box. The proof pile underneath the false bottom was reserved only for those dreams that had been *fully* realized. In spite of my drive, it remained to be seen what type of upperclassman I would be.

My new bed in my new squadron next to my new roommate . . . I was trying very hard to perpetuate my feeling of personal safety, but here, alone in the darkness, it was a challenge. I was once again 100 percent responsible for my own physical and emotional safety.

Stop stop stop stop stop.

I punched myself in the thigh while I whispered it out loud so that if my brain missed it my ears would hear it.

Come on, Po. Come on.

Things were *different* this year. I had the chance to start in the present tense. I turned my atomic focus toward only that. In that vein, I rewarded myself with thoughts of Hopper—not Booker—on this, the first night in my new squadron. I had changed the default settings on my brain's screen saver. Hopper's laugh, his smell, his touch was waiting for me when I closed my eyes. I went to sleep with thoughts of him sharing my pillow.

40

THE ACADEMY

Reveille brought a brand-new, inaugural day, and C3C Apple Pie and I helped each other out and meshed well during our morning routines.

Being on the opposite side of the training spectrum, I had fewer restrictions but more daily tasks to accomplish. To start me out gently, my new AOC had assigned my first four-degree to someone else so that I could get my bearings in this new squadron—and I was happy for the delay. As much as I wanted to be able to mentor, I first had to exemplify. And besides, in order to catch up with my class I was saddled with *twenty-one credits* in addition to volleyball, military duties, squadron duties, finding my social niche, and learning to make safe and buoyant memories in this haunted place. It was a challenging sophomore gauntlet, to say the least. The brass had already put me on ac-pro . . . and it wasn't because I needed another extracurricular.

After what felt like a week's worth of classes crammed into day one, I went down to the field house for practice. It was our team's first of the year and almost everything had changed.

Coaches Hubby and Wifey had resigned. And although they had been responsible for recruiting me, the incident had caused them to lose their star captain. Our team had been through so much, and it broke my heart that I had never gotten to say good-bye to them.

Our new coach was a civilian who brought fresh ideas and a new philosophy with her, but she was still trying to wrap her head around life at a service academy. The men's head coach—whom I respected—stayed on as our assistant coach to help her get acclimated. Our team had seen some substantial turnover as well. Besides Her Horrible Her, several other girls had left due to honor violations, flagging grades, and loss of focus. Linny had quit to pursue a squadron military position; on impulse, Mo-Mo had decided over the summer to become a cheerleader. Quinner and I were the only ones left from our recruiting class, which made everything different. Exciting, but totally different. I had missed my sport, my team, my sense of athletic normalcy, and could not wait to return to it.

To kick off the new volleyball season, Mickey, Hopper, Quinner, and I decided to have dinner together. Hopper's roommate was on a flight-training "hop" out of town for the weekend, so we took advantage of his empty room to have a picnic on his floor, ordering in from our favorite pizza parlor.

As the boys picked over the last of the food, Quinner ran her hand through Mickey's hair, and I could sense his heart growing thrice in size like a Dr. Seuss character. She stood up and pulled Mickey to his feet.

"C'mon, Mickey Mouse, you're taking me on a walk."

And just like that, they left. Hand in hand.

Hopper and I looked at each other with raised eyebrows. God, he was beautiful. My sweet crush. He smiled and got up to throw the food containers away. I hopped into his rolly desk chair and turned up the music coming out of his computer speakers. Before I could turn back around, his hand had found the back of my neck. He caressed it. I closed my eyes, concentrating on the electric current emanating from his huge hand and lanky fingers into my neck, then all through my body. I let my head fall back against his stomach, feeling the rippled muscle beneath his shirt.

He sat down in his roommate's matching rolly chair and spun me around to face him. The soft desk lamp caught his eyes, which exploded into intricate blue fractals. They were stunning. I couldn't look away. He *didn't* look away. His gaze bounced from my eyes to my lips and back again. I wanted him to kiss me. We sat like this until taps intruded and we both jumped—then laughed off the fact that we'd been startled.

He moved his hands from my chair to my thighs one by one and pulled me closer. He raised one large, athletic hand slowly to my cheek. I closed my eyes and felt it.

I am unbreakable.

His thumb grazed my lips, stopping under my chin to lift it gently. His firm, velvety lips found my neck. He started in the nape and moved slowly upward with his mouth. When he reached my ear, he breathed softly, slowly into it.

Places inside of me that had felt only scary, searing, panicky pain for so long were now throbbing from something infinitely more pleasurable. I was safe. I was completely in the moment and unafraid. My hand made a trail from his neck up behind the back of his head. I ran my fingers through his thick, dark, overgrown Princeton haircut. We moved in time. He turned my face with his hand and brought his lips toward mine. Our mouths came together in a perfect fit.

We kissed and kissed and kissed and kissed. He held me. I let him. I pulled him even closer.

In one fluid movement, Hopper was on top of his bed unit. He reached his hand down to me. I flashed him a look that felt as if it carried a full year of pain.

I was not ready.

Without knowing, he understood, no questions asked. I smiled. I breathed. He was safe. I took his hand and climbed up to him.

We kissed and cuddled. And kissed and cuddled. I ran my hands along his warm, muscular torso. His arms were my armor. His shoulders were my shield. I let him guard me, protect me. I let him have as much as I could give. As much as I could give.

Please don't let go.

And he didn't, until the next day.

41

THE ACADEMY

In order to move forward, I turned myself into a building with many floors and rooms. Just as each building along the terrazzo served a unique function, each floor and room within me served its own purpose. The basement stored all that I had done, felt, seen, and experienced since arriving for basic training the year before. It housed the past, both glorious and wretched. Many of the rooms belowground were flooded with cold, dirty water. I had done my best to stay out of them all summer, and I made sure they were locked up tight as I rose up to ground level for my three-degree year.

I started assigning new rooms as I made the rounds alongside my fellow cadets, most of whom simply picked up where they had left off the year before.

My classes occupied seven different rooms, and I ran to each of them every day, working to establish good relationships with each teacher. In the room reserved for volleyball and my team responsibilities, I dove, passed, set, hit, and escaped into my sport—my salvation.

I ran to the two-room suite I had set up for my military duties. In the first, I made my uniform shit-hot and caught up on my knowledge. I exemplified. In the other, I showed, taught, coached, led my assigned four-degrees through their first-year military gauntlet.

I ran to the floor reserved for my new squadron and tended to each room: my roommate, squadron mates, and chain; my duties and chores; my events and obligations.

After making the rounds to all of the spaces I'd created for my duties, I ran to the cluster of rooms that held Mickey, Hopper, Quinner, Mo-Mo, and all who made me believe in a better USAFA.

I sidestepped the rooms in which Her Horrible Her's remaining friends dwelled. I sidestepped her residual path of destruction, the mocking graffiti she'd sprayed over the walls that I couldn't reach to paint over.

I avoided—at all costs—the attic lair inhabited by Him Horrible Him. I tried to avoid his residual violence, devastation, threats. I tried to avoid the sickening, haunting potential of his presence. He was back on campus. But I had not seen him. Yet.

For the next two months I ran from room to room to room to room to room. In each, I fulfilled every duty. I tended to every person. I studied every waking moment. I gave 200 percent to every single thing. And it was paying off.

Until the day my past caught up with me.

Danno, Beansy, and Paulson, three boys from my old squadron, were walking across the terrazzo with two female three-degrees— Baker and Daisy. I was escorting two four-degree Wild Weasels over to Fairchild Hall.

"So, how do you guys feel about the knowledge for this week?" I chatted. "Are you finding the information easily? You don't have to sound off. . . ."

I walked loosely beside them as they walked the strips at

attention. Escorting them allowed me to check in and allowed them to walk instead of run. C4C Scooter answered first.

"Yes, ma'am. Ma'am, may I ask a question?"

"Yes, of course—"

WHAAP!

Something pelted me, hard, on the shoulder.

"YOU DON'T DESERVE TO BE CALLED *MA'AM*, FUCKING CITY GIRL!"

I stopped dead in my tracks. My four-degrees stopped and immediately fell in. The apple core that had hit me rolled to a stop near their feet. Paulson, Beansy, and Danno elbowed one another and pointed at me.

"See, I told you that good-for-nothing cunt-bag was back."

"What the FUCK is she doing wearing a uniform?!"

I turned toward my freshmen.

"Go on ahead, you guys."

They hesitated, unsure what to do, but I insisted, showing them only relaxed strength. Inside, my blood boiled.

Paulson yelled again at the top of his lungs. "HEY, TATE! HEY . . . *SLASH!* WHO DID YOU HAVE TO *FUCK* TO BE ABLE TO COME BACK AS AN UPPERCLASSMAN, HUH?!"

His veins were bulging from his neck and forehead, his face was as red as his words were vulgar. I just stared, taken completely aback by his . . . vitriol . . . *hatred*. He was angry to his . . . *soul*. I looked past him at the other boys. I looked at the girls. I had considered them *friends*. We had been through . . . a hell of a lot together, both in real time and in military time. Baker was the first of the girls to jump on the bandwagon.

"DON'T COME CRYING TO ME, *WHORE*. I'VE SEEN ENOUGH OF YOUR FAKE-ASS TEARS! GO HOME, BITCH!"

It was Paulson's turn again. "YEAH, DIDN'T YOU GET THE MESSAGE THE FIRST TIME AROUND? YOU DON'T BELONG HERE! GET YOUR FAT FUCKING TRAITOR ASS OUTTA HERE!"

Jesus. I stood there, speechless, trying not to let them see me shake. Their animosity honestly shocked me. I didn't understand that kind of hate. People on the terrazzo started to gather to see what was going on, but I just stood. I muttered to him in a low volume, feeling scared for my safety and reputation in that moment.

"It's too bad becoming an upperclassman didn't allow you to grow up, Paulson." Lots of things were too bad about that situation. Too bad and too sad.

Paulson, livid, waved to his buddies. "C'mon, you guys, we've already left the money on the bedside table. . . . It's time for this fucking *whore* to leave."

And with that, they walked by me. I waited until it was clear that I was not retreating because of them and I turned and burned to Mickey's room. I leaned my forehead against his door, staving off a wave of nausea until I could take in enough oxygen to edge out the fear, adrenaline, and sadness coursing through me.

Mickey let me in, no questions asked. He defused my swirling emotions and helped me calm down by letting me be. I was not alone, and I was most appreciative.

I breathed and got back to a slightly bruised but buoyant place.

Then I kept on running.

One morning we woke to find that a new edition of *Cadet X Letters* had been placed under our doors. These wing-wide flyers detailed every major disciplinary action that the administration had taken against delinquent cadets in the prior year. The names were replaced with big bold Xs to ensure the "anonymity" of all involved—hence the title.

The brass distributed them as learning tools, as a warning about making the same mistakes. Needless to say, more than one of my disciplinary exploits was featured in the latest edition, but it was my infamous frat hit—the unauthorized visit to the Chapel Hills Mall with Her Horrible Her—that some found the most seditious. Our identities were obvious.

So much for a clean slate.

I didn't even realize how bad it was until the next day.

Apple Pie, her BF, and I were walking across the terrazzo to the cadet store talking about Mo-Mo having joined the cheerleading squad. She had made it to the top of the pyramid.

"She has learned everything so fast!" said Apple Pie. Then she stopped talking and tapped us both on the thighs before saluting. Taking her cue, we both looked to our right and saluted as well.

"Good afternoon, ma'am!" we said in unison to the second lieutenant walking past us. Apple Pie immediately resumed her praise of Mo-Mo.

"I mean, she said she had cheered in high—"

"HEY!" The second lieutenant's voice detonated in the middle of our conversation like a time-delayed bomb. We stopped and turned to face her.

"YOU! *TATE!*"

My stomach bottomed out, and I instinctively put my hand over it. *Medusa*—now a second lieutenant stationed *at USAFA*—was rocking back and forth on the balls of her feet, pointing at me like a fighter in the ring.

"HOW THE *FUCK* ARE YOU WALKING AROUND AT REST?! HEY! I'M AN OFFICER! FALL IN, *CADET!*"

I did as ordered. C3Cs Apple Pie and BF looked at each other, puzzled, then fell in next to me.

"HEY! FRECKLES AND BEEFCAKE—GET THE FUUUUCK OUTTA HERE! NOWWW! GOOO!"

Apple Pie and BF about-faced and left as I geared up for round three with Her Horrible Her's good friend.

"I READ ABOUT YOUR CELEBRITY CADET CAREER YESTERDAY, CADET X!"

She was an *officer* screaming at a *cadet* on the terrazzo. A crowd gathered immediately to witness the spectacle.

"YOU RUINED THE FUCKING CAREER OF A BETTER OFFICER THAN YOU WILL *EVER* BE, DO YOU HEAR ME?!"

I wanted to scream. I wanted to ask her what the fuck she wanted from me. But I couldn't. She was an officer. I was a cadet. And here we were again. We were standing in the middle of a crowd. I was guilty by rank alone. If a superior flames you, you take it. You shut your hole and you take your punishment. I stood there at attention.

She closed the gap between us. She put her mouth to my ear, her breath hot against my cheek.

"You do not deserve to be here. You do not deserve to be walking around at all." She paused, then continued, threateningly, "And I am not the only one who feels this way."

She stopped talking but stayed right next to my ear. I said nothing. I felt her fury raise the hairs on the back of my neck.

"GET YOUR SORRY, SAD-SACK SELF THE FUCK OUTTA MY FACE, CADET! NOW!"

I did not look her in the eye. I did not engage her at all. Covering my blown-out eardrum with my hand, I simply turned ninety degrees and walked off. I broke through the crowd that had gathered and kept going until I found a restroom and ducked into a stall. I locked the door. I fell to my knees, and I got sick for the first time in weeks.

After rinsing my mouth, splashing water on my face, I went back into the bathroom stall and sat on the toilet. I rested my head in my hands. My head was light; my thoughts were heavy.

This feels familiar.

STALLED.

"Regulatooors . . . *mount up!*"

Our basketball team captain, Dutch, shouted to us as our school bus stopped outside Everett High School—Magic Johnson's alma mater—in Lansing, Michigan. They were one of our biggest rivals, and in my sophomore season we had lost to them, so *this* season—as a junior—I was determined to help us *beat them* for the conference title.

We clambered off the bus into their away-team locker room, changed into our uniforms, warm-ups, and high-tops, then took a knee. I kissed my junior dog tags, wrapped them around my left leg, and stuffed them into my sock. After a moment of silence, we all put our hands into the center of the circle, with Dutch's on top.

"'Aww, team' on three, ready? One, two, three . . . !" Dutch pumped all of our hands.

"AWWWW, TEAM!" we cheered in tight unison.

We all high-fived and smacked asses before breaking apart and running into the gym to begin our warm-up drills. Every home team had its own warm-up music that they played over the loudspeaker before games. Everett had a mash-up playlist starting with Naughty by Nature. It blared over the PA system as the Vikings jogged out to start their layup drills. Four songs in, I felt my stomach drop before my ears could even *hear* the tune that had sent it plunging.

"When Doves Cry."

I lost nine years within the first three bars of Prince's song. Without even thinking, without even blinking, I sprinted from the gym, burst through the locker room door, and barricaded myself in the last stall of the bathroom. I bent over and put my hands on my knees, trying to catch my breath. I could not catch my breath.

Every note, every beat, every word, gave me chronological whiplash.

I was seven years old in an instant.

I smelled fresh paint. I had been banished from our bedroom, and I could smell fresh paint. Sary and I had shared a bedroom for our whole lives. Three days ago, the world stopped, and now our bedroom door was locked. And I didn't know where I was supposed to be, or what I was supposed to do.

The downstairs was full of people. They brought food. They wore black. Some came alone; some came in packs. They brought presents, and sadness and cards in the madness. But I just wanted my sister back.

Finally, the door swung open. The new paint, new furniture, new clothes, new toys. There was nothing I recognized until I heard my voice.

Where did my world go?

My aunt came upstairs and found me in the closet. She put headphones on me and told me, "Don't pause it." So I listened to it on repeat for as long as I could. For hours and days and weeks and months. It was the *Purple Rain* album by Prince. And I hadn't heard "When Doves Cry" since. I hadn't heard it since. Until we did layups and sprints.

Where did my world go?

I sat on the toilet in the bathroom stall. I pulled my legs up underneath me. I closed my eyes without closing my eyes. I plugged my ears without plugging my ears. I retreated without retreating. My heart rate slowed, my options became clear. I could either cower inside that stall, hiding from the ghosts of childhood past, or I could make my sister proud, and try to honor her legacy in the present. She had always been my biggest fan. She had always cheered me on the loudest.

I opened my eyes without opening them. I unplugged my ears without unplugging them. I returned without ever having left. I slapped my knees, came back into my body, and unlocked the door. I jogged toward the gym just as Dutch was coming to find me.

"You okay, Popo?" she asked, putting her hands on both of my shoulders.

"I'm good, Dutchie." I looked her deep in the eyes. "Let's go crush it."

We took the conference title that year, that night. I felt the world at my back. It was my life, multiplied by the power of two.

42

THE ACADEMY

I had never lashed out, argued, or fought with anyone besides the Horribles—and yet I could feel backs turning all around me. With the exception of my very closest friends—Mickey, Hopper, Quinner, and Apple Pie—I watched my colleagues *follow the crowd* rather than make up their own minds. It baffled me. This wasn't a training exercise. No one had been ordered to follow the leader. This was *me*—my life. The mass abandonment broke my heart.

Despite everything, despite it all, I kept going to class. I kept taking care of my duties. I tried my best to eat. And I kept running from room to mental room of my metaphorical building.

Until Him Horrible Him found me. Again.

43

THE ACADEMY

There is an immediate and innate pinpoint-sized tunnel vision that takes over at the very moment your senses register grave physical danger. It is this acute, cellular hyperawareness that forces out all else. All other matters flee to the periphery in an instant. They fall below the priority of your impending harm. In an instant, there is nothing; no story, no adventure, no make-out session, no training session, no friendship—nothing—that can compete for your mind and body's attention, when the sudden and overwhelming thought of life-or-death survival is upon you. This state of hypervigilance takes an all-consuming toll; it drains you of all energy.

This is the feeling of being hunted.

I was jogging between the athletic fields when I saw him approaching. I spied him early enough to run in the opposite direction over the flat terrain, calling out to a freshman boy, who jogged over. Him Horrible Him disappeared.

Even with my careful plotting, planning, routing, rerouting, and run, run, running between rooms, he found me two days later.

I had been walking under the terrazzo, along a hidden fifty-foot strip of sidewalk. I was hoping that it might be a safer route—but I was wrong.

He cornered me before I even saw him. At first paralyzing glance, I could see no escape. I tried to run. He caught me. He caught me with his whole body, as if I were one of those rubber player pads attached to a football sled. He punched me in the solar plexus, and I doubled over.

I have no air. I cannot breathe. I don't want to die.

While I was still bent in half, he tried to maneuver over me. Despite my lack of oxygen, I managed to stand up. I tried to pry his hands from their death grips around my arm and throat.

"I thought I told you to keep your fucking mouth shut."

He started to run his hands over me once again.

No, no, no, no, no, no, no.

I found my air. I could not let this happen again.

"NO. NEVER AGAIN, YOU FUCK. NEVER AGAIN!"

"You little bitch, you fucking little bitch. That's right . . . fight, you little fucking whore. I dare you to fight, bitch. . . ."

He was whispering against my face, his breath hot and hoarse. His spit dripped down my cheek.

NO, NO, NO. He is trying to take what he has taken already. NO. NEVER AGAIN.

"I dare you to scream, you fucking little cunt."

This is NOT happening again.

He growled into my ear and ran his wretched hands over me. And then, without my thinking about it, a window popped open. Running his hands over my body was his mistake, because it meant that he wasn't completely restraining me.

I drove my head back against his face so hard that the impact bounced me forward, and as my hands fell to the concrete, I kicked my right leg up and behind me like a mule. My heel hit him squarely in the groin, and he doubled over. He fell to the ground, holding his own horrible flesh.

I ran.

I ran and ran and kept on running. I could not live like this anymore. I could not live like someone being hunted. I could not spend every waking and sleeping moment looking, listening, smelling, and touching everything in anticipation of danger. I could not protect myself all of the time. I used to think that I could until Him Horrible Him found me again.

NEVER. AGAIN.

The vomit, blood, and bile spewed out of me in thick, ropy streams as I bent over the toilet in Fairchild Hall. Old, familiar, treacherous waters had flooded almost every room in my building.

I was the hunted one, but I knew that I could not tell a single soul. The brass, my chain of command, the angels who had helped me get back to USAFA, they warned me that I had already used my mulligan.

I'm scared, but I cannot succumb to my fear again. I cannot.

I have already used my mulligan.

Intellectually, I knew that there was no reason for me to feel unspeakable shame.

But I felt unspeakable shame.

I slipped under the water's surface. Choking on the salty unworthiness lapping over me.

Over the next couple of weeks, my body, my mind, my heart, my soul—they all fell apart. What had taken months the first time now happened much more quickly. I crumbled into rubble. I didn't sleep.

I couldn't keep food down. My grades took a nosedive. And because of my injuries—a couple from when he had found me again, and a couple self-inflicted as a result of it—I was demoted to the junior varsity volleyball team. I was hardly setting an example for the underclassmen.

I was caught in a riptide.

Officially submerged and drowning.

After Sary's death, I had spent most of my life numb to pain great and small. Nothing could eclipse the pain that I had felt the day I lost my world—my darling, blond-haired, blue-eyed world—in the blink of an eye. Had I been there, as I was supposed to be, *had I been there*, I could have, would have, *should* have prevented the death of my sister.

Had I been there.

I should've prevented it.

However, the losses and pain that I had experienced at USAFA had done more to stir up that deep sorrow, and dredge that throbbing river of grief than any other thing I had experienced since her death. It had mingled the waters—both old and new. Both cold and hot. And I was no longer numb anymore. Instead, I felt *everything*. Everything even more intensely in this riptide-filled whirlpool.

I didn't know how to navigate these waters.

I was completely lost.

I could not separate myself from my emotions, orchestrate a game plan, or follow through. Nothing was working. My brain, my body, my soul; they weren't working together—or at all. I had no control.

I was drowning.

Sary? I have no control. I'm drowning. Sary?

Help me. I'm scared.

44

THE ACADEMY

I was afraid to leave my dorm room and simultaneously afraid that Him Horrible Him would find me there and turn it into yet another crime scene. Hopper had given up and yanked the ejection seat handle on our relationship by pulling away, and then eventually starting to see a civilian girl. I started camping out in Mickey's room.

Hopper's ejection had hurt. Badly. But the worst part about it was that I understood why he'd left. He was a thriving, overloaded firstie thinking about graduation and beyond. He wanted something easy, into which he didn't have to put much effort. I'm sure I seemed like effort. I was a screwed-up former smack drowning in a whirlpool of dysfunction. I did not blame him. But it broke my heart just the same. It broke my heart. Just the same.

I lost all ability to sleep unless I was within Mickey's reach. But the last thing I wanted to do was jeopardize his cadethood. Something had to change—and quickly.

———————

"Popo . . . Popo . . . Look at me. C'mon, baby girl, look at me."

I saw Mickey's face, his eyes. I felt his touch, his hand. I had lost time. Again. I was shaking.

"That's it . . . that's it, c'mon, ba—"

I came back to the present. Something was heavy. In my hand. I looked down at the Swiss Army Explorer I had taken out of my pocket.

I remember now.

I had needed a physical distraction to keep me in the present while Mickey and I talked about the *Cadet X Letters*. I looked down at my hand. The corkscrew was pulled out and I was trying to balance the tool on it, trying to spin it like a top. I needed a distraction. To stay in the present. My hand shook at Richter levels. And I was losing at *both*. Both the balancing trick and staying in the present.

"Look, this place is not like other places. . . . It makes people . . ."

I tried to hear Mickey's voice. But all I heard was pain.

I opened the knife.

Will I ever feel anything again?

I ran the blade across my hand.

Will I ever feel anything but hurt again? Will I ever feel anything other than eviscerated, again?

I dragged the blade across my hand and watched the blood flow. I tried to feel the physical pain as I watched the red river bubble up, but I couldn't feel anything at all.

"NO! Aww, Popo . . . NO!"

Mickey grabbed the blade. "C'mon . . . I gotcha, c'mon."

In one fluid move, Mickey scooped me off the ground. I tried to watch the blood, to feel the pain, but all I saw was Him Horrible Him. And all I felt was fear. I lost time.

"Yes, she . . . ahh . . . fell and cut it on a piece of glass. . . ."

I came to on a hospital table. Mickey was talking to a doctor.

"No, she's okay. It just scared her."

I heard him speak for me without betraying me. I felt his body behind me, propping me up.

"I think blood makes her woozy—she'll be okay in a little bit."

I felt the tug of the stitches being sewn into my hand. I saw the shiny-headed snake weave its thick black tail in and out, in and out of my skin, leaving a tightly closed zipper in its wake. I tried to feel the pain.

"Popo?"

We were back in Mickey's car. His hand was on my head. I heard his voice above the engine drone, above the quiet song coming out of the speakers. I heard him say my name again and again. I felt his hand. His huge, heavy, healing hand on my light and hurting head.

He put me in his bed.

I woke fully present. I had finally snapped out of it. Mickey's face was drained of color. The fear in his eyes ran as deep as the truth of what had happened: the truth that I couldn't share with anyone, not even him.

I needed help.

I needed help, and I was going to ask for it. Finally. I had been trying to protect those around me, but I had just hurt the one closest.

I needed to protect myself first.

45

THE ACADEMY

I made the decision to leave the United States Air Force Academy for good.

I could not stay, as prey, for the hunter. I would self-destruct. Or worse, get caught.

I could not tell the brass. I was already on their *unprecedented* second chance.

I could not tell my friends. If Him Horrible Him heard anything, I would not survive it.

I could not tell *anyone*. If the process was even half as lengthy or stressful as the Her Horrible Her investigation and trial, I feared I wouldn't make it. I could barely stay conscious as it was.

I didn't tell anyone about Him Horrible Him. I would not survive the aftermath.

I'm scared I won't survive.

I needed to *save* my own life and then *salvage* it, and in order to do that I *had to leave* the first home that I had made on my own.

It was simple. Either stay . . . or *live*.

I showed up at Captain Jag's office in the middle of duty day. She knew by the dark, puffy circles under my eyes. By the hollow, battered look on my face. She knew that I had just made a difficult decision. She took me into her office. She reassured me that it was either *stay* or *live* and that *my life trumped all.*

She submitted the paperwork, and I began outprocessing. I was walking away from this haunted and hallowed place. I was leaving some people that I loved. Telling them was one of the most difficult duties I had to carry out. USAFA was an all-encompassing institution. I found out firsthand that cadets had difficulty making time for other *cadets*, let alone friends who attended other *schools*. Saying good-bye to my buoys carried with it the gravity of a soldier off to war; there was a strong likelihood that we would never see each other again.

Some members of my chain questioned why I would go. Some teachers wanted me to stay. My coaches saw more of me. And more of why I had to leave.

Once my signature was on the resignation form, all of the pressures to perform academically, militarily, and athletically were lifted off of my shoulders. I should have felt light, airy, and free, but I didn't. I felt the opposite. As I walked over the grounds that I had been trying to make my home for almost two years, my body ached and creaked and cracked and shook. I had been liberated from my restrictive duties, but in place of the restrictions, a familiar and overpowering feeling of paralysis set in. By the time I reached the field house to clean out my volleyball locker, it struck me that the lethargy weighing down my extremities was actually a deep and profound sense of *sadness.*

For the first time in my life, I had withdrawn from a challenge, and it was one that could have had a profound bearing on my future. I could not shake the awful feeling of powerlessness. It was as if my strength had been insidiously leaking from some fissure in my soul.

Perhaps this was failure. Perhaps this was what it felt like. *Failure.* The very word, its connotation, twisted my insides into a knot. I had failed my school, my squadron, my team, my parents, my community, my sister, and myself. I felt a stifling grief for all that I was losing by choosing to leave.

I reached up to the top shelf of my volleyball locker. I pulled down my Ralph Lauren baseball cap—a replacement for the one that had been taken from me. I reached inside the upturned cap and pulled out the last picture ever taken of Sary and me. I looked at the two of us, our arms wrapped around each other. My cheeks were still chubby, and my eyes still sparkled with innocence. For the first time, I really *saw* how truly *young* a seven-year-old child is. I would *never, ever, in a zillion years* blame a seven-year-old baby child for an accident like my sister's. And yet I blamed *myself* for hers, from the moment I knelt beside her lifeless body.

I would *never* blame a child. I would scoop her up and tell her as many times as she needed to hear it that it was not her fault. It was not her fault.

Oh my God. It was not my fault.

I had immediately assumed responsibility for Sary's death, and ever since, I had shouldered an extraordinary amount of pain, sadness, and humiliation in order to spare those around me from feeling those things. Those feelings were familiar to me—they were mine—so what was a bit more pain, a bit more sadness?

Oh my God.

I think that I deserve *this pain. I deserve it as punishment for not saving my sister. As punishment for* surviving.

I had always felt responsible. I had always felt I deserved to be disciplined—that I had to discipline myself. But as ridiculous as it sounds, I had never before entangled the two thoughts, or realized that they were codependent. Subconsciously, I was always expecting pain. I had conditioned myself to take it, devour it, and conquer it. And, because I didn't think that I was worthy of living my life, when my sister could not live hers, pain had become an ever-present force for me.

If I wasn't dragging the blade across my skin myself, then I was unconsciously inviting someone else to do it. As protective and supportive as I had been to so many others—including Her Horrible Her—I had been sacrificing my own safety and my own happiness. I had tried to save Her—*but she was not my sister.*

I had waded into the water in an attempt to save Her Horrible Her, but I didn't know how to swim on my own. She pulled me under. I was already drowning when Him Horrible Him yanked me beneath the surface.

I had always expected to have to *pay* for my failure in order to *earn* my happiness.

But *there is no failure.* And . . .

Happiness is and should always be free.

———————

As I returned to my room from the field house to continue packing, I felt a fundamental shift taking place.

I am not responsible for my sister's death.

I do not deserve to be punished for surviving.

I do not deserve the pain that has been inflicted on me here.

I do not deserve to be hurt. By anyone.

One of the greatest gifts that my parents ever gave me was the belief and knowledge that I could be anything that I wanted to be. So why was I choosing to be a victim? *I am so much more than that. We are all so much more.*

I loved people. I adored finding, cultivating, and celebrating friendships. But I had lost my ability to do that, because I had not taken care of myself first. Like an oxygen mask on an airplane. I could not help others unless I'd helped myself. It was time to move forward, *move on*, and help myself. *First.*

I could feel the grand chasm gaping in my heart and soul finally closing. My emotions had reunited with my physical, intellectual, and spiritual being. My heart, though still damaged, was finally whole. *It was finally whole.* And *healing.*

I packed up my uniforms and standard-issue items, still folded into tiny origami patterns and starched to high hell. Among them I found a lone beige sock from which I had tried to bleach the massive bloodstains from That Night. I thought about all of the punishment, all of the pain that I had inflicted onto myself. I thought about the fact that people who have been hurt are the ones who hurt others.

Hurt people hurt people.

Her Horrible Her was hurt people.

Him Horrible Him was hurt people.

Hurt people hurt people.

I understood pain.

As broken and manipulative and maniacal as my two tormentors had been, their words and horrible deeds had come from a place of hurt. It didn't excuse their actions, but it did help explain what had caused them.

I do not deserve to be hurt. I refuse to be held hostage by the actions of sick, damaged people. I have to unlock their chains and break free because I deserve to be free.

I have to forgive them.

My stomach winced.

Okay, it doesn't have to be now.

I have to forgive me.

I have to forgive me.

I forgive me.

Oh my God.

I am free.

I felt myself breathing deeply. I heard myself drawing in huge lungfuls of air. *In through my nose, out through my mouth. In and out. In and out.* I felt the shackles crack and break and fall to the floor. I felt the weight of the past two years, the weight of a lifetime fall with them. I felt lighter, freer.

I felt freer. Free.

Oh my God. I am free.

For the first time in my life I could feel all of myself moving forward in one piece. No part of my heart stayed behind, imprisoned by guilt from my childhood. No part of my intellectual or physical self turned around to flagellate me. No part of me deserved to be hurt. I was moving *on*. I finally realized that the most important question to ask myself was, "How do I feel?" knowing where you are in any given moment is the only way to know how to get to where you want to go. It is the only way to move forward toward a better . . . everything.

Even if it takes me years to be all that I am, I know I am finally on my way.

The last thing I packed was my dream box. I ran my fingers over the top of it, and it felt as smooth and soft as a lamb's ear. I opened the lid. There were two dreams waiting just inside next to my junior dog tags. I took out my dog tags first.

POLO REO TATE
USAFA, 15 MAY, O-NEG
NO ONE CAN TAKE YOUR JOY

The words were under my thumb from the very beginning.
The answer. Right there. In my hands. From the very beginning.
No one can take your joy.
Not Her Horrible Her, not Him Horrible Him, not those in my chain, or squadron, or those on my team could take my joy. Not even my sister, and all that had happened. No one could take my joy . . . *without my consent.*

I took out the first dream and unfolded it. The thick paper resisted, as if it wanted to shield me from what was written inside. I pried it open and read the heavy, dark lines.

To survive.

I felt a rush of heat rise up my neck. A sprinkling of goose bumps followed. My cheeks flooded with pigment and my eyes with hot, salty tears. It was such a simple dream, yet it had been one of the hardest to realize during my time here.

I folded it back up and returned it, this time to the belly of the box, with the other dreams that had been fulfilled. I reached for the other piece of paper, which held words I had written just after high school graduation. I had been saving this one for after USAFA graduation. I had not looked at it since. I opened it up and let my eyes skim over the dark writing.

I am so happy and appreciative that I was a stellar cadet—one who served honorably,

**touched a great number of people, and stood
out as a beacon of bright shiny light.**

I read it again and again and again. I thought about the times that I had tried to handle my indignities with dignity. I thought about my time on the witness stand. I thought about having chosen to tell the truth, my truth, above all else. I thought about every opportunity I'd had to retaliate and how that wasn't true to who I am. I thought about the incredible bonds I had been able to form, despite my dysfunction. I thought about how much had happened since I had arrived. A *lifetime* had happened since I'd arrived.

I had not failed at USAFA. Just like I had not failed my sister. How could I fail, when life is about the journey . . . and my journey—all of our journeys—lasts a lifetime. Being a USAFA cadet would always be a part of me. I would still have the chance to live honorably, to touch a great number of people, to stand out as a beacon of joy.

I folded the dream back up and put it beside the other one in the belly of the box. My mission was clear. I had new dreams to fulfill. And there was no going back.

I am alive right now. And I am appreciative. I am so appreciative.

I had signed my paperwork. I was all packed. I had officially disentangled myself from USAFA. Disentangling my mind and my heart from here would take much more time.

EPILOGUE

I left USAFA feeling as if I had just come out of open-heart surgery.

I had gotten so sick, so wounded, so twisted, hurt, and dysfunctional, that both emotional and physical triage were critical for my survival. I was finally able to see the gaping fissure that had severed my heart the moment that my sister had died. And just like every other deep cut, if the blade of life slices over the same wound—or pulls the scab off—over and over and over again, it will never have the opportunity to heal. My experiences at the air force academy had run that blade over the cut in my heart so often and so deep, that by the time I was on the emotional gurney, they had to sew nearly two separate hemispheres of my *soul* together. Her Horrible Her and Him Horrible Him had left me bleeding out on the floor of Mickey's bedroom, and had I not asked him for help, had I not finally decided to leave, I would have died there, at the United States Air Force Academy.

But I did not.

The road to recovery was not pain-free. Months after leaving USAFA for good, I received a call from Captain Policy. He told me that Tip had appealed the decision all the way up the chain of command until it was overturned at the very last moment. Less than two weeks after she was reinstated to the air force, she died in an accident. His words knocked the wind out of me. For months. Even after everything, I felt deep sorrow for her family. No family should have to endure the loss of a child.

I had been so damaged, so disconnected in order to survive, that I had to literally relearn simple emotional cause and effect. It took practice to learn how to *feel* things in real time. It took practice to learn how to ask myself *how I felt* instead of how I *should* have felt. I had to establish and discover a whole new lexicon for my feelings. Like physical therapy after major surgery, I had to learn how to use my heart as it related to my *own* life—not just others' lives—on a moment-by-moment basis. One step at a time. Painful and slow, but forward nonetheless. It took me a full year to recuperate enough from my experience at USAFA to be able to start my college career over at the University of Notre Dame. I was offered the same place on the volleyball team as I had been out of high school, and even though I was not completely healed, I had gained strength and functionality enough to start over.

My tenure at Notre Dame was excruciating at times. I popped several metaphorical sutures when I blew my knee out—repeatedly—playing volleyball. Life's blade ripped the scab off my mending heart on a few occasions with dating, friendships, and relationships. And I suffered a few painful reminders that happiness must be priority one. And that it was not my job to try to save anyone else before I got better myself. However, just as my buoys at USAFA bobbed over to offer their rescue and respite, I had some extraordinary people come into my life at the perfect time to help me work through each challenge, one of whom was a sports psychologist, as instrumental in my survival as he was in my recovery.

It took patience for me to learn that recovery does not happen in an instant. It is a process. The distance between my intellectual under-standing and emotional understanding seemed vast at times. And it took much longer than anticipated to earn my undergraduate degree, but I did.

I graduated.

And by the time I graduated from the University of Notre Dame, I had my diploma as documentation of my perseverance, and signifi-cant scars as documentation of what was now only the *memory* of emotional open-heart surgery.

I moved out to New York City shortly after graduation.

Perhaps the most important thing that came out of my decision to leave the academy and its surrounding epiphanies and instru-mental life changes was my artistic deepening. It provoked from me the most in-depth exploration of my life, my mind, my heart, my soul, and my spirit. It revealed in me a desire to study people, to study behavior, to observe, to ingest, and then to re-create experiences as vast and wide as the human condition would allow. Instead of study-ing human behavior to help the Federal Bureau of Investigation profile criminals as I had originally intended, I kept the process and curiosity the same, and changed the outcome. I studied acting. I studied the exploration of myself so that I could explore others, and it has been one of the most therapeutic journeys that I have ever undergone. I had not allowed myself to really validate just how impactful the performing arts had been on my life since toddlerhood. Watching people re-create reality in film or on television or on the stage had always been so cathartic, so healing, so inspiring to me.

As I started to study the craft, I realized that the biggest gift that someone can give another is the opportunity to *feel*, the opportunity to grieve, to laugh, to cry in pain, to scream in fear, to roll on the floor with laughter . . . to *get it out. To emote. To feel.* The biggest gift is to tap into the incredibly deep, shared well of what makes us human. To drop the bucket down the long, dark, personal fount within each of us in search of that crystal clear, pure mountain runoff of emotion, the very distinguishing feature that makes us human. It connects all of us to one another and lets us know that we, too, have felt deeply. We, too, have feared, have laughed, have loved, have hurt. We, too, have hurt and you are not alone.

You are not alone.

I have had the opportunity to do so many things since moving to New York City. And I am—as we all are—so much more than just one thing. But no matter how many things I take pleasure in doing, there is none more challenging, nor more fulfilling, than being able to provide an emotional vehicle for others to connect with on the deepest, rawest, most basic human level that exists. At the core of my very being, I am an artist. It was a calling that I had marginalized my entire life, thinking that its frivolity would not—should not—put bread on the table in a noble way.

Except if you are doing what lights you up, then that, by nature, is noble.

In order to truly relate to one another in a deep, soul-shifting, spiritually expansive way, you have to know how you feel and be willing to share it. As heart-palpitatingly scary as it may seem at times, it is the most profoundly rewarding thing that I have been able to do for myself and my relationship with others. Through whichever medium I choose to express my unique point of view—that which we all have—I know now that there is no more noble calling for me in my life. To live heart first.

I live heart first.

I am many things. And I am capable of being many more. But at the heart of it all, I am an artist. The moment that I discovered, recognized, and acknowledged how my sister's death had affected me, was the moment I realized that my heart was and will always be the only brush with which I can paint the never-ending canvas of my life. It is the single most powerful artistic utensil that we all have to process our experience and find joy in anyone and anything we encounter along the winding, crazy, devastating, amazing, unfathomably rich and delicious journey through life . . . and I have found my joy. Everyone has one—at least one—thing that truly lights them up.

I have found my joy.
And no one can take it from me.

For those of you who are struggling or need help, please know that there are those who care about you only a phone call away. Following is a list of organizations full of people who know that we are all in this together. All you need to do is pick up the phone, tablet, or computer. There is nothing that is worth more than your life and your happiness. You are surrounded by love. All you need to do is reach out. You are not alone.

RESOURCES & SUPPORT

1 in 6—For men whose lives have been disrupted by unwanted or abusive sexual experiences, working through it can help turn things around. 1in6.org

Anti-Violence Project—Serves LGBTQ and HIV-affected survivors of all forms of violence.
avp.org/get-help/get-support or call 1-212-714-1141

End Rape on Campus
endrapeoncampus.org

Forge—A national organization that provides direct services to transgender, gender non-conforming, and gender non-binary survivors of sexual assault. forge-forward.org/anti-violence/for-survivors

National Sexual Violence Resource Center (NSVRC)
nsvrc.org/resources

National Suicide Prevention Lifeline
Call 1-800-273-8255

Rape, Abuse, & Incest National Network

rainn.org or call 1-800-656-HOPE (4673)

Safe Horizon

safehorizon.org or call 1-800-621-HOPE (4673)

Teen Librarian Toolbox—Using YA to talk with teens about sexual violence and consent.

teenlibrariantoolbox.com/2014/02/svyalit-project-index

ACKNOWLEDGMENTS

Everybody has to find something—at least one thing—that lights them up, that ignites a fiendish passion fueling a soul-nourishing, blood-burning, brilliant wildfire of desire inside of them. People are one of the things that light me up. They are endlessly fascinating, mind-blowing, surprising, and amazing in every possible way. The following people exemplify all of that and more. They have made my life joyful, inspiring, yummylicious, and worth living:

To Kal, my lighthouse. You helped save my life. Quite literally. And to Mike, Sam, and Ben, thank you for taking in my wayward ship way, way back when. I love you.

To Alma, and all of the "bouys" at USAFA . . . thank you for keeping me afloat in a sea of blue.

To Jill, Liz, and Laura, I could not have asked for a more motivating group of powerful, knowledgeable, and amazing women to bring this book to life. Thank you, truly, for believing in this project, and in me. Thank you for my master class in authorship. I adore all of you.

To Johanna, Abby, and Carrie, to think of you is to bask in a perpetual childhood up at Charlevoix. I love you, sweet, gorgy girls.

To Mickey Franco, thank you for taking me by the heart—and at times even defibrillating it—so that I could earn my diploma from the University of Notre Dame. You were my village. Love you.

To Scott Rodeo, thank you for putting my body back together again and again . . . and again, after playing Division I ball . . . you are a brilliant surgeon, an incredible man, and I so appreciate you.

To Alicia and Sweet Bear Blu, thank you for showing me what a strong, loving, happy, healthy, cooperative, vegan, rich, and wonderful life can look like. You inspire me every day, sweet, brilliant, amazing you.

To Casey, thank you for showing me that brilliant, funny women who live heart first can find love, family, and a beautifully successful life in this industry. I love you, hunny, so much.

To Alicia, Casey, Selma, Amy, Jordan and Lauren, Nancy and Pete, Josh, Lori and Jonas, and Jay, thank you for supporting and believing in me getting this book out to the world. It would not have happened without your help. I love you.

To The Upright Citizens Brigade, the UCB Four, and to Eric Morris and Anthony, thank you for opening my protected heart and allowing me to have a career doing what I love. I love you all profoundly.

To Esther, Abraham, Tracy, Dave, Kate and Luke, Jeremy, Joe, and Thomas, thank you for holding space for us to experience incandescent joy together, for provoking expansion, and for continuously redefining the meaning of generosity in the perpetual now of our creation. My heart is so, so full of love for you, now and always.

To Kimber, Becky, and Betsy, may we always share a bowl full of belly laughs between moments of epic, epiphanic expansion. Cannot express how much I appreciate you. So much more to come, beautiful brilliant beings . . . luv, luv, luv you.

To Michele and Megsy, my chosen family, thank you for so many years of laughing and loving through life . . . cannot wait for every moment more. I love you.

To Mark and Sonya, Chris, Kye, Jared, Richard, Peter, Brian and Carolyn, Victoria and Paul, Charlie, Camelia, Christian, Mikey and Lynner, my vibrational family. I am so appreciative for the incredibly rich, abundant, and amazing experiences we have had together . . . and I'm eager for every moment more with all of you. I love you infinitely.

To sweet Michael McPeak for the gorgeous photos that adorn this book, thank you for the beautiful light you carry with you. . . . And to sweet Heather Nelson, for being my amazing one-woman glam squad for said photos, luv you, hunny. :)

For all of those who have shared, enriched, and inspired my life that I did not have a chance to mention, please know that I hold you close to my heart and am incredibly appreciative for all that you bring into my life. . . . I love you. Here's to more, more, more. :)